Date Due

		JUL	2000
OCT 3 '68			
OCT 14 '68			
NOV 4 '68		JUL 0 9	
		JUN	2004
		JUL X X 2015	

Date Due

PRINTED IN U.S.A.

Paul Elmer More's Shelburne Essays on American Literature

Paul Elmer More's
Shelburne Essays on

HARCOURT, BRACE & WORLD, INC.
NEW YORK · BURLINGAME

American Literature

SELECTED AND EDITED BY

Daniel Aaron

A Harbinger Book

ACKNOWLEDGMENTS

The editor wishes to thank the following for their permission to reproduce material in this book:

Houghton Mifflin Company: The selections from Paul Elmer More, *Shelburne Essays*, Fifth Series (1908) and Eleventh Series (1921), are reprinted by permission of and arrangement with Houghton Mifflin Company, the authorized publishers.

Princeton University Press: The essay "A Note on Poe's Method," reprinted from *The Demon of the Absolute*, New Shelburne Essays, Volume I (1928), by Paul Elmer More, by permission of Princeton University Press. Copyright, 1928, Princeton University Press.

Contents

Contents

Paul Elmer More's Shelburne Essays on American Literature

Paul Elmer More: Biographical and Biobligraphical Note

Paul Elmer More was born in St. Louis, Missouri, in 1864. He attended Washington University, receiving his B.A. in 1887 and his M.A. in 1892. After four years of teaching at a boys' preparatory school in St. Louis and a ten-month sojourn in Europe, he entered Harvard University in the fall of 1892 for graduate study in Sanskrit and Indian philosophy. He received his Harvard M.A. degree in 1893. It was during his second year at Harvard that a lifelong friendship with Irving Babbitt began. In 1894 and 1895, More was an assistant in Indo-Iranian languages at Harvard, and then in the fall of 1895, he accepted a position as associate in Sanskrit and classical literature at Bryn Mawr College. In 1897 More abandoned academic life and retired to a cottage in Shelburne, New Hampshire, which served as a spiritual as well as physical retreat. Then, drawn to journalism, he moved to New York and became in turn literary editor of the *Independent* (1901–1903), of the New York *Evening Post* (1903–1909), and of the *Nation* (1909–1914). He was elected to the American Academy of Arts and Letters in 1915. In 1914 More settled down in Princeton, New Jersey, to devote the rest of his life to writing and, until 1934, lecturing occasionally on philosophy and the classics at Princeton University. More died in 1937.

The essays on American literature included in this volume are with one exception selected from More's *Shelburne Essays*, published in eleven volumes from 1904 to 1921. One essay is from *The Demon of the Absolute*, the first volume in the *New Shelburne Essays*, published in 1928. More's participation in the "New Humanism" controversy which enlivened the late 1920's is not reflected in the critical essays printed here; that episode is treated, albeit with considerable partisanship, by Robert Shafer, in an emotional and highly eulogistic monograph, *Paul Elmer More and American Criticism* (New Haven, Yale University Press, 1935). A more balanced and authoritative account of More's life

1

and work is Arthur H. Dakin's *Paul Elmer More* (Princeton, Princeton University Press, 1960). No complete bibliography of More exists, but the reader should consult Malcolm Young's *Paul Elmer More: A Bibliography* (Princeton University Press, 1941) and Dakin's *Paul Elmer More Miscellany* (Portland, Maine, Anthoensen Press, 1950). More's preoccupation with the culture of New England has been most recently explored in Francis X. Duggan's essay, "Paul Elmer More and the New England Tradition" (*American Literature*, January, 1963).

2

Paul Elmer More: Introduction

⟨～∂⟩ Literary reputations are notoriously short-lived in America, and this generalization holds for critics as well as for novelists, poets, and playwrights. Although the name of Paul Elmer More is listed in most surveys of American letters and although histories of American literary criticism treat him with respectful consideration, he is now regarded pretty much as an "imperfect critic," to borrow T. S. Eliot's phrase in his note on More—erudite and intelligent but primarily a moralist, only incidentally concerned with the richer complexities of art. Usually More is bracketed with his close friend and philosophical ally, Irving Babbitt, an identification that has done him a double disservice. First, it has tended to obscure the remarkable differences between the two men simply as practicing critics, and second, it has placed him so squarely in the center of the Humanist–anti-Humanist controversy of the late 1920's that his literary opinions have been overshadowed by his philosophical and political ones.

More entertained certain views about ethics and social relations to which both the aesthetes and the radicals of the 1920's were antipathetic. He was a mordant foe of romanticism[1] and naturalism; he distrusted humanitarianism as a literary impulse (unless it was transmuted by deep emotion into art); and he was a great believer, as we shall see, in character, discipline, and responsibility. But even his strong moral predilections rarely distracted him entirely from his task of literary evaluation—a task to which he brought

[1] "Romanticism [signified for More] the infinitely craving personality, the usurpation of emotion over reason, the idealization of love, the confusion of the sensuous and the spiritual, the perilous fascination that may go with these confusions. It is like a dream of fever, beautiful and malign by turns; and, looking at its wild sources, one can understand why Goethe curtly called romanticism disease and classicism health. He might have added that disease is infection, whereas health may be acquired or preserved by the effort of the individual." Quoted in Dakin, *Paul Elmer More*, p. 140.

3

an extensive learning, an eye for the happy analogy, and a talent for succinct and pungent phrasing.

Readers accustomed to a more detached and objective kind of critical writing may be amused or irritated by More's frequent interpolations, autobiographical or theological, but upon reflection they will see these intrusions as neither the preenings of an egoist nor the pronouncements of a pundit. More was first and last the "engaged" critic. Literary experience for him was always bound up closely with other private experiences; literature was always a very serious business, what Matthew Arnold called a "criticism of life." Now this may be a "facile phrase," as Eliot remarked, but I think More interpreted it to mean that literature should be at once moral and aesthetic. Any writer risked his censure by neglecting either aspect. A solicitous if partisan reader, he paid to every serious writer the compliment of his closest attention, praising and reproving by turn and never yielding to him an iota more of his esteem than he thought the writer deserved.

But whether More momentarily identified himself with the ideas of one writer or withdrew frostily from the errors of another, he seldom lost sight of his main purpose, the exegesis of the man and his works. He had, to be sure, obvious favorites among the American writers included in this volume. A Hawthorne, a Thoreau, a Whittier appealed to him as literary companions more than did a Whitman or a Poe, yet he would not withhold his qualified acclaim from the flawed but gifted reprehensibles.

Consider the case of Whitman, whom More somewhat gingerly confronts in one of the Shelburne essays. We see immediately that Whitman is not a congenial subject for our fastidious moralist. How testily he approaches this (to More) dirty, garrulous, half-educated loafer, touched with insincerity and "speaking in the patois of the pavement." Yet despite his irritation and even disgust with Whitmanism, the critic triumphs over the prig. Whitman can be tedious, his "ejaculatory language" a bore; much of his poetry is of the "rudimentary sort." But *Specimen Days* remains for More "one of the most remarkable autobiographies ever written," and the author of that "incomparable rhapsody, *Out of the Cradle Endlessly Rocking*," stands "with the great and not the minor poets."

4

This essay first appeared in 1906 when many critics of the genteel persuasion still treated Whitman as an obscene old man and excluded him from their hygienic Parnassus. More, a discriminating literary patriot, was never conventional in this sense, however, and accepted or rejected literary candidates according to his private standards. Mark Twain and Henry James apparently operated outside his mental wave lengths; at least they are not dignified by full-dress analyses in the Shelburne essays. The same is true for the twentieth-century literary rebels who violated almost every regulation in More's artistic and moral code. He was quite at home, on the other hand, with the traditional American writers, and in discussing them his moral preconceptions (which occasionally obscured particular literary virtues apparent to less ethical-minded critics) usually deepened more than constrained his outlook. Perhaps a didactic literature requires a moralist to celebrate it properly. In any case, he was at ease with what one of Henry James's characters calls "the New England expression, the air of Puritanism reclaimed and refined." The carping note in his critical voice faded out when he expatiated on the excellencies of his beloved company (slighted by his impatient younger contemporaries) and sketched the winter, spring, and Indian summer of the New England mind.

Doubtless More never thought of his essays as constituting a systematic or linked account of American letters. He wrote them at intervals and for different purposes and occasions, but these random pieces tell a story: the development of one literary strain from the harsh-tongued Puritan ministers—those "oracles of God" with their "appalling energy and straightforwardness of the imagination"—to the disconsolate and restless searcher, Henry Adams, who had rejected his ancestors' faith in the "providential purpose in history" and whose life was a long walk through "the corridors of chaos." Between the exultant beginning and the pessimistic finale, the Golden Day intervened, the supreme achievement, but More found something rare and precious in each period.

It is not hard to understand why the Puritan view of life appealed to him. More was a kind of Puritan himself, albeit a somewhat Anglicanized and Platonized variant, and the Puritan's inhibitions—a sense of the immutable One lying behind and beyond material phenomena, together with a refusal to blend heavenly and earthly categories, a distrust of the unchecked imagination, and the moral criteria by which one judged both life and art—were not dissimilar to his own. More may have regretted certain narrow and repressive features of Puritanism, particularly its morbidity and its antisecular literary bias. The grim divines who carried a "desolated sanctity" into their homes, whose God was splashed with the blood of His delinquent children, suffered from a defective sympathy. Their "sincerity of vision," as he remarked of Edwards, sometimes amounted to a species of cruelty. This harshness, however, was mitigated by a tenderness and serenity of spirit that seemed to More entirely admirable, and if the Puritans ruthlessly sacrificed half of their cultural heritage by detaching themselves from the "main current of English literature," they restored to English letters "that sense of something central and formative in man, of character as distinguished from the mere portrayal of unrelated passions."

"Character" is the key word here. It is character, More feels, that gives weight and solidity to New England literature, that disciplines the passions and provides a counterforce to the antinomian tendencies of its writers. The Puritan's "hardness of character" sometimes ground down the gentler affections (New England, More says, may "have been snow-bound in creed as well as in climate"), but out of the harshness and bleakness came a special kind of pale and fragile beauty that More particularly relished. It was character, finally, that preserved Emerson and Thoreau from the romantic excesses of the German Transcendentalists and gave to the verses of Whittier, often bordering so "perilously near to the trivial and the mean," their sturdiness and refinement.

How the "asthmatic Muse" of Puritanism made the most of her limitations and how "the flowering of New England" (as More called the age of Emerson some years before Van Wyck Brooks did) was foreshadowed in its craggy beginnings provoke some of More's most illuminating speculations. Few critics before or after him have written so suggestively about the impact of brute nature on the American literary imagination. The forest world, More believed, intensified the Puritan's conviction "that life is a perpetual battle with the doers of evil, to whom no concession must be granted." For Cotton Mather and others, "the dark unredeemed forests" were the devil's playground—the "Synagogues of Satan," in Mather's words—and all of their traditional superstitions, transported from the old world, darkened in the precincts of the American wilderness.

More saw both the Salem mania and the horrendous visions of evil in the sermons of the Calvinist preachers as consequences of the colonial confrontation with "the great unsubdued forces of the world." What fascinated him, however, was the way in which this ancestral memory of "man's struggle with the primeval woods" continued to haunt American writers long after the seventeenth century. By Thoreau's time, the New England forests were no longer looked upon as the suburbs of hell, but, even so, Thoreau never contemplated nature in the spirit of Byron, Shelley, or Wordsworth; "she was still an alien creature who succumbed only to his force and tenderness, as she had before given her bounty, though reluctantly, to the Pilgrim fathers." Thoreau, More continues, had a "certain intimacy" with plants and beasts, but he retained a dread and awe of what he called "pure Nature . . . vast and drear and inhuman." And More comments:

The loneliness of the mountains such as they appeared to the early adventurers in a strange, unexplored country; the repellent loneliness of the barren heights frowning down inhospitably upon the pioneer who scratched the soil at their base; the loneliness and terror of the dark, untrodden forests, where the wanderer might stray away and be lost forever, where savage men were more feared than the wild animals, and where superstition saw the haunt of the Black Man and of all uncleanness,—all this tradition of sombre solitude made Nature to Thoreau something very different from the hills and valleys of Old England.

The aftereffects of old terrors and superstitions could be traced even more clearly in the "dark psychology" of Hawthorne and Poe.

More's most systematic and original treatment of this idea is in his essay "The Origins of Hawthorne and Poe," which first appeared in 1902. Here as elsewhere More's wide and eclectic reading shows to good advantage, for he was able to compare and contrast the English and continental Gothic writers with their American equivalents and to make his claim that the Americans, because of their inherited "moral experience," were able to achieve a more profound and meaningful terror than the Europeans.

American literature properly begins, perhaps, after religion had passed from something "real and urgent," as More says, into "an intoxicant of the imagination." But the "long contemplation of things unearthly" had encouraged the literary imagination "to fasten upon the sombre effects of guilt and reprobation." This "constant meditation on death and decay," More believed, ultimately affected classical American literature and especially the tales of Poe and Hawthorne, "whose minds were absorbed by the weirder phenomena of life." By "weird," More meant

not the veritable vision of unearthly things, but the peculiar half-vision inherited by the soul when faith has waned and the imagination prolongs the old sensations in a shadowy involuntary life of its own; and herein too lies the field of true and effective symbolism. If Hawthorne and Poe, as we think, possess an element of force and realism such as Tieck and the German school utterly lack, it is because they write from the depths of this profound moral experience of their people.

Other critics since More have offered other and sometimes ingenious explanations to account for the domestication of the Gothic tradition in America, but More's emphasis on "moral experience" helps us to understand why and how such writers as Philip Freneau, Charles Brockden Brown, Cooper, Poe, Hawthorne, Melville, and Faulkner converted a literary tradition that is so often ridiculous or merely melodramatic in English fiction into something serious and disturbing.

The other essays in this volume are generally more grudging in their praise of American writing than the above quotations would indicate. More, as I have said, was not given to unqualified celebration, and he was too well read in world literature to exaggerate the importance of the American literary achievement.[2] At a time when many of our writers, both the lesser ones and the "classical," are being smothered by the excessive solicitude of American scholars and critics, it is instructive to read his tempered praise and strictures and to see how justly and aptly he measured the attainments of his subjects.

Occasionally More's prejudices led him astray, as when he dismissed Baudelaire as a feeble and degenerate imitator of Poe. It seems, at times, as if he considered literature as a kind of quasi-religious vocation too often profaned by unclean practitioners. More's religious and ethical preconceptions and his self-imposed role of scholar-priest insulated him from the kinds of experience open to less rigorously moral writers. In a passage on Sainte-Beuve (which may have autobiographical implications) More attributed Sainte-Beuve's failure as a "creative" artist and his success as a critic to his early disillusionment and his "passion for truth." This "passion for truth" produced in More something akin to the "defective sympathy" he detected in the Puritans. One feels that he never confronted directly what Coleridge called the Jacobinical impulses that the artist must struggle with, imaginatively entertain, even if he finally subdues them by self-discipline. What kept More from becoming a "creative" writer, and what limited him as a critic, was his inability to face up to the abhorrent or to identify himself vicariously with sensual, feckless, and untidy human nature. His sardonic rejection of humanitarianism (whose canting exponents and whose shams he enjoyed deflating) would have seemed more convincing if he had not contrasted it with his

---

[2] American literature, More wrote to a correspondent, is "a subject which we must sorrowfully admit is for the greater part of trivial magnitude. Eight or ten names, none of which reaches the very first rank, do not make a literature." In another letter, he listed the following writers as probably the best: Edwards, Emerson, Hawthorne, Poe, Whitman, and Parkman (see Dakin, p. 85). At the same time, More believed no critic need apologize for frequenting "the byways as well as the highways" of literature: "Is there not room for a perfectly legitimate criticism which deals with lesser names and tries to lend them interest by adventitious aids of various sorts?" (Dakin, p. 102).

9

own laundered asceticism. He professed to know "real, unadulterated, undisciplined human nature." If so, this knowledge must have seeped out of books or have come by hearsay from his Puritan heritage. Mark Twain, who found no place in More's pleached garden, would have agreed with More that man is "a poor, restless, animal, evil thing," but because Mark Twain never separated himself from "the damned human race," because he really had seen it in all of its undraped imperfection, he could write about mankind with a certain indulgence.

Within his charted domain, however, More moved with ease and authority, and any student of American literature who is reading More for the first time will be struck again and again by his underivative judgments, often less dated today than the literary opinions of his progressive contemporaries who were in revolt against a Puritan tradition they did not always understand.

In H. L. Mencken's amusing tirades, in Theodore Dreiser's fulminations, and even in the gentler animadversions of the young Van Wyck Brooks, Puritanism stood for everything mean, narrow, and repressive in American life. To Dreiser and the rebels of the Wilsonian era, it was simply another name for the public censor (Mencken's "smut-hound") or the "frozen perverted religiosity that would make a sin of sex."[3] Their contempt for many

---

[3] Reviewing More's *A New England Group and Others* (Houghton Mifflin, 1921), Mencken wrote: ". . . undismayed by the winds of anarchic doctrine that blow down his Princeton stovepipe, [More] continues to hold fast to the notions of his earliest devotion. He is still the gallant champion sent against the Romantic Movement by the forces of discipline and decorum. He is still the eloquent fugleman of the Puritan ethic and aesthetic. In so massive a certainty, so resolute an immovability there is something almost magnificent. These are somewhat sad days for the exponents of that ancient correctness. The Goths and the Huns are at the gate, and as they batter wildly they throw dead cats, perfumed lingerie, tracts against predestination, and the bound files of the *Nation*, the *Freeman* and the *New Republic* over the fence. But the din does not flabbergast Dr. More. High above the blood-bathed battlements there is a tower, of ivory within and solid ferro-concrete without, and in its austere upper chamber he sits undaunted, solemnly composing an elegy upon Jonathan Edwards, 'the greatest theologian and philosopher yet produced in this country.'" (*Prejudices: Third Series*, Knopf, 1922, p. 176.) For all the vigor of the assault against what

of the writers More cherished as well as their insensitiveness to what he considered the autochthonously American may have prompted his prim and often ungenerous response to the new.

But for all of his old-fogyism, More had at least read—and read with critical attention and sympathy—the writers the Menckenians unreflectively patronized or ridiculed. To him, Jonathan Edwards was no mere preacher of hell-fire sermons, but "an earlier and perhaps greater Emerson," superior even to Calvin "in subtle resourcefulness of reasoning and still more in the scope of his spiritual insights." He maintained, as Van Wyck Brooks did, "that there was . . . a stretch of humanity beyond Franklin's victorious good sense," that his "renovating intellect" could not plumb "the treacherous obscurities" of the imagination, but no one, I think, has indicated more perceptively Franklin's "clearness, force, and flexibility." Few if any of More's contemporaries were capable of detecting the less obvious parallels between Edwards and Emerson, Hawthorne and Edwards, Freneau and Poe, Poe and Hawthorne, Henry Adams and Henry James, or, for that matter, the significant distinctions that divided them. When he remarks, for example, that in Hawthorne's tale *Ethan Brand* the effect is "ghostly," where in Poe it would have been "ghastly," the point has wider implications than its succinct expression might indicate. And his essays on Hawthorne and Thoreau (in some ways among the most impressive in this volume) abound with trenchant and quotable observations that show, among other things, how deeply More had immersed himself in their private worlds. The larger figures evoke a richer response than the lesser ones (the essay on Thoreau's journal, in addition to being a searching analysis of Thoreau, also contains a brilliant elucidation of the differences between the German and the American Transcendentalists), but he says enough that is interesting about Longfellow or Whittier or Charles Eliot Norton to make us reconsider our fashionable and perhaps superficial prejudices.

More stood for, Mencken considered him the best of all the Humanists. Both men, it should be noted, shared a dislike for "uplifters" and a taste for good eighteenth-century English prose. In one of his relaxed moments, More wrote to a friend: "Mencken says I should be a good fellow if I had drunk more whiskey and begotten more bastards." (Quoted in Dakin, p. 278.)

It is worth noting, in conclusion, that these selections from More's essays on American literature were not chosen because of their factual accuracy or comprehensiveness. Recent scholarship has developed and deepened many of his casual insights and has proved him wrong or at least inadequate on a number of important points. Whitman's alleged liaison with a New Orleans woman which More takes for granted is now dismissed by most authorities as poppycock. The discovery of the poems of Edward Taylor (a poet More would have read with delight and appreciation) of necessity invalidates some of his conclusions about seventeenth-century New England poetry. One can only regret, moreover, that he felt no interest in Cooper and Mark Twain, disliked Henry James, and that he omitted Herman Melville, still virtually forgotten when More was writing his Shelburne essays.

Nevertheless, the pieces included in this volume—discursive, seemingly random, opinionated, personal—constantly surprise us by their force and incisiveness. Sometimes they begin with commonplaces and appear to be overloaded with irrelevant asides, but then suddenly the critic, in a paragraph or even a sentence, will throw into sharp relief what is unique or idiosyncratic.

In revealing the writer, More as often revealed himself, for he never tried to separate his private emotions from his literary interests. He was "in the best sense of the word, the man of culture, the ripe scholar, to whom the lessons of the past had become personal experience." So More wrote of Charles Eliot Norton, whom he esteemed because of his "utter veracity," because he "never swerved aside to be funny or wise or profound or original, but was concerned to say with unflinching precision just what he thought and felt." These are not necessarily the most ingratiating attributes of a critic, as More himself admitted. To set oneself up as a check to the "ranging enthusiasms of the soul," as a rein on the antinomian impulses of one's contemporaries, is not to court popularity. More defended Norton and, by implication, himself by saying that character is "always in some way negative."

There is something a bit self-righteous, almost smug, in More's image of the critic stanchly holding to his course, unmoved by the "winds of folly," the "dust of pedantries," and the foul smell of "cant and sentimentalism." This must have been the way he conceived of himself; but we who read him today can appreciate him rather as the consecrated man of letters attuned to the finer vibrations of our national literature.

DANIEL AARON

Smith College
1963

The Spirit and Poetry of Early New England

The refuge of the Puritans on this side of the ocean was not exactly a nest of singing birds; but it had a character and self-conscious spirit which sought expression in verse as well as in sermons, and, at least, if not poetical, it resounded with the psalmody of the saints. In judging the strength and weakness of those early poets, to grant them the title by courtesy, we should remember first of all that for the most part they belonged to the class who were leaders in breaking away from the full current of English life, and spoke for a people who brought with them to these lands a civilization rent and shorn by what rightly may be called one of the huge mischances of history.

It is, I know, the teaching of a certain school of scientific historians that the changes of civilization are produced by large impersonal laws under whose sway the will of the individual sinks into insignificance. That theory is, perhaps, not quite so common now as it was a few years ago. And surely, if any great event can be referred to the character of individual men, it was the crime of the seventeenth century in England, with its consequent train of evils. In that month of spring in the year 1603 when James Stuart was riding south to take up his crown in London, a prophetic eye might have foreseen the troubles he and his son were to cause. On the way the so-called Millenary Petition was presented to him by a band of moderate and conforming Puritans, who desired only a few unimportant changes in the service and Prayer Book; one of the first acts of James at Hampton Court was to deny the Petition and to abuse the petitioners with a threat to "harry them out of the land." After that the history of England for two generations was a series of *ifs*, depending on the actions of a small group of

From A *New England Group and Others*, Shelburne Essays, Eleventh Series (Boston and New York, Houghton Mifflin Company, 1921), pp. 3–32.

men. Thus, if Prince Henry, with his objection to a Catholic marriage, had not imprudently overheated himself on the tennis court, and so left the throne to his brother Charles; if Charles at the beginning of his reign had not been bribed to accept the Petition of Right and so to bind his hands; if Wentworth had been kept in England to raise a standing army, instead of being called back from Ireland when too late, and if Henrietta Maria by meddling with the soldiers had not brought him to the scaffold; if Charles had married a Protestant instead of a Bourbon princess; if he had chosen a wiser prelate than Laud; if he had not attempted to seize the five members of Parliament, or had planned the attempt more secretly; if the navy had not been wantonly alienated;—If, in a word, James and Charles had not been at once so obstinate and so weak, either they might have succeeded in establishing, for a time at least, a monarchy like that raised in France on the ruin of the Fronde and the Reformation, or they might have guided their people through a bloodless and healthy revolution. But for the fanaticism of the King the opposing fanaticism of Pym and Lilburne and Cromwell would never have come to the top, crushing between them the moderate men who were the real strength and, in the end, the salvation of England. And so I, for one, cannot look back upon that period without shuddering at its passion of violent extremes, and without a feeling of amazement that so much evil in the world can be traced to the temper of a few fanatics who, by the whim of Fortune, had the destiny of the English people in their hands.

Old England, though her richer and completer development was perhaps forever marred by the harsh divisions of that age, did nevertheless in a manner quickly shake herself into balance. But we must remember that the New England colonists, driven from their homes by the Laudian persecution, came almost exclusively from one of the national factions. They did not bring with them the full temper of the English people, or even that part of its character which has given us Chaucer and Shakespeare and Dryden and Swift and Johnson and Byron and Tennyson. Their poetry therefore must be criticised, not as belonging to the main current of English literature, but as a slender branch, so to speak, running to one side, and deprived of the broader nourishment of tradition. It is the prolongation of a mood that had been tortured into excess by the goading stings of Accident; nor must we forget that at home under the sway of this same mood the imagination was distrusted, the theatres were closed, the picture collections of Charles dispersed or destroyed, the churches made barren of their beauty, the courtly poets silenced or driven into obscure places— that the land was for a time, in the language of Strafford, "frequent in combustions, full of massacres and the tragical ends of princes."

It would be unjust, of course, to say that with this iconoclasm all the charm of life was banished by the Puritans. Even leaving out of account the supreme achievement of Milton, no one can go through the writings of these men without finding passages that have a grace entirely their own. One recalls, for instance, the scene in Bunyan's pilgrimage, when Christian, having twice climbed the Hill Difficulty, comes to the Palace Beautiful, and is there entertained by the maidens Piety, Prudence, and Charity. "Thus they discoursed together till late at night," the narrative proceeds, "and after they had committed themselves to their Lord for protection, they betook themselves to rest. The Pilgrim they laid in a large upper chamber, whose window opened towards the sunrising; the name of the chamber was Peace, where he slept till break of day; and then he awoke and sang." I shall not repeat the words of the Pilgrim's song, for Bunyan, with all his genius, endured the confinement of Bedford Gaol better than the shackles of rhyme; but no candid reader will fail to respond to the peculiar beauty of that chamber of peace. In this chastened loveliness, won by the exclusion of a whole half of life, the Puritan literature is not wanting. One foresees in it much that long afterwards will charm the ear in the poems of Longfellow and Whittier.

And in one respect the Puritans brought no diminution to the field of art and literature, but effected rather a return to the main line of tradition from which England for a while had been partially diverted by the seductions of the Renaissance. I mean that sense of something central and formative in man, of character as distinguished from the mere portrayal of unrelated passions, which was so lamentably lacking in most of the dramatists, and which since the advent of Puritanism has been the chief honour of British letters. . . . it is highly important to remember this positive side

16

of Puritanism when reckoning up the devastating effects of its rigid and combative morality on the imagination.

Now the very conditions of existence in New England exaggerated the seclusions of the half-civilization which the people brought over with them in their exile. Not only were the colonists withdrawn from contact with the secular tradition which makes itself so deeply felt in the art of a Milton, but the inevitable hardships of their state intensified their belief that life is a perpetual battle with the powers of evil, to whom no concession must be granted. In the dark unredeemed forests that surrounded them there lurked tribes of savage people whose appearance and habits were such as to warrant the notion that here indeed Satan was unchained and held undisputed sway. One of the first voyagers to the new continent, William Strachey, carried back this report of devil worship to credulous ears. "There is yet in Virginia," he wrote in 1618, "no place discovered so savadge and simple, in which the inhabitants have not a religion and the use of bow and arrows. All things they conceive able to do them hurt beyond their prevention, they adore with their kind of divine worship, as the fire, water, lightning, thunder, our ordinaunce pieces, horses, etc.; but their chief god they worship is no other, indeed, than the devill, whom they make presentments of, and shadow under the form of an idol, which they entitle Okeus." Naturally the settlers, looking out into the infinite wilderness, saw visions of dread and heard sounds of preternatural portent. Even the redoubtable Captain John Smith was sufficiently troubled to express his apprehensions in doggerel rhyme:

> But his waking mind in hideous dreams did oft see
> wondrous shapes
> Of bodies strange, and huge in growth, and of stupendous makes.

This may have been a passing sentiment in Virginia, but in Massachusetts it became a rooted conviction. It is the excuse, if any excuse be possible, for the wild delusion of witchcraft that for a time drove the leaders of Boston and Salem into a mania of fear and persecution. "The New Englanders," wrote Cotton

Mather, "are a people of God settled in those which were once
the devil's territories. . . . An army of devils is horribly broke in
upon the place which is the centre and, after a sort, the first-born
of our English settlements; and the houses of the good people
there are fill'd with the doleful shrieks of their children and servants, tormented by invisible hands, with tortures altogether preternatural." If we were discussing the prose of America as well as the
poetry, we should find in the after-effects of this superstition, this
deisidaimonia in the true sense of the word, turned now from a
religious conviction into a kind of haunting mood of the imagination, the sources of Hawthorne's dark psychology and no small part
of that awe which Thoreau felt in the presence of the mountains
and lonely forests.

Meanwhile we can see something of its influence in contracting
the poetry of the colonists within still narrower bounds of religious
sentiment. The first volume printed in this country was the Bay
Psalm Book, translated from the Hebrew by Richard Mather,
Thomas Welde, and John Eliot in 1640. In the preface Mather
made this candid statement: "If therefore the verses are not al-
waies so smooth and elegant as some may desire or expect, let
them consider that God's altar needs not pollishings." And indeed
the polishings are conspicuous by their absence, as any specimen
of this notable book will show. For instance, the great nineteenth
Psalm is thus rendered for the satisfaction of the faithful:

> The heavens doe declare
>   The majesty of God:
> also the firmament shows forth
>   his handy-work abroad.
> Day speaks to day, knowledge
>   night hath to night declar'd.
> There neither speach nor language is
>   where their voyce is not heard.

It would not be easy outside of Puritanism to find a great religion
divesting itself so heroically not only of the smoothness and elegance but of the manifold traditions of life. But if the oracles of
God were thus delivered through the nose, they could convey the

menace of wrath as well as the upliftings of holiness. Perhaps the best known of the early New England poets is that Michael Wigglesworth who, for one fearless theological line, has obtained a kind of immortality in obloquy. Possibly a few of my readers will be unacquainted with Master Wigglesworth's picture of the terrors of the damned, when God at the Day of Doom has pronounced judgment upon them, and a merciful Christ has begun to consume the universe in fire:

Then might you hear them rend and tear
    The air with their outcries;
The hideous noise of their sad voice
    Ascendeth to the skies.
They wring their hands, their caitiff-hands,
    And gnash their teeth for terror;
They cry, they roar, for anguish sore,
    And gnaw their tongues for horror.

But get away without delay;
    Christ pities not your cry:
Depart to hell, there you may yell
    And roar eternally.

         〜 〜 〜

With iron bands they bind their hands
    And cursed feet together;
And cast them all, both great and small,
    Into that lake forever;
Where day and night, without respite,
    They wail and cry and howl,
For torturing pain which they sustain,
    In body and in soul.

For day and night, in their despite,
    Their torment's smoke ascendeth;
Their pain and grief have no relief,
    Their anguish never endeth.
There must they lie and never die,
    Though dying every day;
There must they, dying, ever lie,
    And not consume away.

Say what one will, there is a grim sincerity in these lines which lifts them out of the commonplace and gives them something of the ring of poetry; and after all, if you are going to depict an eternal hell, there's no use in being finicky about the benevolence of your deity. It is only when our prophet of the New World vouchsafes to make concessions to human sympathy that he becomes odious. You know the words with which the Almighty Judge is supposed to condemn the little pleading souls of unbaptized infants:

> You sinners are, and such a share
>   As sinners, may expect;
> Such you shall have, for I do save
>   None but mine own elect.
> Yet to compare your sin with their
>   Who lived a longer time,
> I do confess yours is much less,
>   Though every sin's a crime.
>
> A crime it is; therefore in bliss
>   You may not hope to dwell;
> But unto you I shall allow
>   The easiest room in hell.

We shudder at that concession, "the easiest room in hell"; it really is odious. And yet, again, if we are to permit logic to deal with these matters, what possible difference does it make whether those chosen by God of His own free will for eternal damnation pass into this state after a few days of life or after many years? In either case their evil fate was imposed upon them at their birth. The only condemnation we can pronounce upon Wigglesworth is that, having allowed his natural human emotions to enter into the question at all, he stopped short halfway and did not revolt from the whole logical scheme of Calvinistic theology. I am disposed to feel a certain respect for this doggerel Dante of the New England meeting-house; though his power of expression was crude, there is in him, as in Jonathan Edwards and others of the line, an appalling energy and straightforwardness of the imagination. And if a late New Englander, Oliver Wendell Holmes, thought no decent man could really hold the doctrine of free grace and election without going mad, we must remember that Wigglesworth spoke the honest and deep-rooted conviction of his contemporaries—and they were not mad. And there is this, too, to be said for his un-flinching sense of the awful consequences of sin, that it bears on the actual problems of life. One recalls that story of a farmer of the present day who was asked by a troubled clergyman why the village churches were left empty, and who replied with Yankee candour and shrewdness: "Wall, sir, I callate it is about like this: since you preachers have stopped preaching hell fire, we country folk have made up our minds that we might as well take our chances on t'other world."

But if the older theological taste had about it a prevailing odour of the pit, we must not infer that life in the colonies, gray in colour though it may have been, was entirely bleak and without those chambers towards the sunrise. Much of the verse produced may have been of the kind described by Captain Edward Johnson:

> From silent night true Register of moans,
> From saddest soul consum'd in deepest sin,
> From heart quite rent with sighs and heavy groans,
> My wailing muse her woful work begins,
> And to the world brings tunes of sad lament,
> Sounding naught else but sorrow's sad relent—

Much of the verse produced was of this nasal quality; but not all. Cotton Mather, he of the witchcraft fame, tells of a certain friend whose custom it was, "when he first arose in the morning, to re-pair into his study: a study well perfumed with the meditations and supplications of an holy soul." Can any scholar to-day hear that sentence without a thrill of envy at the thought of the long un-interrupted hours which those old divines contrived to pass in the earnest and unrepentant searching of mighty books? Ah, that study well perfumed with the meditations and supplications of an holy soul—how many a student of our age, distracted by the multitude of conflicting intellectual interests, disturbed by doubts of the value of learning in itself, when he enters his work-room of a morn-ing, can breathe that atmosphere of assured content, as it were the

21

palpable memory greeting him of similar days past? And this quiet satisfaction of a life devoted to retired scholarship and public teaching found due expression in literature. Nothing is more characteristic of the prose and poetry of the day than the innumerable eulogies of good men and women, to some of which the *pax theologica* lends an element of passionate sincerity. One of the best known of these is Urian Oakes's *Elegy on the Death of Thomas Shepard*, a saintly minister of Charlestown, who died in 1677. A few of the concluding stanzas will indicate the quality of the piece:

> If to have solid judgment, pregnant parts,
> A piercing wit, and comprehensive brain;
> If to have gone the round of all the arts,
> Immunity from death could gain; . . .

> If holy life, and deeds of charity,
> If grace illustrious, and virtue tried,
> If modest carriage, rare humility,
> Could have bribed Death, good Shepard had not
>   died. . . .

> ∾　∾　∾

> Farewell, dear Shepard! Thou art gone before,
> Made free of heaven, where thou shalt sing loud
>   hymns
> Of high triumphant praises evermore,
> In the sweet choir of saints and seraphims. . . .

> My dearest, inmost, bosom-friend is gone!
> Gone is my sweet companion, soul's delight!
> Now in an huddling crowd I'm all alone,
> And almost could bid all the world—Good-night.
>   Blest be my Rock! God lives; O let him be,
>   As He is All, so All in All to me!

We need not magnify the virtues of such an elegy as this, which would in fact appear poor enough if compared with Milton's superb lines on the reception of Edward King into the

> . . . solemn troops, and sweet societies,
> That sing, and singing in their glory move,

or with Cowley's learned lament for his Cambridge companion in philosophy. Yet we shall miss the truth if we fail to discover in Oakes's less polished muse the charm of a friendship built upon a sure sympathy in the hopes of the spirit. As he himself wrote in one of the Latin verses whose elegance won the applause of his contemporaries,

Parvum parva decent, sed inest sua gratia parvis.*

From these by-products of the theological laboratory we may turn aside to say something of the first and most ambitious of the professional poets of the age, the stupendous Anne Bradstreet, whose volume of verse was heralded to the world with this overwhelming title-page:

The Tenth Muse lately sprung up in America; or Several Poems, compiled with great variety of wit and learning, full of delight; wherein especially is contained a complete discourse and description of the four elements, constitutions, ages of man, seasons of the years; together with an exact epitome of the four monarchies, viz., the Assyrian, Persian, Grecian, Roman; also, a dialogue between Old England and New concerning the late troubles; with divers other pleasant and serious poems. By a gentlewoman in those parts. Printed at London, for Stephen Bowtell, at the sign of the Bible, in Pope's Head Alley, 1650.

Well, Mistress Anne was in sooth a memorable and characteristic figure of the New World. Though born and married in England, she migrated at the early age of eighteen to this country, and through her children became the fountain head of one of the purest streams of the so-called Brahminism. One of her descendants was Richard Henry Dana, another Oliver Wendell Holmes. John Norton of Hingham, ancestor of the present Nortons and Adamses, whose line also was to intermarry with the Eliots, gave vent to his admiration of the dead poetess in resounding couplets:

---

* [Small things befit a small person, but small things too have their own grace.]

Virtue ne'er dies: time will a poet raise,
Born under better stars, shall sing thy praise.
Praise her who list, yet he shall be a debtor;
For Art ne'er feigned nor Nature framed, a better.
Her virtues were so great, that they do raise
A work to trouble fame, astonish praise.

I do not know that time has yet raised a poet to celebrate her works to the taste of the pastor of Hingham, but one of his descendants, the late Charles Eliot Norton, edited the poems of the matchless gentlewoman, and in his introduction wrote of her character in his most genial vein.

All, indeed, that we know of Anne Bradstreet from contemporary sources and from her own autobiographical sketch justifies us in revering her as one of those large-minded women of the seventeenth century who managed somehow, in ways that seem inexplicable to their daughters, to combine the manifold cares of a household with indefatigable study and sober unhurried reflection. But the outpourings of her muse, it must be acknowledged, remind us too forcibly of one of her own aphorisms: "A ship that bears much sail, and little or no ballast, is easily overset." She is seen perhaps at her best in such stanzas as these:

I heard the merry grasshopper then sing,
    The black-clad cricket bear a second part,
They kept one tune, and played on the same string,
    Seeming to glory in their little art.
Shall creatures abject thus their voices raise?
And in their kind resound their Maker's praise:
Whilst I, as mute, can warble forth no higher lays.

〰 〰 〰

When I behold the heavens as in their prime,
    And then the earth (though old) still clad in green,
The stones and trees, insensible of time,
    Nor age nor wrinkle on their front are seen;
If winter come, and greenness then do fade,
A spring returns, and they more youthful made;
But man grows old, lies down, remains where once
        he's laid.

24

〜 〜 〜

O Time, the fatal wrack of mortal things,
    That draws oblivion's curtains over kings,
Their sumptuous monuments, men know them not,
    Their names without a record are forgot,
Their parts, their ports, their pomps all laid in th'
        dust,
Nor wit, nor gold, nor buildings 'scape time's rust;
But he whose name is grav'd in the white stone
Shall last and shine when all of these are gone.

Professor Barrett Wendell, who quotes these stanzas, remarks
aptly that in seventeenth-century New England the author "stands
alone, without forerunners or followers; and if you compare her
poetry with that of the old country, you will find it very much
like such then antiquated work as the *Nosce Teipsum* of Sir John
Davies, published in 1599, the year which gave us the final version of *Romeo and Juliet*." The female prodigy of New England,
in fact, belongs to that strain of literary Puritanism which is more
distinctly British than American, and which was already becoming
outworn in the old home.

The names of Mrs. Bradstreet's more poetical descendants serve
to remind us how intimately all this New England society was
knit together, and how its spirit was handed down from generation
to generation as a kind of family possession. Her own contemporary
fame may call our attention to the fact that women played no
inconsiderable part in creating the peculiar tone of the New World
literature. And their influence was felt in two ways. In the first
place that sturdiness and uprightness of character, which was one
of the great, the very great, compensations of Puritanism, not only
made itself heard in the eulogies pronounced over those who died
in the harness of virtue, but was active in the family relations of
the living. Saintliness, I know, does not invariably make for comfort. Sometimes the Puritan hardness of character dominated too
tyranically the softer traits of affection and compliance, bringing
what might be called a desolation of sanctity into the home. But
there were other households—and these I believe the majority—
in which the tenderness to every duty, the sense of due subordina-

25

tion, the competence of training, the repose of a clear conscience, must have evoked an atmosphere of serene and equitable joy. The very discipline of the passions, the renunciation of the wider sweep of human experience, would put a stamp of sacredness on those chaster pleasures which knit a family together in contented unison. In a way all of New England may be said to have been snow-bound, in creed as well as in climate, but in the shelter of the hearth there was warmth for the body and there was comfort for the soul. Whittier was recalling a true incident of his childhood, and was writing also an allegory of New England's inner life, when he described that night of storm and snow:

> Shut in from all the world without,
> We sat the clean-winged hearth about,
> Content to let the north-wind roar
> In baffled rage at pane and door,
> While the red logs before us beat
> The frost-line back with tropic heat.

One can find in the older literature abundant evidence of these protected comforts of the home. Take for instance Cotton Mather's life of John Eliot. There, if anywhere, you have one of the stalwarts. So diligent was Eliot in study that he took to sleeping in his library, in order that he might get to his beloved books at some unearthly hour in the morning without disturbing the household. So fervid was he in piety that he is described as "perpetually 'jogging the wheel of prayer.'" Now the habit of perpetually jogging the wheel of prayer does not, I admit, sound alluring to our modern unsanctified ears; the appearance of a reverend jogger in our parlour would probably cause a little constraint, but then— other times other manners. And of Eliot we are assured by his biographer that "he was indeed sufficiently pleasant and witty in company, and he was affable and facetious in conversation." His affability, I doubt not, was only a part of the large charity of his nature. When an old man he said to one who questioned him about his state: "Alas, I have lost everything; my understanding leaves me, my memory fails me, my utterance fails me; but, I thank God, my *charity* holds out still; I find that rather grows than fails!" And his charity and affability, as well as his prayerfulness, were exercised at home, as sometimes in this strange world they are not. Of his relations with his wife it is said: "His whole conversation with her had that *sweetness*, and that *gravity* and *modesty* beautifying it, that every one called them Zachary and Elizabeth." The biographer continues: "God made her a rich blessing, not only to her *family*, but also to her *neighborhood*; and when she died, I heard and saw her aged husband, who else very rarely wept, yet now with tears over the coffin, before the good people, a vast confluence of which were come to her funeral, say, 'Here lies my dear, faithful, pious, prudent, prayerful wife; I shall go to her, and she not return to me.' " These are the commonplaces of life, you may think, and perhaps they are, although I am not sure that peace and self-control are ever quite commonplace; but it is just these softer aspects of the old New England that we are likely to forget.

Now in the making of this home spirit the women naturally played an important rôle. Thomas Shepard, for example, he whose own elegy was sung so enthusiastically by Urian Oakes, had written a *Character of Mistress Joanna Shepard*, his wife, wherein he had portrayed her as "a woman of incomparable meekness of spirit, toward myself especially, and very loving; of great prudence to take care for and order my family affairs, being neither too lavish nor sordid in anything, so that I knew not what was under her hands. She had an excellency to reprove sin, and discern the evils of men." Incomparable meekness of spirit may not be precisely the sort of eulogy a modern wife would desire in her epitaph, however some husbands might desire it in her life—but, again, other times other manners. And if one is inclined to shudder a little at the thought of her excellency to reprove sin and discover the evils of men, one may suspect that this sharp-edged knowledge was useful in protecting her bookish and busy husband from the inroads of fraudulent beggars and evil mischief-makers. At any rate one may be certain that the house of Mistress Joanna Shepard much resembled the Palace Beautiful of Bunyan, where the maidens Piety, Prudence, and Charity kept watch and ward, and where there was a large upper chamber of peace whose window opened towards the sunrising. Certainly also the peaceful affections of home, the cool and quiet places of rest out of the turmoil of the world's contentions, came to be a marked trait of New England literature. There are traces of it in the early poets; in the works of Whittier and Longfellow it was to blossom into something exceedingly precious, however it may lack the more dazzling qualities of the imagination. The other side of this truth is that you will find no love poetry, as the word is commonly understood, in those primitive days—at least I know of none—and there is a minimum of it in the later age. That is an extraordinary fact, when you stop to think of it, and to some may seem a sad lack. Let such critics turn elsewhere; heaven knows the erotic Muse has been vocal enough in other sections of the world. For my part I still prefer James Russell Lowell's *Under the Willows* to the self-advertised passion of a certain living poetess who bears his family name.*

That was one way in which the influence of women was felt. In another way they brought not peace but conflict into colonial life. The orthodoxy of the New England church was of a hard Calvinistic hue; it was eminently logical and intellectual, the creation and delight of strong men who, however they may have been possessed by a "boiling zeal" for saving souls, yet, like John Cotton, thought twelve hours of continuous study a "scholar's day" and true service to God. Against the virility, and one must add rigidity, of this religious dominion there were inevitably, almost from the beginning, movements of revolt. And it was natural that the good women of the colony should be conspicuous in rebellion as well as in meekness. Not all the great men of the land were as fortunate in their helpmates as were Thomas Shepard and John Eliot. In Winthrop's *History of New England from 1630 to 1649* there is an amusing story of one woman to whom much, and not a little, learning was a dangerous thing. "Mr. Hopkins, the governor of Hartford upon Connecticutt," we there read, "came to Boston, and brought his wife with him (a godly woman, and of special parts), who was fallen into a sad infirmity, the loss of her understanding and reason, which had been growing upon her divers years, by reason of her giving herself wholly to reading and writing, and had written many books. Her husband, being very loving and tender of her, was loath to grieve her; but he saw his error, when it was too late. For if she had attended her household affairs, and

* [Amy Lowell (1874–1925).]

28

such things as belong to women, and not gone out of her way and calling to meddle in such things as are proper to men, whose minds are stronger, etc., she had kept her wits." I do not know by what stages this learned lady fell into her sad infirmity, but I suspect she betook herself to her books as a refuge from her spouse, the worthy governor, of whom it is related "that he frequently fell a bleeding at the nose, through the agony of spirit with which he laboured in them [his prayers]." Neither do I know what was in her many books—even the all-embracing Tyler does not mention them—but my guess is that she wrote verse and tampered with the man-made mysteries of religion.

At least this second form of audacity was what brought trouble between another "godly woman" and the rulers of the State. The story of the conflict may be read in Thomas Welde's *Heresies of Anne Hutchinson*, from which it would appear that this strong-minded female had the pious, and in those days obligatory, habit of going regularly to meeting, but added the very bad habit of collecting a company of critical folk after service and of expounding to them the sermon in a spirit of contumely and contradiction. Now the colonists had a high sense of the value of liberty, as was natural in men who had suffered so much in its cause—so high a sense that, in the words of Governor Winthrop, they would have it only "maintained and exercised in a way of subjection to authority." But this was not the view of Anne Hutchinson and her coterie. Liberty to them meant the freedom of the individual, not to follow the truth, but to choose the truth; it was the kind described by Winthrop as making "men grow more evil, and in time to be worse than brute beasts: *omnes sumus licentia deteriores*,"* and as "that great enemy of truth and peace, that wild beast, which all the ordinances of God are bent against, to restrain and subdue it."

We will not now enter into the question of truth as it lay between the preachers of the Commonwealth and Mistress Hutchinson, but there is no doubt of the fact that her manner of prophesying did not bring peace. The result of her lectures among the women is thus denounced by Thomas Welde:

* [We are all the worse by reason of licentiousness.]

*Now, oh their boldness, pride, insolency, alienations from their
old and dearest friends, the disturbances, divisions, contentions
they raised amongst us, both in church and State, and in families,
setting division between husband and wife! . . .*

*Now the faithful ministers of Christ must have dung cast on
their faces, and be no better than legal preachers, Baal's priests,
popish factors, scribes, Pharisees, and opposers of Christ himself.*

And it was not only against the persons of the clergy that Anne
Hutchinson lifted her terrible prophetic voice; she struck at the very
dogmatic centre of their authority. She lays a profane hand on
the intellectual and traditional basis of theology;—as the horrified
author of the *Wonder-Working Providence* exclaimed: she is a
"woman that preaches better than any of your black-coats that
have been at the Ninneversity." Her heresy is analysed at length by
Thomas Welde, but it is really summed up in the single charge:
"This witness of the Spirit is merely immediate, without any
respect to the word, or any concurrence with it." That is to say, she
was sent into exile for teaching exactly what two centuries afterwards was to be the doctrine of Emerson's essays and Whittier's
most exquisite work. Her proclamation of the witness speaking in
the breast of each man, and requiring no confirmation from revealed book or ordained interpreter, was a signal of the course
to be pursued by her people, starting with rebellion against institutions and rites and ending in rejection of all authority and
tradition and the very principle of organization. She was the first,
and remains the typical, "come-outer."

Lowell remembered these passages at arms when, in his *Biglow
Papers*, he described the troubles caused by the townswomen of
the good pastor of Jaalam:

*The painful divisions in the First Parish, A.D. 1844, occasioned
by the wild notions of (what Mr. Wilbur, so far as concerned the
reasoning faculty, always called) the unfairer part of creation, put
forth by Miss Parthenia Almira Fitz, are too well known to need
more than a passing allusion. It was during these heats, long since
happily allayed, that Mr. Wilbur remarked that "the Church had
more trouble in dealing with one sheresiarch than with twenty
heresiarchs," and that the men's conscia recti, or certainty of being
right, was nothing to the women's.*

It is a pity, I often think, that Lowell, who could have translated Cotton Mather into puns without depriving him of his
Puritan savour, lived too early to try a fling at New England's
latest *she*resiarch—the feminine counterpart of Emerson's refusal
to face the reality of evil in the world.*

It remained for Whittier, who as a Quaker found it easier to
give free expression to the inner voice which had supplanted
the religion of reason, to do justice, or more than justice, to those
feminine flails of the man-made church. Often in his ballads
Whittier makes use of the heresies that filled the early divines
with terror, as if in prospect of the coming dissolution of their
iron-bound creeds. And it is the women of Boston who are chiefly
remembered by him for introducing the leaven of rebellion.
Cassandra Southwick, who was threatened with exile and slavery
for entertaining Quakers and neglecting divine service, is one of
his heroines. Another is Margaret Brewster, who suffered worse
than threatenings for coming into the South Church barefoot and
in sackcloth, and crying out against the rulers and magistrates of
the town.

> She shook the dust from her naked feet,
>   And her sackcloth closer drew,
> And into the porch of the awe-hushed church,
>   She passed like a ghost from view.
>
> They whipped her away at the tail o' the cart
>   Through half the streets of the town,
> But the words she uttered that day nor fire
>   Could burn nor water drown.
>
> And now the aisles of the ancient church
>   By equal feet are trod,
> And the bell that swings in its belfry rings
>   Freedom to worship God!

So did the spirit and poetry of early New England become an
inheritance; out of the strong was to come sweetness, out of the
uncouth grace. It will be objected, I fear, that in my treatment of
the subject I have said much of the spirit and little of the poetry

---

* [Mary Baker Eddy (1821–1910), the founder of Christian Science.]

31

of the age; but in truth poets in those days were something like the historian's snakes in Ireland: there weren't any. As the first satirist, and not the worst, of the colony, Nathaniel Ward, the Simple Cobbler of Agawam, declared:

> Poetry's a gift wherein but few excel,
> He doth very ill, that doth not passing well.

Enough has been quoted from the primitive verse-makers to show that none of them did passing well; but enough also has been said, I trust, to show that some acquaintance with their spirit is a profitable, almost a necessary, preparation for approaching that fine and ephemeral thing, the flowering of New England in the first half of the nineteenth century.

It is rather the fashion, I am aware, among a certain coterie of enlightened critics to condemn the later poetry of New England as almost equally negligible with that of the men and women we have been considering. And indeed no rightly informed person will rank the outpourings of Concord and Cambridge with the supreme creations of the older centres of civilization. We are not likely to fall into that error of over-praise; but we may be tempted by the clamour of our emancipated youth, hailing largely from strange lands in the dark map of Europe, to miss the more fragile beauty of what after all is the fairest thing this country has produced. At its best the poetry of New England is one of the very desirable possessions of the world, and not to appreciate it is to prove one's self dulled and vulgarized by the strident conceit of modernity. It is limited no doubt, and for reasons which I have tried to set forth. But limitation is not always and altogether a vice. At least out of the limitations fixed by the origin of New England grew the peculiar attitude of the later writers towards nature, the charm of their portrayal of the less passionate affections of the home and the family, the absence of erotic appeal, the depth and sincerity, but the perilous independence also, of their religious intuition, the invincible rightness of their character. We may laugh as we will at old Wigglesworth and at the asthmatic Muse of the other Puritan divines; they have been justified of their children.

Jonathan Edwards

Jonathan Edwards was born at Windsor, Connecticut, in 1703. He belonged, unlike his great contemporary Franklin in this, to the "Brahmin families" of America, his father being a distinguished graduate of Harvard and a minister of high standing, his mother being the daughter of Solomon Stoddard, the revered pastor of Northampton, Massachusetts, and a religious author of repute. Jonathan, one of eleven children, showed extraordinary precocity. There is preserved a letter of his, written apparently in his twelfth year, in which he retorts upon the materialistic opinions of his correspondent with an easiness of banter not common to a boy; and another document, from about the same period, an elaborate account of the habits of spiders, displays a keenness of observation and a vividness of style uncommon at any age. He who could write such a sentence as the following was already a master in his own right: "In very calm and serene days in the forementioned time of year, standing at some distance behind the end of an house or some other opaque body, so as just to hide the disk of the sun and keep off his dazzling rays, and looking along close by the side of it, I have seen a vast multitude of little shining webs, and glistening strings, brightly reflecting the sunbeams, and some of them of great length, and of such a height that one would think they were tacked to the vault of the heavens, and would be burnt like tow in the sun."

He studied at Yale, receiving his bachelor's degree in 1720, before his seventeenth birthday. While at college he continued his interest in scientific observations, but his main concern was naturally with theology and moral philosophy. As a sophomore he read Locke *On Human Understanding*, with the delight of a "greedy miser" in "some newly discovered treasure." Some time

From A *New England Group and Others*, Shelburne Essays, Eleventh Series (Boston and New York, Houghton Mifflin Company, 1921), pp. 35–65.

33

after reading Locke and before graduation he wrote down a series of reflections, preparatory to a great metaphysical treatise of his own, which can only be compared with the *Commonplace Book* kept by Berkeley a few years earlier for the same purpose. In the section of *Notes on the Mind* this entry is found: "Our perceptions or ideas, that we passively receive by our bodies, are communicated to us immediately by God." Now Berkeley's *Principles* and his *Hylas and Philonous* appeared in 1710 and 1713 respectively, and the question has been raised, and not answered, whether this Berkeleian sentiment was borrowed from one of these books or was original with Edwards. Possibly the youthful philosopher was following a line of thought suggested by the English disciples of Malebranche, possibly he reached his point of view directly from Locke; in any case his life work was to carry on the Lockeian philosophy from the point where the Berkeleian idealism left off.

After graduation Edwards remained for two years at Yale, preparing for the ministry. In 1722 he was called to a Presbyterian church in New York. Here he preached acceptably for eight months, returning then to his father's house, and later to New Haven, where he held the position of tutor in the college. In 1727 he went to Northampton as colleague, becoming in due time successor, to his grandfather. Almost immediately after ordination he married Sarah Pierrepont, like himself of the Brahmin caste, whom he had known as a young girl, and whose beauty of body and soul he had described in a passage of ecstatic wonder. "They say," he began, being himself then twenty and the object of his adoration thirteen, "there is a young lady in New Haven who is beloved of that great Being who made and rules the world, and that there are certain seasons in which this great Being, in some way or other invisible, comes to her and fills her mind with exceeding sweet delight." The marriage, notwithstanding this romantic rapture, proved eminently wise. Lying on his deathbed at Princeton, while his wife was far away in Northampton, he could, after a life not without sore trials and difficulties, send her this message: "Tell her that the uncommon union which has so long subsisted between us, has been of such a nature as I trust is spiritual, and therefore will continue forever." They had eleven children, one of whom married the Reverend Aaron Burr, president of Nassau Hall (now Princeton University), and was the mother of a more famous son of the same name.

Like a good many other men of his age Edwards lived his inner life, so to speak, on paper—a custom which may seem morbid to a generation taught to believe that it is better to look out than to look in, but which has the advantage of counteracting the disruptive work of time and of linking the periods of life together into one conscious whole. There is therefore nothing peculiar or priggish in the fact that at the beginning of his religious career he should have written out a set of formal resolutions, which he vowed to read over, and did read over, at stated intervals in order to keep watch on his spiritual progress. A number of these resolutions have been printed, as has also a part of the diary kept at about the same time. Neither of these documents, the time of their writing considered, contains anything remarkable, unless our knowledge of the author's life justifies us in attaching unusual significance to such words as the following, which in themselves might have been set down by a thousand other young men of the age: "I have been to God this morning, and told him that I gave myself *wholly* to him."

But it is quite otherwise with the private reflections which he wrote out some twenty years later (about 1743) at Northampton, apparently on some occasion of reading over his youthful diary. In this we have an autobiographical fragment that, for intensity of absorption in the idea of God and for convincing power of utterance, can be likened to the *Confessions* of St. Augustine, while it unites to this religious fervour a romantic feeling for nature foreign to the Bishop of Hippo's mind and prophetic of a movement that was to sweep over the world many years after Edwards' death. A few extracts from this document (not so well known as it would have been if not printed with the works of a thorny metaphysician) must be given for their biographical and literary interest:

From my childhood up, my mind had been full of objections against the doctrine of God's sovereignty, in choosing whom he would to eternal life, and rejecting whom he pleased; leaving them eternally to perish, and be everlastingly tormented in hell. It

35

used to appear like a horrible doctrine to me. But I remember the time very well, when I seemed to be convinced, and fully satisfied, as to this sovereignty of God. . . . I have often, since that first conviction, had quite another kind of sense of God's sovereignty than I had then. I have often since had not only a conviction, but a delightful conviction. The doctrine has very often appeared exceedingly pleasant, bright, and sweet. Absolute sovereignty is what I love to ascribe to God. But my first conviction was not so.

The first instance that I remember of that sort of inward, sweet delight in God and divine things that I have lived much in since, was on reading those words, Now unto the King eternal, immortal, invisible, the only wise God, be honour and glory for ever and ever, Amen. As I read the words, there came into my soul, and was as it were diffused through it, a sense of the glory of the Divine Being.

Not long after I first began to experience these things, I gave an account to my father of some things that had passed in my mind. I was pretty much affected by the discourse we had together; and when the discourse was ended, I walked abroad alone, in a solitary place in my father's pasture, for contemplation. And as I was walking there, and looking up on the sky and clouds, there came into my mind so sweet a sense of the glorious majesty and grace of God, that I know not how to express. I seemed to see them both in a sweet conjunction; majesty and meekness joined together; it was a sweet and gentle, and holy majesty; and also a majestic meekness; an awful sweetness; a high, and great, and holy gentleness.

God's excellency, his wisdom, his purity and love, seemed to appear in everything; in the sun, and moon, and stars; in the clouds and blue sky; in the grass, flowers, trees; in the water, and all nature; which used greatly to fix my mind. I often used to sit and view the moon for continuance; and in the day spent much time in viewing the clouds and sky, to behold the sweet glory of God in these things; in the mean time, singing forth, with a low voice, my contemplations of the Creator and Redeemer.

I spent most of my time in thinking of divine things, year after year; often walking alone in the woods, and solitary places, for meditation, soliloquy, and prayer, and converse with God.

Holiness, as I then wrote down some of my contemplations on it, appeared to me to be of a sweet, pleasant, charming, serene, calm nature; which brought an inexpressible purity, brightness, peacefulness and ravishment to the soul. In other words, that it made the soul like a field or garden of God, with all manner of pleasant flowers; all pleasant, delightful, and undisturbed; enjoying a sweet calm, and the gentle vivifying beams of the sun. The soul of a true Christian, as I then wrote my meditations, appeared like such a little white flower as we see in the spring of the year; low and humble on the ground, opening its bosom to receive the pleasant beams of the sun's glory; rejoicing as it were in a calm rapture; diffusing around a sweet fragrancy; standing peacefully and lovingly, in the midst of other flowers round about.

This is not the Edwards that is commonly known, and indeed he put little of this personal rapture of holiness into his published works, which were almost exclusively polemical in design. Only once, perhaps, did he adequately display this aspect of his thought to the public; and that was in the *Dissertation on the Nature of Virtue,* wherein, starting from the definition of virtue as "the beauty of the qualities and exercises of the heart," he proceeds to combine ethics and æsthetics in an argument as subtle in reasoning as it is, in places, victorious in expression. One cannot avoid the feeling when his writings are surveyed as a whole, despite the laxness of his style, that in his service to a particular dogma of religion Edwards deliberately threw away the opportunity of making for himself one of the very great names in literature.

It should seem also that he not only suppressed his personal ecstasy in his works for the press, but waived it largely in his more direct intercourse with men. He who himself, like an earlier and perhaps greater Emerson, was enjoying the sweetness of walking with God in the garden of earth, was much addicted to holding up before his people the "pleasant, bright, and sweet'" doctrine of damnation. Nor can it be denied that he had startling ways of impressing this sweetness on others. It is a misfortune, but one for which he is himself responsible, that his memory in the popular

* [More properly, "The Nature of True Virtue," in *Two Dissertations* (first published in 1765).]

mind to-day is almost exclusively associated with certain brimstone
sermons and their terrific effect. Best known of these is the discourse on *Sinners in the Hands of an Angry God*, delivered at
Enfield, Connecticut, in the year 1741. His text was taken from
Deuteronomy: "Their foot shall slide in due time"; and from these
words he proceeded to prove, and "improve," the truth that "there
is nothing that keeps wicked men at any moment out of hell, but
the mere pleasure of God." He is said to have had none of the
common qualities of the orator. His regular manner of preaching,
at least in his earlier years, was to hold his "manuscript volume
in his left hand, the elbow resting on the cushion or the Bible,
his right hand rarely raised but to turn the leaves, and his person
almost motionless"; but there needed no gesticulation and no
modulation of voice to convey the force of his terrible conviction,
when, to an audience already disposed to accept the dogma, he
presented that dogma in a series of pictures beside which the
Inferno of Dante seems like the naïveté of a child:

> How awful are those words, Isaiah lxiii, 3, which are the words
> of the great God: "I will tread them in mine anger, and trample
> them in my fury, and their blood shall be sprinkled upon my gar-
> ments, and I will stain all my raiment." It is perhaps impossible to
> conceive of words that carry in them greater manifestations of these
> three things, viz., contempt and hatred, and fierceness of indigna-
> tion. If you cry to God to pity you, he will be so far from pitying
> you in your doleful case, or showing you the least regard or favour,
> that instead of that he will only tread you under foot: and though
> he will know that you cannot bear the weight of omnipotence
> treading upon you, yet he will not regard that, but he will crush
> you under his feet without mercy; he will crush out your blood,
> and make it fly, and it shall be sprinkled on his garments, so as to
> stain all his raiment. He will not only hate you, but he will have
> you in the utmost contempt; no place shall be thought fit for you
> but under his feet, to be trodden down as the mire in the streets.
>
> There is reason to think, that there are many in this congregation
> now hearing this discourse, that will actually be the subjects of this
> very misery to all eternity. We know not who they are, or in what
> seats they sit, or what thoughts they now have. It may be they

JONATHAN EDWARDS

*are now at ease, and hear all these things without much dis-
turbance, and are now flattering themselves that they are not the
persons; promising themselves that they shall escape. If we knew
that there was one person, and but one, in the whole congregation,
that was to be the subject of this misery, what an awful thing it
would be to think of! If we knew who it was, what an awful sight
it would be to see such a person! How might all the rest of the
congregation lift up a lamentable and bitter cry over him! But
alas! Instead of one, how many is it likely will remember this discourse in hell! And it would be a wonder, if some that are now
present should not be in hell in a very short time, before this
year is out. And it would be no wonder if some persons, that now
sit here in some seats of this meeting-house in health, and quiet
and secure, should be there before to-morrow morning.*

The congregation of Enfield, we are told, was moved almost to
despair; "there was such a breathing of distress and weeping" that
the speaker was interrupted and had to plead for silence. Sincerity
of vision may amount to cruelty, and something is due to the
weakness of human nature. Dr. Allen, the biographer of Edwards,
is right in saying that "he was almost too great a man to let loose
upon other men in their ordinary condition. He was like some
organ of vast capacity whose strongest stops or combinations
should never have been drawn."

The result was inevitable. Life is made up of ordinary men in
their ordinary condition. The people of Northampton listened to
Edwards for a time; were rapt out of themselves; suffered the re-
lapse of natural indolence; grew resentful under the efforts to keep
them in a state of exaltation; and freed themselves of the burden
when it became intolerable. That, in brief, is the explanation of
the difference between Edwards and the people of his parish, ending in his dismissal from Northampton. So at least it would be if
we judged from the contemporary point of view; from another
point of view it may be described as the certain outcome of a
combat between inhuman logic and common sense.

At first all went well. Mr. Stoddard, in whose declining years
the discipline of the church had been somewhat relaxed, died in
1729, and the fervour of his successor soon began to tell on the

people. In 1733, as Edwards notes in his *Narrative of Surprising Conversions*, there was a stirring in the conscience of the young, who had hitherto been prone to the awful sin of "frolicking." The next year the sudden conversion of a young woman, "who had been one of the greatest company keepers in the whole town," came upon the community "like a flash of lightning"; the Great Awakening was started, which was to run over New England like a burning fire, with consequences not yet obliterated. The usual accompaniments of moral exaltation and physical convulsions showed themselves. Edwards relates with entire approbation the morbid conversion of a child of four. The poor little thing was overheard by her mother in her closet wrestling with God in prayer, from which she came out crying aloud and "wreathing her body to and fro like one in anguish of spirit." She was afraid she was going to hell! And so, "she continued thus earnestly crying and taking on for some time, till at length she suddenly ceased crying and began to smile, and presently said with a smiling countenance—Mother, the kingdom of heaven is come to me!" This was the beginning of "a very remarkable abiding change in the child"; thereafter she loved "to hear Mr. Edwards preach," delighted in religious conversations, and had "a great concern for the good of other souls." Like saints of an older age she could not always distinguish between rapture and despair:

At some time about the middle of winter, very late in the night, when all were in bed, her mother perceived that she was awake, and heard her as though she was weeping. She called to her, and asked her what was the matter. She answered with a low voice, so that her mother could not hear what she said; but thinking it might be occasioned by some spiritual affection, said no more to her; but perceived her to lie awake, and to continue in the same frame for a considerable time. The next morning she asked her whether she did not cry the last night: the child answered yes, I did cry a little, for I was thinking about God and Christ, and they loved me. Her mother asked her, whether to think of God and Christ's loving her made her cry: she answered yes, it does sometimes.

It was inevitable that such a wave of superheated emotion should subside in a short time. In fact the enthusiasm had scarcely

40

reached its height when it began to show signs of indubitable per-
version, and decay. Immediately after the story of the young
convert Edwards notes that "the Spirit of God was gradually with-
drawing" and "Satan seemed to be let loose and raged in a dreadful manner." An epidemic of melancholy and suicidal mania
swept over the community, and multitudes seemed to hear a
voice saying to them: "Cut your own throat, now is a good opportunity." Strange delusions arose and spread, until common
sense once more got the upper hand.

It was an old tale, told in New England with peculiar fury. The
saddest thing in the whole affair is the part played by Edwards.
Other leaders saw the danger from the first, or were soon aroused
to it; but Edwards never, either at this time or later, wavered in
his belief that the Awakening, though marred by the devil, was in
itself the work of the Divine Spirit. His *Thoughts on the Survival
of Religion* and his *Marks of a Work of the True Spirit* are both
a thoroughgoing apology for the movement, as they are also an
important document in his own psychology. The jangling and
confusion he admits; he recognizes the elements of hysteria that
were almost inextricably mixed up with the moral exaltation of
conversion; but his defence is based frankly on the avowal that
these things are the universal accompaniments of inspiration—
they attended the founding of the church in the Apostolic age,
they were to be expected at the reinstauration of religion. Often
the reader of these treatises is struck by a curious, and by no means
accidental, resemblance between the position of Edwards and the
position of the apologists of the romantic movement in literature.
There is the same directness of appeal to the emotions; the same
laudation of expansiveness, at the cost, if need be, of judgment or
measure or any other restraint. Prudence and regularity may be
desirable in the service of God, yet it is still true that "the cry of
irregularity and imprudence" has been chiefly in the mouths of
those who are enemies to the main work of redemption. Perturbation, in truth, is not properly so called when it is the means of
rousing the cold and indifferent from their lethargy; we are bound
to suppose that not even the man "of the strongest reason and
greatest learning" can remain master of himself if "strongly impressed with a sense of divine and eternal things." And thus the

religious apologist rises into the equivalent of "Titanism": "When God is about to bring to pass something great and glorious in the world, nature is in a ferment and struggle, and the world as it were in travail." It comes in the end to this, that, notwithstanding his verbal reservations, Edwards had no critical canon to distinguish between the order and harmony governed by a power higher than the tumultuous sway of the emotions and the order and harmony that are merely stagnation.

One factor in his confidence was a belief that the discovery of America, coinciding as it did with the beginning of the Reformation, came by Providence for "the glorious renovation of the world"; nay more, that the humble town in which he was preaching might be the cradle of the new dispensation, from whence it should spread over the whole earth. His language may even seem to betray a touch of spiritual pride over the part he himself should be called upon to play as the instrument of Grace in this marvellous regeneration. That vice of the saints was indeed a subject much in his meditations, and one of the finest pieces of religious psychology in his works is the passage of the *Revival* in which he tracks it through the labyrinthine deceits of the human heart. Pride no doubt was a sin against which he had to keep particular ward in these years, but we should not say that he ever, in any proper sense of the word, lapsed from the virtue of Christian humility. If he seemed to set himself above other men as an exigent judge, this was rather due to a faulty sympathy, an inability to measure others except by the standard of his own great faculties. Thus, for all his emotionalism, he lived under the control of an iron will, and he could not comprehend how the over-stimulation of terror and joy in a weaker disposition would work moral havoc. Nor from his own constant height could he understand how brief and fitful any mood of exaltation must be among ordinary men in their ordinary condition. Hence he not only failed to see the gravity of the actual evils at the time of the Awakening, but failed also, with more grievous results for himself, to recognize the impossibility of flogging the dead emotion into new life.

The issue came on a point of church discipline. Edwards believed that religion was essentially a matter of the emotions, or affections. A man might have perfect knowledge of divine things, as indeed the devil had, but unless the love of God was implanted in his heart by the free act of Grace he had no lot with the faithful. To develop this theme he wrote his great *Treatise Concerning Religious Affections*, a work which without exaggeration may be said to go as far as the human intellect can go in the perilous path of discriminating between the purely spiritual life and the life of worldly morality. The hard kernel of the argument is stated thus:

From these things it is evident, that those gracious influences which the saints are subjects of, and the affects of God's Spirit which they experience, are entirely above nature, altogether of a different kind from any thing that men find themselves by nature, or only in the exercise of natural principles; and are things which no improvement of those qualifications, or principles that are natural, no advancing or exalting them to higher degrees, and no kind of composition of them, will ever bring men to; because they not only differ from what is natural, and from every thing that natural men experience, in degree and circumstances, but also in kind; and are of a nature vastly more excellent. And this is what I mean, by supernatural, when I say that gracious affections are from those influences that are supernatural.

From hence it follows, that in those gracious exercises and affections which are wrought in the minds of the saints, through the saving influences of the Spirit of God, there is a new inward perception or sensation of their minds, entirely different in its nature and kind. . . .

. . . And even in those things that seem to be common, there is something peculiar; both spiritual and natural love cause desires after the object beloved; but they be not the same sort of desires: there is a sensation of soul in the spiritual desires of one that loves God, which is entirely different from all natural desires: both spiritual love and natural love are attended with delight in the object beloved; but the sensations of delight are not the same, but entirely and exceedingly diverse. Natural men may have conceptions of many things about spiritual affections; but there is something in them which is as it were the nucleus, or kernel of them, that they have no more conception of, than one born blind, has of colours.

Now even this simple statement of the difference between the condition of Grace and the condition of nature is hard for the natural man to follow; but when Edwards, with the acumen of a genius and the doggedness of a scholar, imposed his distinction on all the intricate feelings of life, the natural man was dazed; and when he attempted to make it the criterion of admission to the Lord's Table, the natural man who called himself a Christian rebelled. Stoddard had thought it right to admit to communion all those who desired honestly to unite themselves with the church. Edwards protested that only those who had undergone a radical conversion and knew the affections of supernatural love should enjoy this high privilege. His congregation sided with their old guide against him.

The quarrel was further embittered by another issue. It came to light that certain young folk of the church were reading profane books which led to lewd conversations. Edwards called for public discipline of the sinners; the congregation supported him until investigation showed that the evil was widespread and would bring discredit on most of the better families of the town, and then they blocked further proceedings. If tradition is correct in naming *Pamela* as one of the guilty books, we may admire the literary taste of youthful Northampton, yet think that their pastor was justified in condemning such reading as incendiary.* However that may be, when, on the 22nd of June, 1750, a public vote was taken whether Mr. Edwards should be dismissed from his pastorate, a large majority was counted against him. Northampton has the distinction of having rejected the greatest theologian and philosopher yet produced in this country. As Socrates taunted the ancient politicians for the injuries they suffered at the hands of those they were supposed to have trained in civic virtue, so perhaps the townsmen of Edwards might retort upon any accuser that, if they failed in religious duty, it was the business of their pastor to have instructed them more effectively.

The behaviour of Edwards when the crisis actually came was simple, dignified, and even noble. His *Farewell Sermon*, with its

* [For an account of the "bad book" episode, see Ola E. Winslow, *Jonathan Edwards, 1703–1758: A Biography* (New York, Macmillan, 1940) and Perry Miller, *Jonathan Edwards* (New York, Sloane, 1949).]

dispassionate and submissive appeal from the tribunal of men to that final judgment which shall be given in knowledge and righteousness, cannot be read to-day without a deep stirring of the heart: "And let us all remember, and never forget our future solemn meeting on that great day of the Lord; the day of infallible decision, and of the everlasting and unalterable sentence. Amen."

At the age of forty-six Edwards was thrust upon the world, discredited, in broken health, with a large family to support, undaunted. Then befell a strange thing. This philosopher, whose thoughts and emotions ranged beyond the ken of most educated men, was sent to the frontier town of Stockbridge as a missionary to the Indians. There for six years he laboured faithfully and, at least in the practical management of affairs, successfully. It must have been one of the memorable sights of the world to have seen him returning on horseback from a solitary ride into the forest, while there fluttered about him, pinned to his coat, the strips of paper on which he had scribbled the results of his meditations. His days were little troubled, and not overburdened with work, peaceful it is thought; and now it was he wrote the treatise on the *Freedom of the Will* upon which his fame chiefly depends.

In 1757 his son-in-law died, and Edwards was chosen by the Trustees of the College of New Jersey to succeed him as president. Edwards hesitated, stating frankly to the Trustees his disabilities of health and learning; but finally accepted the offer. He left his family to follow him later, and arrived in Princeton in January of 1758. Small-pox was in the town and the new president was soon infected. His death took place on the 22nd of March, in the fifty-fourth year of his age. His last recorded words were: "Trust in God and ye need not fear."

The child was indeed father of the man, and it was peculiarly fitting that he who from youth upward had been absorbed in the idea of God should have died with the sacred word on his lips. But what shall be said of the fearlessness of one who had made terror the chief instrument of appeal to men and had spent his life in fighting for a dogma which the genial author* of *The One-*

* [Oliver Wendell Holmes (1809–1894).]

Hoss Shay thought no decent man could hold without going crazy?

Now the Edwardian theology was a part of the great deistic debate which took its root in the everlasting question of the origin of evil in the world. It was a three-cornered contest. The Calvinists and the infidels both believed in a kind of determinism, but differed over the nature of the determining cause. The Calvinists found this cause in a personal Creator, omnipotent and omniscient, to whom they did not scruple to carry up all the evil as well as the good of the universe—"c'est que Dieu," as Calvin himself states categorically, "non seulement a preveu la cheute du premier homme, et en icelle la ruine de toute sa posterité, mais qu'il l'a ainsi voulu."* The Deists, who at this time formed the fighting line of the infidels, while verbally acknowledging the existence of God and theorizing on the nature of evil, virtually regarded the universe as a perfectly working machine in which there was no room for a personal governor or for real sin. To the Arminians, including the bulk of the orthodox Churchmen, the alliance between Calvinism and Deism seemed altogether to outweigh the differences. As Daniel Whitby declares in the preface to his discourses *On the Five Points of Calvinism*, to hold God responsible for evil is to play directly into the hands of the atheists. And so the age-old dispute between Augustinian and Pelagian, and between Calvinist and Arminian, took on a new life from the deistic controversy, and there sprang up a literature which undertook to preserve the idea of an omnipotent personal Creator and at the same time to save His face, if the expression may be tolerated, by attributing to man complete free will and accountability for his actions. Dr. Whitby, whose discourses appeared in 1710 (reprinted in America), was a man of considerable learning but of no great metaphysical acumen, and a writer, as one of his critics said, of "disgusting tautology." His argument consists mainly in heaping up quotations from the philosophers and early Fathers, typical of which are these two, chosen with cunning application to his opponents from St. Augustine himself: "It is the height of madness and injustice to hold any person guilty because he did not that

---

* [God has not only foreseen the fall of the first man, and within the same the ruin of all his posterity, but he has also willed it.]

which he could not do," and "Who will not pronounce it folly to command him who is not free to do what is commanded?" The clear moral inference follows: God does punish men, therefore they have in themselves the power to live righteously; and God does command and exhort men, therefore their will is free to obey or disobey.

It was in answer to Whitby's book and one or two others of the kind that Edwards composed his *Freedom of the Will*. His argument has a psychological basis. In the *Treatise Concerning Religious Affections* he had divided the soul into two faculties: one the understanding, by which it discerns, views, and judges things; the other called the heart or will, being nothing else but the inclination of the soul towards, or the disinclination from, what is discerned and judged by the understanding. In the *Freedom of the Will* he starts with Locke's statement that "the Will is perfectly distinguished from Desire, which in the very same action may have a quite contrary tendency from that which our Wills set us upon." This theory Edwards analyses and rejects, and then proceeds to show that a man's desire and will are virtually the same faculty of the soul. It follows from this that the will at any moment is determined by the strongest motive acting upon the soul; we are free in so far as no obstacle is presented to our willing in accordance with our inclination, but our inclination is determined by what at any moment seems to us good. In his attack on the common arguments for the freedom of the will Edwards is magnificently victorious. If the psychology by which the Arminians sought to relieve God of the burden of evil in human life is pushed into a corner, it shows itself as nothing more than this: Man's will is a faculty absolutely indeterminate in itself and entirely independent of his inclinations. When, therefore, a man errs, it is because, the choice between evil with its attendant suffering and good with its attendant happiness being presented to him, the man, having full knowledge of the consequences and being impelled by no momentary preponderance of the one or the other from his innate disposition, deliberately and freely chooses what is evil and painful. Such an account of human action is monstrous, inconceivable; it offered an easy mark for so sharp a logician as Edwards.

But whence arise the conditions by which a man's inclination is swayed in one direction or the other? Edwards carries these unflinchingly up to the first cause, that is, as a Christian, to God. Berkeley had made the world to consist of ideas evoked in the mind of man by the mind of God; Edwards accepts the logical conclusion, and holds God responsible for the inclination of the human will which depends on these ideas. To the charge that such a theory makes God the author of evil he replies in these terms:

If, by the author of sin, is meant the permitter, or not a hinderer of sin; and, at the same time, a disposer of the state of events, in such a manner, for wise, holy, and most excellent ends and purposes, that sin, if it be permitted or not hindered, will most certainly and infallibly follow: I say, if this be all that is meant, by being the author of sin, I do not deny that God is the author of sin (though I dislike and reject the phrase, as that which by use and custom is apt to carry another sense). . . . This is not to be the actor *of sin, but, on the contrary, of holiness.*

Calvin, as we have seen, did not hesitate to attribute the source of evil to God's will in franker words than these, but at the same time he warned men against intruding with their finite reason into this "sanctuary of the divine wisdom." The mind of Edwards could not rest while any problem seemed to him unsolved. Confronted with the mystery of the divine will, he undertakes to solve it by applying his psychology of man to the nature of God. (He himself would put it the other way about: "Herein does very much consist that image of God wherein He made man.") The passage in which he most explicitly develops this thesis, though generally overlooked by his critics, is of the first importance:

We must conceive of Him as influenced in the highest degree, by that which, above all others, is properly a moral inducement, viz., the moral good which He sees in such and such things: and therefore He is, in the most proper sense, a moral Agent, the source of all moral ability and Agency, the fountain and rule of all virtue and moral good; though by reason of his being supreme over all, it is not possible He should be under the influence of law or

*command, promises or threatenings, rewards or punishments, coun-
sels or warnings. The essential qualities of a moral Agent are in
God, in the greatest possible perfection; such as understanding,
to perceive the difference between moral good and evil; a capacity
of discerning that moral worthiness and demerit, by which some
things are praiseworthy, others deserving of blame and punishment;
and also a capacity of choice, and choice guided by understanding,
and a power of acting according to his choice or pleasure, and
being capable of doing those things which are in the highest sense
praiseworthy.*

In other words, the will of God is precisely like the will of
man; it is merely the inclination, or *moral inducement,* to act as
He is *influenced* by an external power. The fatal mystery of good
and evil, the true cause, lies somewhere above and beyond Him;
He is, like ourselves, a channel, not the source. The only difference
is that God has complete knowledge of the possibilities of being,
and therefore is not moved by threats and blind commands, but
immediately, by what Edwards elsewhere calls the "moral necessity" of governing in accordance with the best of the "different
objects of choice that are proposed to the Divine Understanding."
By such a scheme God is really placed in about such a position as
in the Leibnitzian continuation of Laurentius Valla's *Dialogue on
Free Will and Providence,* where He is naïvely portrayed as looking
upon an infinite variety of worlds piled up, like cannon balls, in
pyramidal form before Him, and selecting for creation that one
which combines the greatest possible amount of good with the
least possible admixture of evil.

From this pretty sport of the imagination Edwards would no
doubt have drawn back in contempt, and, indeed, in his ordinary
language God is merely the supreme Cause, without further
speculation. One of the Leibnitzian inferences, moreover, is utterly excluded from his philosophy. He was no optimist; was in
fact the last man to infer that, because this world is the best
possible conceivable, evil is therefore a small and virtually negligible part of existence. On the contrary the whole animus of his
teaching springs from a deep and immediate hatred of evil in
itself and apart from any consideration of its cause. "The thing," he

says, "which makes sin hateful, is that by which it deserves punishment; which is but the expression of hatred. . . . Thus, for instance, ingratitude is hateful and worthy of dispraise, according to common sense; not because something as bad, or worse than ingratitude, was the cause that produced it; but because it is hateful in itself, by its own inherent deformity."

To the charge of the Arminians that the doctrine of predestination leaves no place for the punishment of sin, this is an adequate reply; but the consequences are, in another way, disastrous to the Edwardian theology. If we are right, as we indubitably are right, in detesting evil in itself and wherever seen, and if we hold with Edwards that the will of God, like the will of man, is merely the inclination towards the best object presented to its choice, and there is no power either in God or in man above the will, in what essential way, then, does the act of God in creating a world mixed with evil differ from the act of Judas in betraying God, and how are we relieved from hating God for the evil of His work with the same sort of hatred as that which we feel for Judas? Edwards had terrified the people of Enfield with a picture of God treading down sinners till their blood sprinkled His raiment, and exulting in His wrath. The retort is obvious, and unspeakable. Nor can he, or any other Predestinarian, escape the odium of such a retort by hiding behind the necessity of things which all men must, in one way or another, admit. There is a war between the nations, he will say, and suddenly a bomb, dropping upon a group of soldiers, themselves innocent of any crime, horribly rends and mangles them. Here is a hideous thing, and by no twisting of the reason can you or I avoid carrying the responsibility for this evil back to the first great cause of all. Shall I be held impious for saying metaphorically that the blood of these soldiers is sprinkled on the raiment of that Cause?—Aye, but the difference to us morally if we leave that cause in its own vast obscurity, unapproached by our reason, untouched by our pride; or if we make it into an image of ourselves, composed only of understanding and inclination like our own, and subject to our reprobation as surely as to our love!

Edwards had riddled and forever destroyed the arguments for free will commonly employed by the Arminians; is there no alternative for the human reason save submission to his theological determinism or to fatalistic atheism?

One way of escape from that dilemma is obvious and well known. It is that which Dr. Johnson, with his superb faculty of common sense, seized upon when the Edwardian doctrine came up in conversation before him. "The only relief I had was to forget it," said Boswell, who had read the book; and Johnson closed the discussion with his epigram: "All theory is against the freedom of the will, all experience for it." That is sufficient, no doubt, for the conduct of life; yet there is perhaps another way of escape, which, if it does not entirely silence the metaphysical difficulties, at least gives them a new ethical turn. Twice in the course of his argument Edwards refers to an unnamed Arminian[1] who placed the liberty of the soul not in the will itself, but in some power of suspending volition until due time has elapsed for judging properly the various motives to action. His reply is that this suspension of activity, being itself an act of volition, merely throws back, without annulling, the difficulty; and as the argument came to him, this refutation is fairly complete. But a fuller consideration of the point at issue might possibly indicate a way out of the dilemma of free will and determinism into a morally satisfying form of dualism within the soul of man himself. At least it can be said that the looseness of the Arminian reasoning leaves an easier loophole of escape into a human philosophy than does the rigid logic of the Predestinarians.

Yet for all that, though we may follow Edward's logical system to the breaking point, as we can follow every metaphysical system, and though we may feel that, in his revulsion from the optimism of the Deists, he distorted the actual evil of existence into a nightmare of the imagination,—yet for all that, he remains one of the giants of the intellect and one of the enduring masters of religious emotion. He had not the legal and executive brain of Calvin, upon whose *Institutes* his scheme of

[1] Edwards, it should seem, had immediately in mind the *Essay on the Freedom of Will in God and the Creature* of Isaac Watts; but the notion had been discussed at length by Locke (*Essay* II, xxi), and at an earlier date had been touched on with great acumen by John Norris in his correspondence with Henry More.

51

theology is manifestly based, but in subtle resourcefulness of reasoning and still more in the scope of his spiritual insight he stands, I think, above his predecessor. Few men have studied Edwards without recognizing the force and honesty of his genius. To Hazlitt he ranked with Hobbes, Berkeley, Butler, Hartley, Hume, and Leibnitz as a metaphysician. To Crabb Robinson the reading of his book on *Original Sin*, in early youth, was "an irreparable mischief." Let us take our leave of him with one of his more gracious meditations impressed on our memory:

All the truly great and good, all the pure and holy and excellent from this world, and it may be from every part of the universe, are constantly tending toward heaven. As the streams tend to the ocean, so all these are tending to the great ocean of infinite purity and bliss.

Benjamin Franklin

There is a certain embarrassment in dealing with Franklin as a man of letters, for the simple reason that he was never, in the strict sense of the word, concerned with letters at all.[1] He lived in an age of writers, and of writing he did his full share; but one cannot go through the ten volumes of his collected works, or the three volumes of the admirable new edition now printing under the care of Mr. Smyth,[2] without feeling the presence of an intellect enormously energetic, but directed to practical rather than literary ends. Were it not for the consummate ease with which his mind moved, there would indeed be something oppressive in this display of unresting energy. Politics, religion, ethics, science, agriculture, navigation, hygiene, the mechanical arts, journalism, music, education—in all these fields he was almost equally at home, and every subject came from under his touch simplified and enlarged; on his tomb might have been engraved the epitaph, *Nullum quod tetigit non renovavit.** He had perhaps the most clarifying and renovating intellect of that keenly alert age, and to know his writings is to be familiar with half the activities of the eighteenth century. Yet his pen still lacked that final spell which transmutes life into literature. He was ever

---

From *Shelburne Essays*, Fourth Series (Boston and New York, Houghton Mifflin Company, 1906), pp. 129–55.

[1] In celebration of Franklin's Bicentenary, January 17, 1906, the *Independent* printed a number of papers on the various aspects of his activity. The subject allotted to me was *Franklin in Literature*.

[2] *The Writings of Benjamin Franklin*. Collected and Edited, with a Life and Introduction, by Albert Henry Smyth. 10 vols. (Three only were published at this date.) New York: The Macmillan Co., 1905–6. The text is here amended much for the better. But an undue squeamishness has led the editor to omit writings important for a right knowledge of Franklin, and the notes are unsatisfactory.

* [Nothing which he touched did he fail to improve.]

engaged in enforcing a present lesson or producing an immediate result, and his busy brain could not pause long enough to listen to those hidden powers that all the while murmur in remote voices the symbolic meaning of the puppets and the puppet-actions of this world. Like his contemporary Voltaire, and to a far higher degree, his personality was greater than any separate production of his brain. And so, as the real charm of Voltaire is most felt in the Correspondence, where there is no attempt to escape from his own personal interests, in the same way the better approach to Franklin's works is through the selected edition so arranged by Mr. Bigelow as to form a continuous and familiar narrative of his life.[3]

But something is still wanting. Franklin the man is so much larger than Franklin the writer that, like his other contemporary, Dr. Johnson, he needs a Boswell to give him his true place in literature. Some indication of what such a work might be we have in Parton's solid and self-respecting volumes.[4] Here the practical achievements of the man, the supreme versatility of his mind, his dominance over the world, and his own powers of expression are so brought together as to create a figure almost comparable to the great personalities that arise from the memoirs of Boswell and Lockhart and Froude. But Parton laboured under certain disabilities. He had, in the first place, to proceed from a very imperfect edition of Franklin's writings, which did not even include a good text of the Autobiography; and he lacked something of the finished literary skill and psychological insight required for his task. His Life is, I venture to say, despite certain misapprehensions of Franklin's character, the most interesting work of its kind yet produced in this country, vastly superior to the mutilated lives of Franklin that have since been turned out for flighty readers, but it still leaves room for a book which might be a possession forever, an honour to American letters. And I have in mind at least one of our younger historians who could thus, if his other

[3] *The Life of Benjamin Franklin, Written by Himself.* By John Bigelow. 3 vols. Philadelphia: J. B. Lippincott Co. Fifth Edition, 1905.
[4] *Life and Times of Benjamin Franklin.* By James Parton. 2 vols. Boston: Houghton Mifflin Co., 1897. (First published 1864.)

BENJAMIN FRANKLIN

self-imposed tasks did not prevent, enroll his name among the memorable biographers.[5]

For Franklin would meet such a biographer more than half way. Whether from some histrionic instinct in his own nature, or from some secret sympathy between his individual will and the forces that play upon mankind, the supreme moments of his career follow one another like the artificial tableaux of a drama. As a man of science his prime achievement was to discover the identity of lightning and the electric fluid. *Eripuit cælo fulmen sceptrumque tyrannis,** wrote Turgot of that famous event, having in mind the tyrant superstitions of both heaven and earth; and it is peculiarly appropriate that this step in what may be called the secularisation of celestial phenomena should have come from the champion of political liberty. Who was better fitted than this prophet of common sense to give an answer to Virgil's question:

An te, genitor, cum fulmina torques,
Nequiquam horremus, cæcique in nubibus ignes
Terrificant animos et inania murmura miscent?****

Not from himself but from others comes the story of his dramatic experiment. The time is a day in June of 1752, when a thunderstorm is threatening. The scene is in the purlieus of Philadelphia. Thither Franklin and his son, fearing the ridicule of their neighbours, steal out unobserved. There they send up a silk kite constructed for the purpose and then seek the shelter of an open abandoned cowshed. The cord of the kite, except the end of non-conducting silk which they hold in their hands, is hempen, and will become, when wet, an excellent conductor. At the juncture of the hemp and the silk is a metal key, which is connected with a Leyden jar. The storm breaks and a thunder-cloud passes directly over the kite, but still there is no sign of electricity. The

[5] As certain humorous critics have intimated that only modesty prevented the naming of this gentleman, I may say that I had in mind Mr. William Garrott Brown.

* [He seized thunder from the sky and the scepter from the tyrants.]

** [Are we afraid in vain, O Father, on whom you cast the lightning, and do blind fires in the clouds terrify our minds and produce empty murmurs?]

philosopher is in despair and begins to fear that the fine theories he has spread abroad will end in mockery, when, suddenly, the fibres of the hempen cord stand on end. He applies his knuckle to the key, feels the customary shock, and knows that he can justify himself in the eyes of Europe.

Even more striking, if less picturesque, is the scene which may stand as the climax of his long struggle to preserve the union of England and the colonies. It happened in 1774, when he was in London as Commissioner for Pennsylvania and Massachusetts, and when the feeling of irritation on both sides was at the fever point. A friendly member of Parliament had put into Franklin's hands certain letters in which Governor Hutchinson, of Massachusetts, though a native-born American, had urged the most exasperating measures of oppression against the colonies. These letters Franklin, by permission, had transmitted to Boston, where they naturally raised a tempest of indignation. Complications ensued in London, a fatal duel was fought, and Franklin, though his part in the affair was perfectly honourable, had given an occasion to his enemies for abusive defamation. And they did not miss the opportunity. A petition had been laid before the Privy Council to remove Governor Hutchinson, and Franklin was summoned to meet that exalted body in the so-called Cockpit. "All the courtiers," Franklin wrote home afterward, "were invited, as to an entertainment, and there never was such an appearance of Privy Councillors on any occasion, not less than thirty-five, besides an immense crowd of other auditors. . . . The Solicitor-General [Mr. Wedderburn] then went into what he called a history of the province for the last ten years, and bestowed plenty of abuse upon it, mingled with encomium on the governors. But the favourite part of his discourse was levelled at your agent, who stood there the butt of his invective ribaldry for near an hour, not a single Lord adverting to the impropriety and indecency of treating a public messenger in so ignominious a manner. . . . If he had done a wrong, in obtaining and transmitting the letters, that was not the tribunal where he was to be accused and tried. The cause was already before the Chancellor. Not one of their Lordships checked and recalled the orator to the business before them, but, on the contrary, a very few excepted, they seemed to enjoy highly the entertainment, and frequently burst out in loud applause.

This part of his speech was thought so good, that they have since
printed it, in order to defame me everywhere, and particularly to
destroy my reputation on your side of the water; but the grosser
parts of the abuse are omitted, appearing, I suppose, in their
own eyes, too foul to be seen on paper." It would be interesting
to know what the Council thought worthy of expunge. As printed,
the speech of Wedderburn was sufficiently vituperative, one would
think:

*I hope, my Lords, he exclaimed, with thundering voice and
vehement beating of his fist on the cushion before him—I hope,
my Lords, you will mark and brand the man, for the honour of
this country, of Europe, and of mankind. . . . He has forfeited
all the respect of societies and of men. Into what companies will
he hereafter go with an unembarrassed face, or the honest in-
trepidity of virtue? Men will watch him with a jealous eye; they
will hide their papers from him, and lock up their escritoirs. He
will henceforth esteem it a libel to be called* a man of letters; homo
trium literarum *(i.e., fur, thief!). . . . He not only took away the
letters of one brother; but kept himself concealed till he nearly
occasioned the murder of the other. It is impossible to read his
account, expressive of the coolest and most deliberate malice,
without horror. . . . Amidst these tragical events, of one person
nearly murdered, of another answerable for the issue, of a worthy
governor hurt in his dearest interests, the fate of America in
suspense; here is a man who, with the utmost insensibility of
remorse, stands up and vows himself the author of all. I can compare it only to Zanga, in Dr. Young's Revenge:*

> "Know then 't was —————— I.
> I forged the letters—I disposed the picture—
> I hated, I despised, and I destroy."

*I ask, my Lords, whether the revengeful temper attributed, by
poetic fiction only, to the bloody African is not surpassed by the
coolness and apathy of the wily American?*

The scene is dramatic in the extreme—the vociferous, malignant
accuser, the lords gloating over their victim, nodding approval
to the bully and breaking out into laughter when the slander

57

was most virulent; and Franklin, all the while standing at one end of the room in the recess by the chimney, erect, motionless, with countenance, so an eyewitness described it, as unchangeable as if carved out of wood. He would seem almost to have had in view the vicissitudes of his own life, when years before, as a young man, he had written his character of "Cato" for the *Weekly Mercury:* "His aspect is sweetened with humanity and benevolence, and at the same time emboldened with resolution, equally free from a diffident bashfulness and an unbecoming assurance. The consciousness of his own innate worth and unshaken integrity renders him calm and undaunted in the presence of the most great and powerful, and upon the most extraordinary occasions." But Franklin had his malicious side. In the Cockpit he wore, we are told, a full dress-suit of spotted Manchester velvet. On a memorable day, just four years later, when the treaty with France was to be signed, he took pains to appear in the same conspicuous garb—he was ever a humourist, this *wily American!* For the rest, the epigram of Horace Walpole is sufficiently well known:

> Sarcastic Sawney, swol'n with spite and prate,
> On silent Franklin poured his venal hate.
> The calm philosopher, without reply,
> Withdrew, and gave his country liberty.

Franklin, I believe, never met Dr. Johnson; and this is a pity, for the clash between the dictator's burly insolence and Franklin's irresistible wit would have furnished an unforgettable pendant to the ignominy of the Cockpit. He was, however, brought face to face with the only other personality entirely of that age which was comparable to his own. In 1778 Voltaire, an old man tottering to the grave, revisited Paris to accept the homage of the city, and to die. The American envoys were received in his chamber, and there the patriarch of the terrible new faith that was permeating society pronounced a solemn blessing upon the representative of the rising generation. "When I gave my benediction," he wrote a few days later, "to the grandson of the sage and illustrious Franklin, the most honourable man of America, I spoke only

these words, *God and Liberty!* All who were present shed tears."
But the petted spokesmen of the century were to meet on a more
eminent stage and in a more noteworthy scene. At a public session
of the Academy of Sciences the two "philosophers" sat together
on the platform, the lodestone of all eyes. What happened can
best be related in the words of John Adams, a curious and jealous
observer:

*Voltaire and Franklin were both present, and there presently
arose a general cry that M. Voltaire and M. Franklin should be
introduced to each other. This was done, and they bowed and
spoke to each other. This was no satisfaction; there must be
something more. Neither of our philosophers seemed to divine
what was wished or expected. They, however, took each other by
the hand; but this was not enough. The clamour continued until
the exclamation came out, "Il faut s'embrasser à la Française!"
The two aged actors upon this great theatre of philosophy and
frivolity then embraced each other by hugging one another in their
arms and kissing each other's cheeks, and then the tumult sub-
sided. And the cry immediately spread throughout the kingdom,
and I suppose over all Europe, "Qu'il était charmant de voir
embrasser Solon et Sophocle!"*

This great theatre of philosophy and frivolity! Dear sir, it is the
world of the eighteenth century you are naming so petulantly,
the stage on which you are yourself playing a lesser but no mean
part. Nor would it be easy to find a tableau more strikingly significant of the powers that had already given freedom to America and
were soon to set France and all Europe ablaze. It might seem as
if the Dæmon of history had chosen Franklin to be the protagonist
in the successive acts of that drama of mingled tragedy and comedy
wherein the people of the nations were shuffled about as super-
numeraries.

Other scenes might be quoted as minor episodes in that
stupendous drama—the presentation of Franklin to his Majesty
Louis XVI., when Franklin's wig played so comical a part; the
receipt of the news of Burgoyne's surrender; and, long before
these, the interrogation of Franklin before the British Parliament.
For the last and most beautiful scene we must pass on to another

59

parliament which was sitting in a far less sumptuous hall. It was in September of 1787, and the Convention of the States at Philadelphia had, after long uncertainties, drafted the Constitution which was to justify and make perpetual the labours of which Franklin had borne so heavy a share. The story is related by Madison that, while "the last members were signing, Dr. Franklin, looking toward the president's chair, at the back of which a rising sun happened to be painted, observed to a few members near him that painters had found it difficult to distinguish in their art a rising from a setting sun. 'I have,' he said, 'often and often, in the course of the session, and the vicissitudes of my hopes and fears as to its issue, looked at that behind the president, without being able to tell whether it was rising or setting; but now, at length, I have the happiness to know that it is a rising and not a setting sun.'" So it was the venerable man pronounced upon the work of his generation and saluted those who were about to take up the burden.

Franklin was not precisely a man of letters, yet his life is almost literature, and out of it might be made one of the great books. Not only do the salient events of his career take on this dramatic form which is already a kind of literary expression, but he goes further than that and leaves the task of the biographer half done, by using language as one of his chief instruments of activity. Even the sallies of his wit were a power, often consciously used, in the practical world. So in Paris, during the dark days of the war, a well-placed jest here and there was surprisingly effective in keeping up the confidence of our French friends. When some one told him that Howe had taken Philadelphia, he was ready with the retort: "I beg your pardon, sir, Philadelphia has taken Howe." And again when the story of another defeat was disseminated by the British Ambassador, and Franklin was asked if it were true, he replied: "No, monsieur, it is not a truth; it is only a Stormont." And throughout Paris a "stormont" passed for a lie. At another time some one accused the Americans of cowardice for firing from behind the stone walls of Lexington: "Sir," said Franklin, "I beg to inquire if those same walls had not two sides to them?" Best known of all is his pun, bravest of all puns, in the Continental Congress when there was hesitation over signing the Declaration of Independence. "We must be unanimous," said

Hancock; "there must be no pulling different ways; we must all hang together." "Yes," added Franklin, "we must, indeed, all hang together, or, most assuredly, we shall all hang separately."

But his pen was as ready a servant as his tongue, and how diligently he trained himself to this end every reader of the Autobiography knows. From childhood he was an eager and critical student, and few pages of his memoirs are written with more warmth of recollection than those which tell of the books he contrived to buy, Bunyan's works first of all. He seems to think that the *Spectator* had the predominating influence on his style, and apparently he was still under sixteen when an odd volume of that work set him to studying systematically. His method was to read one of the essays and then after a number of days to rewrite it from a few written hints, striving to make his own language as correct and elegant as the original; or, again, he turned an essay into verse and back again into prose from memory. "I also," he adds, "sometimes jumbled my collections of hints into confusion, and after some weeks endeavoured to reduce them into the best order, before I began to form the full sentences and complete the paper. This was to teach me method in the arrangement of thoughts. By comparing my work afterwards, with the original, I discovered many faults and amended them; but I sometimes had the pleasure of fancying that, in certain particulars of small import, I had been lucky enough to improve the method or the language, and this encouraged me to think I might possibly in time come to be a tolerable English writer, of which I was extremely ambitious." His method—on the whole one of the best of disciplines, better, I think, than the system of themes now employed in our colleges—could scarcely have been anything for Franklin save a precocious discovery, although it had, of course, been used long before his day. Cicero tells how the orator Crassus had begun to form himself on a plan not essentially different, but turned from this to the more approved exercise of converting the Greek writers into equivalent Latin. *Vertere Græca in Latinum veteres nostri oratores optimum judicabant,** said Quintilian; and Franklin's language would have gained in richness if he, too, had

* [Our orators of old considered it best to turn Greek works into Latin.]

proceeded a step further and undergone the discipline of comparing his English with the classics.[6] As it is, he made himself one of the masters of that special style of the eighteenth century which concealed a good deal of art under apparent, even obtrusive, negligences. He professed to model himself on Addison, but his language is really closer to the untrimmed and vigorous sentences of Defoe. And in spirit his actual affinity is more with Swift than with the *Spectator;* or, rather, he lies between the two, with something harsher than the suave impertinence of Addison yet without the terrible savagery of the Dean. In particular he affected Swift's two weapons of irony and the hoax, and, if he did not quite make literature with them, he at least made history, which his predecessor could not do. Sometimes he was content to borrow an invention bodily—" 'convey,' the wise it call"—as when he badgered a rival almanac maker by foretelling the date of his death and then calmly proving the truth of the prophecy out of the poor fellow's angry protestations. And entirely in the vein of Swift, if not so palpably stolen, are a number of his political pamphlets, notably, in the way of irony, the *Rules for Reducing a Great Empire to a Small One.* As for his hoaxes they were innumerable and astonishingly successful. They all point back to the incorrigible Dean of St. Patrick's, although one of the most famous of them was probably suggested by Walpole's fictitious letter of Frederick the Great, which drove Rousseau one stage further into lunacy. To expose the hollowness of Great Britain's claim to

[6] That venerable schoolmaster, Roger Ascham, had his way of elaborating this method: "First, let him teach the childe, cherefullie and plainlie, the cause, and matter of the letter [of Cicero's]: then, let him construe it into Englishe, so oft, as the childe may easilie carie awaie the vnderstanding of it: Lastlie, parse it ouer perfitlie. This done thus, let the childe, by and by, both construe and parse it ouer againe: so, that it may appeare, that the childe douteth in nothing, that his master taught him before. After this, the childe must take a paper booke, and sitting in some place, where no man shall prompe him, by him self, let him translate into Englishe his former lesson. Then shewing it to his master, let the master take from him his latin booke, and pausing an houre, at the least, than let the childe translate his owne Englishe into latin againe, in an other paper booke. When the childe bringeth it, turned into latin, the master must compare it with *Tullies* booke, and laie them both togither.

absolute ownership of America because that country had been colonised by Englishmen, Franklin took advantage of the ancient German settlement of England and published a so-called *Edict of the King of Prussia*. The result he tells in a letter to his son (October 6, 1773):

What made it the more noticed here was, that people in reading it were, as the phrase is, taken in, till they had got half through it, and imagined it a real edict, to which mistake I suppose the King of Prussia's character must have contributed. I was down at Lord Le Despencer's, when the post brought that day's papers. Mr. Whitehead was there, too [Paul Whitehead, the author of Manners], *who runs early through all the papers, and tells the company what he finds remarkable. He had them in another room, and we were chatting in the breakfast parlour, when he came running in to us, out of breath, with the paper in his hand. Here! says he, here's news for ye! Here's the King of Prussia, claiming a right to this kingdom! All stared, and I as much as anybody; and he went on to read it. When he had read two or three paragraphs, a gentleman present said, Damn his impudence, I dare say we shall hear by next post that he is upon his march with one hundred thousand men to back this. Whitehead, who is very shrewd, soon after began to smoke it, and looking in my face, said, I'll be hanged if this is not some of your American jokes upon us. The reading went on, and ended with abundance of laughing, and a general verdict that it was a fair hit: and the piece was cut out of the paper and preserved in my Lord's collection.*

Other hoaxes were not so readily detected, and have even crept into sober history and criticism. There is the notorious *Speech of Polly Baker*, which the Abbé Raynal quoted to illustrate a point of law in his *Histoire des Deux Indes*, and which he refused to expunge when informed of its source. "Very well, Doctor," said he with perfect nonchalance; "I had rather relate your stories than other men's truths." And there is the no less notorious proposal for a *New Version of the Bible*, in which Franklin, under the plea of modernising the text, altered the first six verses of Job into a satire on monarchical government. The solemn comment of

Matthew Arnold on the passage is a delightful piece of unconscious humour:

> *I remember the relief with which, after long feeling the sway*
> *of Franklin's imperturbable common sense, I came upon a project*
> *of his for a new version of the Book of Job, to replace the old*
> *version, the style of which, says Franklin, has become obsolete and*
> *thence less agreeable. "I give," he continues, "a few verses, which*
> *may serve as a sample of the kind of version I would recommend."*
> *We all recollect the famous verse in our translation: "Then Satan*
> *answered the Lord, and said, Doth Job fear God for naught?"*
> *Franklin makes this: "Does your Majesty imagine that Job's good*
> *conduct is the effect of mere personal attachment and affection?"*
> *I well remember how, when I first read that, I drew a deep breath*
> *of relief, and said to myself, "After all, there is a stretch of hu-*
> *manity beyond Franklin's victorious good sense."*

Alas for the proud wit of man! These stumblings of a great critic
may be a lesson in humility for us, the children of a later day.
And after all, to use his own phrase, it was only a slight misplace-
ment of sarcasm; he did not mean Franklin's merry skit, but was
speaking, prophetically, of that pretentious humbug, the *Revised
Version*.

Later in life, especially during his stay in Paris, Franklin's satire
became even mellower, and he took up again a form of writing in
which he had early excelled. This was the *Bagatelle*, as he called
it, the little apologue written in the lightest vein, yet containing
often the very heart of his genial philosophy. Such were the
*Epitaph on Miss Shipley's Squirrel, The Ephemera, The Whistle,
The Handsome and Deformed Leg*, and the *Dialogue between
Franklin and the Gout*, to name no others. How neatly turned
they all are, how wise and gracious and tender; how they show
what was lost to pure literature by the exigencies of his busy life.
I cannot pass on without quoting the least of these, the letter
to a young friend *On the Loss of Her American Squirrel*. It belongs with that long list of poems and epitaphs, half playful and
half pathetic, on the pets of dear women, beginning with Lesbia's
sparrow:

I lament with you most sincerely the unfortunate end of poor Mungo. Few squirrels were better accomplished, for he had a good education, travelled far, and seen much of the world. As he had the honour of being, for his virtues, your favourite, he should not go, like common Skuggs, without an elegy or an epitaph. Let us give him one in the monumental style and measure, which, being neither prose, nor verse, is perhaps the properest for grief; since to use common language would look as if we were not affected, and to make rhymes would seem trifling in sorrow.

EPITAPH
Alas! poor Mungo!
Happy wert thou, hadst thou known
Thy own felicity.
Remote from the fierce bald eagle,
Tyrant of thy native woods,
Thou hadst naught to fear from his piercing talons,
Nor from the murdering gun,
Of the thoughtless sportsman.

Safe in thy wired castle,
Grimalkin never could annoy thee.
Daily wert thou fed with the choicest viands,
By the fair hand of an indulgent mistress;
But, discontented,
Thou wouldst have more freedom.
Too soon, alas! didst thou obtain it;
And wandering,

Thou art fallen by the fangs of wanton, cruel
Ranger!
Learn hence,
Ye who blindly seek more liberty,
Whether subjects, sons, squirrels, or daughters,
That apparent restraint may be real protection,
Yielding peace and plenty
With security.

You see, my dear miss, how much more decent and proper this broken style is than if we were to say by way of epitaph—

Here Skugg
Lies snug
As a bug
In a rug.

And yet, perhaps, there are people in the world of so little feeling as to think that this would be a good enough epitaph for poor Mungo.

So it is that speech and action blend together inextricably to form this fascinating literary figure. He moves through the whole length of the eighteenth century, serene and self-possessed, a philosopher and statesman yet a fellow of infinite jest, a shrewd economist yet capable of the tenderest generosities. There was a large admixture of earth in the image, no doubt. His wit was often coarse, if not obscene, and, as his latest editor observes, leaves a long "smudgy trail" behind it. Not a little that he wrote and that still exists in manuscript is too rank to be printed. One might wish all this away, and yet I do not know; somehow the thought of that big animal body completes our impression of the overflowing bountifulness of his nature. If wishing were having, I would choose rather that he had not made of his Autobiography so singular a document in petty prudence and economy. Nothing in that record is more typical than the remark on his habit of bringing home the paper he purchased through the streets on a wheelbarrow—"to show," he adds, "that I was not above my business." And for economy, one remembers his visit to the old lady in London who lived as a religious recluse, and his comment: "She looked pale, but was never sick; and I give it as another instance on how small an income life and health may be supported." Possibly the character of his memoirs would have changed if he had continued them into his later years; but I am inclined rather to think that the discrepancy between the breadth of his activities and the narrowness of his professed ideals would have become still more evident by such an extension. The truth is they only exaggerate a real deficiency in his character; there was, after all, a stretch of humanity beyond Franklin's victorious good sense.

We feel this chiefly in his religious convictions; it is pressed upon us by contrast with the only other American who was intellectually his peer, Jonathan Edwards. The world in which Franklin moved lay beneath a clear, white light, without shadow of concealment, with nothing to cloud the sincerity and keenness of his vision; but far beyond, in the dim penumbra, loomed that other world of his contemporary—a region into whose treacherous obscurities those must venture who seek the comforts and sweet ecstasies of faith, and who find these at times, and at times, also, drink in only strange exhalations of deceit and vapours of spiritual pride. As often as Franklin's path approached that misty shore he drew back as from a bottomless pit. Like other men of his century, he had built up for himself his own private religion, from which the vague inherited emotions of the past were to be utterly excluded. The little book that contains his formulated creed and liturgy may still be read, an extraordinary document in the history of deism. The remarkable point in it is the frankly pagan way in which he relegates the Infinite God to realms beyond our concern, and selects for worship "that particular wise and good God who is the author and owner of our system." Even more remarkable is the *great and extensive project,* divulged in the Autobiography, of creating throughout the world a kind of religious Freemasonry, to be initiated into his own doctrines and to be called *The Society of the Free and Easy*—"free, as being, by the general practice and habit of the virtues, free from the dominion of vice; and particularly by the practice of industry and frugality, free from debt, which exposes a man to confinement, and a species of slavery to his creditors." Who can read this without recalling Lamb's panegyric of the *great race* of borrowers and fearing that he has "fallen into the society of *lenders* and *little men*"?

The same practical views of religion may be traced through many of Franklin's familiar letters. Sometimes they combine with his humour to form a kind of benevolent worldly wisdom, as in this letter to his sister Jane, with its mock exegesis of some religious verses written long ago by an uncle:

In a little book he sent her, called "None but Christ," he wrote an acrostic on her name, which for namesake's sake, as well as the good advice it contains, I transcribe and send you, viz.

"Illuminated from on high,
And shining brightly in your sphere,
Ne'er faint, but keep a steady eye,
Expecting endless pleasures there.

"Flee vice as you'd a serpent flee;
Raise *faith* and *hope* three stories higher,
And let Christ's endless love to thee
Ne'er cease to make thy love aspire.
Kindness of heart by words express,
Let your obedience be sincere,
In prayer and praise your God address,
Nor cease, till he can cease to hear."

. . . *You are to understand, then, that* faith, hope, *and* charity *have been called the three steps of Jacob's ladder, reaching from earth to heaven; our author calls them stories, likening religion to a building, and these are the three stories of the Christian edifice. Thus improvement in religion is called building up and edification. Faith is then the ground floor, hope is up one pair of stairs. My dear beloved Jenny, don't delight so much to dwell in those lower rooms, but get as fast as you can into the garret, for in truth the best room in the house is charity. For my part, I wish the house was turned upside down; 't is so difficult (when one is fat) to go up stairs; and not only so, but I imagine hope and faith may be more firmly built upon charity, than charity upon faith and hope. However that may be, I think it the better reading to say—*

"Raise faith and hope one story higher."

Correct it boldly, and I'll support the alteration; for, when you are up two stories already, if you raise your building three stories higher you will make five in all, which is two more than there should be, you expose your upper rooms more to the winds and storms; and, besides, I am afraid the foundation will hardly bear them, unless indeed you build with such light stuff as straw and stubble, and that, you know, won't stand fire.

In the end one feels that both in Franklin's strength and his limitations, in the versatility and efficiency of his intellect as in the lack of the deeper qualities of the imagination, he was the typical American. If his victorious common sense excluded that thin vein of mysticism which is one of the paradoxes of our national character, he represents the powers that have prevailed and are still shaping us to what end we do not see. In particular one cannot read far in his letters without noting the predominance of that essentially American trait—contemporaneity. One gets the impression that here was almost, if not quite, the most alert and most capacious intellect that ever concerned itself entirely with the present. He was, of course, an exemplar of prudence, and thus in a way had his eye on the immediate future; but it was the demands of the present that really interested him, and the possession of the past, the long backward of time, was to him a mere oblivion.

Parton regarded Franklin as the model Christian, others find no religion in him at all. Their views depend on how they are affected by his absorption in the present, by his relegation of Faith and Hope to the attic and his choice of earth-born Charity. There is, in fact, no more extraordinary chapter in the religious history of the eighteenth century than the episode of the Autobiography which tells how Franklin deliberately set aside all the traditions and experience of the past and set himself to create a brand-new worship of his own, adapted to the needs of the hour. Was this prophetic of our cheerful readiness, long ago observed by Renan, to start a new religion among us every time a man is convicted of sin? Are Christian Science and all the lesser brood merely in the line of Franklin's projected brotherhood of "The Free and Easy"? Some of the more modern sects seem at least to have taken to themselves that society's virtue of "industry," and have made themselves "free of debt."

And it was this overmastering sense of the present that coloured Franklin's schemes of education. Everything should be practical, and look to immediate results. Naturally the Classics, as the very embodiment of the past, received scant sympathy from him. He merely tolerated them in the project which led to the Philadelphia Academy and the University of Pennsylvania, and one of his last pamphlets, written, indeed, from his death-bed, was a diatribe against Greek and Latin.

As a writer he has all the clearness, force, and flexibility that come from attention to what is near at hand; he lacks also that depth of background which we call imagination, and which is largely the indwelling of the past in the present. A clear, steady light rests upon his works; no obscuring shadow stretches out over them from remote days, and also no shade inviting to repose. It is not by accident that his two most literary productions, in the stricter sense of that word, are the Autobiography, which might be called a long lesson in the method of settling problems of immediate necessity, and the Introductions to the Almanacs— those documents in contemporaneity that have so strangely weathered the years. Particularly the Introduction of 1757, known as the *Harangue of Father Abraham*, has been translated into all the languages of the world, and has almost made of Poor Richard a figure of popular mythology:

I found the good man had thoroughly studied my almanacs and digested all I had dropped on these topics during the course of five and twenty years. The frequent mention he made of me must have tired any one else; but my vanity was wonderfully delighted with it, though I was conscious that not a tenth part of the wisdom was my own, which he ascribed to me, but rather the gleanings that I had made of the sense of all ages and nations.

And the sense of all ages is pretty well summed up by Poor Richard in "One to-day is worth two to-morrows."

Philip Freneau

It is a somewhat disturbing thought that the laborious publications most prized by scholars are just those which are likely to deprive an author of a real public. To take recent examples, there is Mrs. Paget Toynbee's superb Walpole in sixteen volumes, the Hazlitt in twelve, the Thoreau in twenty. How many of those who stand between the haphazard and the professional reader, thinking they must have the best, will, if they can afford it, buy the bulky Hazlitt, will scan its pages, packed with ephemeral salvage, place it on a shelf, and never again take it down? They would actually read the old Bohn edition, in its seven comfortable volumes. And this new Freneau[1] will, I fear, suffer the same fate, with the additional drawback that no popular selection of his works is available. I would not appear ungrateful: these elaborate editions are highly desirable, highly useful; but why does not some enterprising publisher give us also the books that we most urgently want—a selected library, for instance, of the literature of the American Revolution. Six or eight compact, uniform volumes, well printed, judiciously annotated, would suffice. One volume might contain the important political speeches of the day, another the more interesting familiar letters, another a taste of the Tory poets. Of single authors, two of Huguenot descent would necessarily be included: Crèvecœur, who represents the moderate party, crushed between the fanatics of both extremes, and whose charming *Letters from an American Farmer*

From *Shelburne Essays*, Fifth Series (Boston and New York, Houghton Mifflin Company, 1908), pp. 86–105.

[1] *The Poems of Philip Freneau, Poet of the American Revolution.* Edited for the Princeton Historical Association by Fred Lewis Pattee. 3 vols. Princeton: The University Library, 1902–7.

were brought out the other day in an excellent reprint[2]; and
Freneau, the shrill spokesman of the ultra-Democrats. Two volumes might well be set apart for Freneau, one for a selection of
his prose and his political poems, the other for his lyrical and
humorous pieces; they would afford a richer mine of reading than
is commonly supposed, and would offer a document of rare historic value.

It has been pointed out more than once that Freneau was a
half-hearted pioneer in that "misty mid region of Weir," from
which Poe, later on, was to bring back such astounding reports.
An idle fancy might even look for a parallel in the circumstances
of their frustrated ambitions, and might stop to compare the
death of Poe with that of the older poet, who wandered one
night into a bog on his way home and was found the next day
dying of exposure—intoxicated, it was rumoured, although that
ugly tradition is denied. Freneau, it need not be said, suffered
from no such disabilities of the flesh as Poe, and the only point
of the comparison would lie in the tragedy of their genius hemmed
in on every side by prosaic surroundings. The later poet, at least,
"amid wreck and sorrow," knew the solace of perfect expression,
whereas the continual complaint of Freneau is that his faculty of
song has been baffled by lack of sympathy. If there is anything
real in the years that follow a man's death, Freneau's was the
harder fate. Not a little of his best prose and verse was contributed
to the *United States Magazine*, a monthly of Philadelphia, which
ran through the year 1779, and then, like so many of the periodi-
cals on which Poe was to lavish his powers, came to a full stop.
A large class of Americans, said the editor in his valedictory,
"inhabit the region of stupidity, and cannot bear to have the
tranquillity of their repose disturbed by the villainous shock
of a book. Reading is to them the worst of all torments, and I
remember very well that at the commencement of the work it
was their language, 'Art thou come to torment us before the
time?' We will now say to them, 'Sleep on and take your rest.'"
And Freneau himself in his verse never misses an opportunity of

[2] *Letters from an American Farmer*. By J. Hector St. John Crèvecœur.
With a Prefatory Note by W. P. Trent, and an Introduction by Ludwig
Lewisohn. New York: Fox, Duffield, & Co., 1904.

girding at the unimaginative age and people into which he was born.

"Before the time" might be taken as the text of Freneau's life. His family was of Huguenot descent, his grandfather having emigrated to New York in 1707. When Philip was born, in 1752, they were prosperous merchants in this city, with something of an estate in New Jersey. In his sixteenth year he went to Princeton, then under the able management of President Witherspoon. In the same class with him was James Madison, whose friendship he retained through life, while just below him were William Bradford and Aaron Burr. Poetry and politics were in the air, and Freneau got his first taste of satire in the rhyming contests between the Whig and Cliosophic societies, which were founded in his sophomore and junior years. Miniature epics, too, such as *The History of the Prophet Jonah*, and solemn dialogues, such as *The Pyramids of Egypt*, with the Horatian *Debemur morti, nos nostraque** duly inscribed above, were not beyond his aspiration in those years, and were printed in the later collections of his works. They are really not so dull as might be supposed. We may smile at the old-fashioned manner of such verses as these, perhaps the earliest of his that have been preserved:

> In ages past, when smit with warmth sublime,
> Their bards foretold the dark events of time,
> And piercing forward through the mystic shade,
> Kings yet to come, and chiefs unborn survey'd,
> Amittar's son perceiv'd, among the rest,
> The mighty flame usurp his labouring breast . . .

but in the work of how many sophomores, aged sixteen, would you find to-day this note of intellectual self-respect? After leaving college he taught school for a while, first at Flatbush, L.I., and then under H. H. Brackenridge, at Princess Anne, Md. In 1775 he is back in New York, writing political pamphlets and poems. He was launched in his career: hatred of the English and of the American Tories was his never-failing theme down to his death in 1832. It is not necessary here to recall the vicissitudes of his

---

* [We owe to death ourselves and all that we have.]

fortune; the various papers he edited, his political animosities, his alternations of literary work with cruising the seas and with farming. "The old hag Necessity has got such a prodigious gripe of me!" he wrote to Madison in 1772, and he never for long shook her off. Those who care to follow the adventures of a poet in the troubled days of "this bard-baiting clime"—and the story is well worth reading—may turn to Professor Pattee's admirable Life in the present edition.

Of two periods in his career, however, a word must be said. In November of 1775 he sailed for Santa Cruz with a West Indian gentleman, who owned large estates on the island. During the voyage the mate of the vessel died, and Freneau was put in his place. A good deal of his life thereafter was passed on shipboard as mate and master, so that he is one of the few poets who write of the sea with complete knowledge of the trade. It was no land-lubber who made the odes, *On the Death of Captain Biddle*, on *Captain Jones's Invitation*, and *On the Memorable Victory*. Nor was his experience of the tropics without influence. The three long poems, *Santa Cruz*, *The House of Night*, and *The Jamaica Funeral*, composed during his visit of two years to the island, are distinctly different in tone from the rest of his work. There is more colour in them, more warmth of imagination. In the midst of much description of the ordinary amateurish sort, one comes upon a perfect image in a single line:

Fair Santa Cruz, arising, laves her waist;

or upon a stanza marred only by his inveterate taste for adjectives in "y":

Among the shades of yonder whispering grove
The green palmettos mingle, tall and fair,
That ever murmur, and forever move,
Fanning with wavy bough the ambient air;—

or upon a whole passage of haunting, if imperfect, beauty, ending with a reflection that foreshadows, so to speak, the most famous line he was afterwards to write:

74

Along the shore a wondrous flower is seen,
Where rocky ponds receive the surging wave;
Some drest in yellow, some array'd in green,
Beneath the water their gay branches lave.

This mystic plant, with its bewitching charms,
Too surely springs from some enchanted bower;
Fearful it is, and dreads impending harms,
And *Animal* the natives call the flower.

From the smooth rock its little branches rise,
The objects of thy view, and that alone;
Feast on its beauties with thy ravish'd eyes,
But aim to touch it, and—the flower is gone.

Nay, if thy shade but intercept the beam
That gilds their boughs beneath the briny lake,
Swift they retire, like a deluded dream,
And even a shadow for destruction take.

Something more than southern warmth enters into the stanzas
of *The House of Night*. It is the fury of the sudden tropic storm
that he tries to express in such lines as these:

Lights in the air like burning stars were hurl'd,
Dogs howl'd, heaven murmur'd, and the tempest
    blew,
The red half-moon peep'd from behind a cloud
As if in dread the amazing scene to view.

Poe himself never imagined anything more grotesquely weird
than this account of the death and burial of Death, nor ever
composed lines of more sombre magnificence than a few of those
scattered through Freneau's poem; the pity of it is that so much
power of imagination should have been wasted through the poet's
provincial training. The *genre* has its risks for the most wary hand,
and how should Freneau escape without a fall? We hardly know
whether to smile or shudder when he writes:

> Each horrid face a grisly mask conceal'd,
> Their busy eyes shot terror to my soul
> As now and then, by the pale lanthorn's glare,
> I saw them for their parted friend condole;

there is, unfortunately, less room for hesitation when he concludes this gruesome burial of Death:

> That done, they placed the carcase in the tomb,
> To dust and dull oblivion now resign'd,
> Then turn'd the chariot tow'rd the House of Night,
> Which soon flew off, and left no trace behind.

These poems were written during the first years of the Revolution, and far away from the scenes of battle, but Freneau was to learn the meaning of war at closer range. On one of his voyages to Santa Cruz, in 1780, his vessel was captured by a British frigate, and crew and passengers were carried to New York. Here for a while he was confined in the horrible prison ships, and immediately on being released by exchange he set himself to describe his experience in rhyme. If he had railed at Great Britain before, he now screamed.

> Weak as I am, I'll try my strength to-day,
> And my best arrows at these hell-hounds play,
> To future years one scene of death prolong,
> And hang them up to infamy, in song.

The descriptive verses and satires that resulted from his travels were the strongest and most telling he ever wrote; as much cannot be said for the product of another period of his life. In August, 1791, he was appointed clerk for foreign languages by Jefferson then Secretary of State, and went to Philadelphia to live. Two months later he issued the first number of the *National Gazette*, a semi-weekly paper devoted to the party of Jefferson against that of Hamilton, not without side thrusts at Washington, and to the favouring of French revolutionary democracy against British monarchy. That was not a day when political writers disguised their feelings, and between the *National Gazette* and *Fenno's Gazette of the United States* there arose as pretty a war of words as one might wish to hear. The attacks of the Federalists are summed up in this anonymous note inserted by Hamilton in *Fenno's Gazette*, July 25, 1792:

The Editor of the National Gazette *receives a salary from Government:*

Quere—Whether this salary is paid him for translations; or for publications, *the design for which is to vilify those to whom the voice of the people has committed the administration of our public affairs—to oppose the measures of Government, and, by false insinuations, to disturb the public peace?*

In common life it is thought ungrateful for a man to bite the hand that puts bread in his mouth; but if a man is hired to do it, the case is altered.

Freneau swore that neither the "*Gazette* nor the editor thereof was ever directed, controlled, or attempted to be influenced in any manner, either by the Secretary of State, or any of his friends"; and Jefferson in a letter to Washington made practically the same protestation. Professor Pattee inclines to defend Freneau through this whole episode, and certainly his virulent abuse can be matched, almost if not quite, by the diatribes of his enemies. On the other hand, it is not easy to defend him against Hamilton's charge, however indirect his relations with Jefferson may have been. His reputation in the end suffers as does that of all barkers at the heels of those who are trying in perilous times to establish order: to Washington he was "that rascal Freneau," to President Dwight [of Yale] he seemed "a mere incendiary, or rather as a despicable tool of bigger incendiaries"; he did not belong to what the Greeks in their days of faction used to call the *agathoi*, the good.

As for Freneau, the writer, those who expect to find in him anything more than a frustrated poet, a poet of hints and anticipations, will be disappointed; but to those who approach him in the right spirit, he will afford a genuine interest. There is a certain charm, a melancholy charm, if you will, in catching the slender

tones of his lyric moods here and there through the noise and
bustle of his political writings. And often in these notes one detects
strange presage of the future. Sometimes these prophetic hints
take a definite form, as in that verse of *The Indian Burying
Ground*—the most famous he wrote—which Campbell appro-
priated bodily: "The hunter and the deer a shade," and which
Hazlitt, in his *Table Talk*, misquoting as "a hunter of shadows,
himself a shade," attributed to Homer's account of Orion. Another line of our poet's, "They took the spear—but left the shield,"
was with the change of "took" to "snatched," borrowed by Scott,
who knew Freneau's work well enough to call *Eutaw Springs* "as
fine a thing as there is of the kind in the language." And a poetess
of Britain went so far as to dignify the whole of one of his poems
with her name. But the real anticipations of Freneau were rather
his own outreachings after the romanticism that was preparing
in England. *On Amanda's Singing Bird*, for instance, sounds like
a faint prelude to Blake. Other poems point further into the future.
A set of verses on *The Power of Fancy*, written in 1770, has a
distinct suggestion of Keats's "Ever let the Fancy roam," which
dates at least forty-eight years later. Another poem, *The Wild
Honey Suckle*, perhaps the most nearly flawless he ever wrote,
combines in its rather languid beauty something of Wordsworth's
moralising love of the less honoured flowers with Keats's relish
of fragility. It is brief enough to quote entire:

> Fair flower, that dost so comely grow,
> Hid in this silent, dull retreat,
> Untouched thy honied blossoms blow,
> Unseen thy little branches greet:
>   No roving foot shall crush thee here,
>   No busy hand provoke a tear.
>
> By Nature's self in white arrayed,
> She bade thee shun the vulgar eye,
> And planted here the guardian shade,
> And sent soft waters murmuring by;
>   Thus quietly thy summer goes,
>   Thy days declining to repose.

From morning suns and evening dews
At first thy little being came:
If nothing once, you nothing lose,
For when you die you are the same;
 The space between is but an hour,
 The frail duration of a flower.

Not flawless, for even a clever journeyman's hand could alter a word here and there for the better; not great in the sense that Wordsworth's and Keats's best work is great; colourless as a whole, yet with a clear, unearthly loveliness of its own. And the last stanza, despite the false "thy" in the second line and the slightly imperfect rhymes, would do honour to any poet of the past century. It has the slender brittleness of a costly vase, marred in the burning.

But Freneau's chief affiliations in the future are undoubtedly with Poe. No one could overlook that quality in such a poem as *The House of Night*; it is no less unmistakable in separate verses and stanzas scattered throughout his works. When he bids farewell to Columbus, in his poem of 1774, he dismisses the discoverer:

To shadowy forms, and ghosts, and sleepy things.

In an earlier poem he writes, in somewhat boyish fashion:

Now, tho' late, returning home,
Lead me to Belinda's tomb;
Let me glide as well as you
Through the shroud and coffin too,
And behold, a moment, there,
All that once was good and fair—
Who doth here so soundly sleep?
Shall we break this prison deep?

Is not this in the very taste of *The Sleeper* although without Poe's power to touch the reluctant nerve of awe? To follow this vein of frustrated romanticism through his writings is as if we should meet with a Poe who had been snatched into the turmoil of aboli-

tionism and the civil war, and all his music set a-jangle by hate.
Freneau, as I have said, was fully conscious of this thwarting bias
of the times:

> On these bleak climes by Fortune thrown,
> Where rigid Reason reigns alone,
> Where lovely Fancy has no sway,
> Nor magic forms about us play,
> Nor nature takes her summer hue—
> Tell me, what has the muse to do?
>
> An age employed in edging steel
> Can no poetic raptures feel;
> No solitude's attracting power,
> No leisure of the noon-day hour,
> No shaded stream, no quiet grove,
> Can this fantastic century move.
>
> The muse of love in no request—
> Go—try your fortune with the rest,
> One of the nine you should engage,
> To meet the follies of the age.
>
> On one, we fear, your choice must fall—
> The least engaging of them all—
> Her visage stern—an angry style—
> A clouded brow—malicious smile—
> A mind on murdered victims placed—
> She, only she, can please the taste!

It is true that a certain inclination toward satire showed itself from
the beginning in Freneau's mind, side by side with his lyrical
moods, and needed only the impulse of circumstances to develop.
By nature, however, this satirical strain was of the more humane
sort, which sends us to the future for comparisons rather than to
the past. Thus, the earliest of these poems, *The Adventures of
Simon Swaugum, a Village Merchant*, would require only a little
more avoirdupois in the rhythm, a little more of psychological
antithesis, to take its place among Crabbe's *Tales*; it contains, in
fact, bits of *genre* painting which might be passed upon any but

the most knowing as actually Crabbe's. Where he differs from the English humourist he tends to forestall the lighter, swifter manner of Lowell and Holmes. Now *Swaugum* was written in 1768 and printed in 1792; *The Library*, Crabbe's first important publication, appeared in 1781, and the *Tales* not until 1812. To appreciate Freneau's originality it must also be remembered that in 1782 John Trumbull, in his *M'Fingal*, was still trying to reproduce the form and wit of Butler's *Hudibras*, tinctured, perhaps, with the more contemporary spirit of Churchill. *Swaugum*, with two or three other *genre* tales, notably *The Expedition of Timothy Taurus, Astrologer*, and *Slender's Journey*, creates a regret that Freneau did not leave a complete picture of American society in this humorous-satiric vein. For, after all, it is not the poet of purest aspiration, nor the harsh denouncer of crime, that hands down his age to us as a breathing human reality; not Virgil or Juvenal, but Horace. It is by his foibles man lives for posterity; his greater virtues and vices make of him an example, not a companion.

But this kindlier satire was swallowed up in the passions of the Revolution, and Freneau produced a long series of dialogues, declamations, and caustic stanzas against poor King George and his servants. Occasionally there is a grudging humour in the ridicule; oftener mere blank invective. Far the strongest of these poems is the lurid account of his detention on *The British Prison Ship*, already mentioned:

> Hunger and thirst to work our woe combine,
> And mouldy bread, and flesh of rotten swine,
> The mangled carcase, and the battered brain,
> The doctor's poison, and the captain's cane,
> The soldier's musquet, and the steward's debt,
> The evening shackle, and the noon-day threat.

Of all his ills the doctor's poison seems to have been the hardest to bear:

> He on his charge the healing work begun
> With antimonial mixtures, by the tun,
> Ten minutes was the time he deign'd to stay,

81

> The time of grace allotted once a day—
> He drencht us well with bitter draughts, 't is true,
> Nostrums from hell, and cortex from Peru—
> Some with his pills he sent to Pluto's reign,
> And some he blister'd with his flies of Spain;
> His cream of Tartar walk'd its deadly round,
> Till the lean patient at the potion frown'd,
> And swore that hemlock, death, or what you will,
> Were nonsense to the drugs that stuff'd his bill.—
> On those refusing he bestow'd a kick,
> Or menaced vengeance with his walking-stick;
> Here uncontroll'd he exercised his trade,
> And grew experienced by the deaths he made;
> By frequent blows we from his cane endured
> He killed at least as many as he cured;
> On our lost comrades built his future fame,
> And scatter'd fate, where'er his footsteps came.

That is legitimate and effective satire; the indignation of the poet is fitted to the abject offensiveness of his theme. But too often he falls into mere shrewish vituperation:

> Said Jove with a smile—
> "Columbia shall never be ruled by an isle. . . .
> Then cease your endeavours, ye vermin of Britain."
> (And here, in derision, their island he spit on) . . .

There is more of the kind, which I shame to repeat, as Freneau himself was confessedly half-ashamed to write. And indeed these explosions of poetic rage have a sad way of losing their force with time, and degenerating into mere ill temper; for what is George III. to you and me that we should understand this hatred? It needs genius to be a good hater in literature. And if we turn with weariness from this scolding of the English, we are affected with something akin to distress at his railing against his own compatriots, Tory and Federalist:

> What is a Tory? Heavens and earth reveal!
> What strange blind monster does that name con-
>   ceal?

There! there he stands—for Augury prepare,
Come lay his heart and inmost entrails bare,
I, by the forelock, seize the Stygian hound;
You bind his arms and bind the dragon down.
Surgeon, attend with thy dissecting knife,
Part, part the sutures of his brazen skull,
Hard as a rock, impenetrably dull.
Hold out his brain, and let his brethren see
That tortoise brain, no larger than a pea—
Come, rake his entrails, whet thy knife again,
Let's see what evils threat the next campaign.

In that slough of civil discord were sunk all his raptures of liberty
and his visions of *The Rising Glory of America*. For not the least
of his anticipations was his prophecy of America's empire, and the
conscious assumption within himself of so many of the traits of the
practical calculating American mind, side by side with its thin
mysticism; as if the temperaments of Poe and Franklin were united
in one person. Here you shall read lines in glorification of commerce and science, such as our national poet to-day, if such existed,
might write; here you shall see the past disparaged in the classics,
and that self-flattering absorption in the present which has sapped
the very roots of the New World's imagination. And here too
is the fullest expression of that spirit of rebellion and mutual
distrust in which the country was unfortunately, if necessarily,
founded, and which has clung to it like an inherited taint in the
blood, marring the harmony of its development, and suffering a
partial expiation in the calamities of the civil war. There is a
lesson for us to-day, and, in more ways than one, a little of hu-
miliation, in the career of our first poet.

But let us rather take leave of Freneau in a different frame of
mind. In 1798 he gave up active participation in editing, and retired to the family estate at Mount Pleasant, N.J., where he
passed the remaining thirty-four years of his life. Politics were not
entirely forgotten, and for a while he contributed to the Philadelphia *Aurora* and other papers a series of amusing letters which
were afterwards brought out in book form—the best of his prose
writings. But for the most part his time was given to farming in a
half-hearted way, and to composing verses under the shelter of a

grove that had been started by his father. "It was a complete grove of locust trees," writes his daughter, "surrounding a house grown old [it was burnt to the ground in 1815] with its time-worn owner, his venerable mother, and maiden sister beloved and respected for her many virtues." Professor Pattee gives a happy picture of the poet in his declining age. He was fond of feeding the farm animals, but, as his daughter says, "when the season came for slaughtering the porkers, he generally managed it so as to have some business in New York, and he was usually absent when poultry was wanted for dinner." One day he and his wife found a slave asleep in the field, and Mrs. Freneau took up the man's hoe, saying she would show him how to work. Her only success was to cut down a hill of the young corn, whereupon the slave chuckled in triumph: "Ho, ho, Missie Freneau, if that's the way you hoe, the corn'll never grow." "No wonder the farm doesn't pay," she exclaimed in disgust, "when even the slaves talk in rhymes!" Of the appearance of the poet in these latter years we get the best description from Dr. John W. Francis in Duyckinck's *Cyclopædia of American Literature*:

He was somewhat below the ordinary height; in person thin, yet muscular, with a firm step, though a little inclined to stoop; his countenance wore traces of care, yet lightened with intelligence as he spoke; he was mild in enunciation, neither rapid nor slow, but clear, distinct, and emphatic. His forehead was rather beyond the medium elevation, his eyes a dark grey, occupying a socket deeper than common; his hair must have once been beautiful, it was now thinned and of an iron grey. He was free of all ambitious displays; his habitual expression was pensive. His dress might have passed for that of a farmer. New York, the city of his birth, was his most interesting theme; his collegiate career with Madison, next. His story of many of his occasional poems was quite romantic. As he had at command types and a printing press, when an incident of moment in the Revolution occurred, he would retire for composition, or find shelter under the shade of some tree, indite his lyrics, repair to the press, set up his types, and issue his productions. There was no difficulty in versification with him. I told him what I had heard Jeffrey, the Scotch Reviewer, say of his

writings, that the time would arrive when his poetry, like that of
Hudibras, would command a commentator like Gray.

That learned commentator has not yet appeared, and is scarcely
needed; but it is agreeable to think of the old poet, in his not
ignoble retirement from the world, hearing such dearly-earned
praise and finding in the future a compensation for the harsh
treatment of the past. Princeton has done well to honour one of
the most distinguished of her sons by publishing his principal
poems in substantial form.

The Origins of Hawthorne and Poe

We are credibly told that in years not so very long past young women and even grave men used to read the Gothic tales of Ann Radcliffe with tense brows and trembling lips; and the essays of Carlyle still stand a voluble witness to prove how seriously the grotesque marvels of German romance were once accepted in England. Mrs. Radcliffe is no doubt read occasionally to-day, and the indefatigable Mr. Lang has even attempted to reinstate her in popular favour. But her most generous admirer could hardly aver that she was anything more to him than a curious amusement; the horror of her tales has vanished away like the moonlight she was so fond of describing. And as for Tieck and Wackenroder and all that dim romantic crew of Teuton *Sturm* and *Drang*—not even an Andrew Lang has arisen for them.

It is a matter for reflection, therefore, that in this country a new life of Hawthorne[1] should be something of a literary event and that there should be a sufficient public to warrant the issue of two new and elaborate editions of Poe;[2] for at first thought it might seem that both Hawthorne and Poe fall in the same class with those forgotten weavers of moonlight and mysticism. What is it, indeed, that gives vitality to their work and separates it from the ephemeral product of English and German Gothicism? More than that: Why is it that the only two writers of America who have won almost universal renown as artists are these romancers, each of whom is, after his own manner, a sovereign in that strange

---

From *Shelburne Essays*, First Series (Boston and New York, Houghton Mifflin Company, 1904), pp. 51–70.

[1] *Nathaniel Hawthorne.* By George E. Woodberry. [American Men of Letters.] Boston: Houghton Mifflin Co.

[2] Published respectively by Thomas Y. Crowell & Co. and by G. P. Putnam's Sons.

region of emotion which we name the weird? Other work they have done, and done well, but when we call to mind their distinguishing productions we think first of such scenes as *The Fall of the House of Usher*, *The Raven*, and *The Sleeper*, or of such characters as Arthur Dimmesdale with his morbid remorse and unearthly sufferings, the dreamlike existence of Clifford, the hideous unexplained mystery of Miriam's wrong, and the awful search of Ethan Brand—scenes and characters which belong to the real world, for they appeal to a sympathetic chord in our own breasts, but which are yet quite overlaid with some insistent shadow of the fantastic realm of symbolism.

Hawthorne ascribes the superiority of Nature's work over man's to the fact "that the former works from the innermost germ, while the latter works merely superficially," and the same explanation may be given of the genuineness of his own work and Poe's in comparison with the unreality of Mrs. Radcliffe or Tieck; the weird, unearthly substance moulded by their genius is from the innermost core of the national consciousness. Their achievement is not like the Gothic novel introduced into England by Horace Walpole, a mere dilettante; there is in them very little of that recrudescence of mediæval superstition and gloom which marked the rise of romanticism in Europe, little or nothing of the knights and ladies, turrets and dungeons and all that tawdry paraphernalia, and, fortunately for their reputation, no taint of that peculiar form of sentimentalism which pervades the German *Herzensergies-sungen** like the odour of Schiller's decaying apples. Their work is the last efflorescence of a tradition handed down to them unbroken from the earliest Colonial days, and that tradition was the voice of a stern and indomitable moral character. The unearthly visions of Poe and Hawthorne are in no wise the result of literary whim or of unbridled individualism, but are deep-rooted in American history. Neither Professor Woodberry in his Life of Hawthorne nor Professor Harrison in his Life of Poe has, it seems to me, brought out with due emphasis these spiritual origins of a school of romance which is so unique in its way as to have made for itself a sure place in the literature of the world.

* [Outpourings of the heart.]

The name of Hawthorne carries us back at once to those grim days of his ancestor in Salem Village when for a season almost the whole community gave itself up to the frenzy of witch hunting. In the earlier days the superstitions of England were concerned chiefly with the fairy folk of hearth and field, a quaint people commonly and kindly disposed, if mischievous. But with the advent of Puritanism came a change; the fair and frolicsome play of the fancy was discredited and the starved imagination had its revenge. In place of the elves and goblins of a freer age, instead of "Robin Goodfellow, the spoorn, the man-in-the-oak, the hellwain, the firedrake, the puckle" and all that antic crew, the imagination now evoked the terrific spectre of the Devil and attributed to his personal agency all the mishaps of life. Hence it is that witchcraft became so much more prominent with the Reformation and reached its height where Puritan feelings prevailed. On the one hand it was employed by the Roman Church as an aid in its exterminating fight with the Waldenses and other heretics—the good monks no doubt being easily persuaded, where persuasion was necessary, that the ascetic revolt against the office of the imagination in worship was of diabolic origin—and, on the other hand, the Protestants, and particularly the Puritans with their morbid horror of sin, were quick to accredit to the author of sin every phenomenon they could not understand. Witchcraft, to be sure, is as old as history, and we need go no further abroad than the classic poets for tales of the most abominable night hags. But there is this difference between such monsters as Lucan's Erichtho and the abortions of Christian demonology: Erichtho may haunt the sepulchres and breathe into the cold mouths of the dead the dark secret she would transmit to the Shades, but in the end she is only a product of the imagination brooding on things unclean and hideous; there is in the dread and repugnance she inspires no such added horror as that which the Christian felt at the thought of a soul leagued for infamous ends with the Prince of Hell and doomed as a rebel against God to everlasting tortures.

Considering the history of the Puritan emigrants we shall not be surprised to find these superstitions breaking out with peculiar virulence in the New World. Persecution and insult at home had not tended to soften their temper, nor did flight across a waste of perilous waters to a wilderness where everything was strange and unexplored bring light and cheerfulness to their imagination. In England at least their morbid intensity was to some extent modified by contact with the worldly life about them; in their new home they were completely given up to the working out of their stern purposes. Terrors and difficulties only added fuel to their zeal. "Our faithers were Englishmen which came over this great ocean and were ready to perish in this wilderness," says old Governor Bradford; and "with what difficulties [they] wrastled in going throug these things," we may read in all our schoolbooks. It is easy to see how these hardships and these bitterly-won victories increased the sternness and unyieldingness of the New England Puritans, but perhaps we do not often consider the influence exerted on their imaginations by the wild country and wilder "salvages," as they called the red men, that now engaged their attention. They no longer beheld about them the pleasant vales and green hills of Old England, which the long habitation of man had rendered almost human, but the vast and pathless forests of the wilderness, where nature appeared under a new and forbidding aspect. There is at the best something weird and uncanny about the great woods into whose depths the eye cannot penetrate and from whose interwoven shadows, especially when night has fallen and the ear has grown painfully alert, come forth at intervals sounds that seem to indicate the activity of some nameless secret life within the darkness. What then must have been the feelings of the New England farmer as perchance he made his way homeward at sundown along the border of the gloomy forest. The kindly fancy of his ancestors who peopled the woods with mischievous goblins had yielded to his belief in the extended powers of evil. In these deep shadows he knew not but the very enemy of God might be lurking to lure him to destruction. It was no pleasant *Waldeinsamkeit* he felt, such as romantic poets love to indulge, but awe and ghostly terror.

And this feeling was exaggerated by the actual savages who inhabited the woods. The settlers were for the most part thoroughly convinced that these poor, brutal denizens of the wilderness were

89

under the special tutelage of Satan. In times of distress the colonists were ready to charge all their calamities to the machinations of an infernal conspiracy.

It was afterward by them [*the Indians*] *confessed,* [*says Cotton Mather in his* Magnalia], *that upon the arrival of the* English *in these parts, the* Indians *employed their* sorcerers, *whom they call* powaws, *like* Balaam, *to curse them, and let loose their* demons *upon them, to shipwreck them, to distract them, to poison them, or any way to ruin them. All the noted* powaws *in the country spent three days together in diabolical* conjurations, *to obtain the assistance of the* devils *against the settlement of these our* English.

It is not strange, therefore, that when the delusion of witchcraft fell upon these people it should have assumed a peculiarly tragic aspect. They were dwelling in the midst of hostile demonic powers, and, feeling themselves attacked, they turned upon the enemy with all the strength and intensity of their souls. And how real and material the phenomena appeared to the bewildered onlookers may be gathered from this sulfurous account written by an eye-witness of the sufferings of one of the victims:

Margaret Rule would sometimes have her jaws forcibly pulled open, whereupon something invisible would be poured down her throat: we all saw her swallow, and yet we saw her try all she could, by spitting, coughing, and shrieking, that she might not swallow; but one time the standers-by plainly saw something of that odd liquor itself on the outside of her neck; she cried out of it, as if scalding brimstone were poured into her, and the whole house would immediately scent so hot of brimstone that we were scarce able to endure it.

Under the stress of this morbid excitement the good people of Salem and the neighbourhood were thrown into a frenzy of fear; crops were abandoned, business stood still, and the only matters considered were the horrible persecutions of Satan in their midst. The general feeling of alarm was aggravated to something like desperation when the Rev. Deodat Lawson in the meeting-house of Salem village preached an inflammatory sermon in which he charged the outburst of the infernal powers directly to the sins of the people.

You are therefore to be deeply humbled, [he said,] and sit in the dust, considering the signal hand of God in singling out this place, this poor village, for the first seat of Satan's tyranny, and to make it (as 't were) the rendezvous of devils, where they muster their infernal forces; appearing to the afflicted as coming armed to carry on their malicious designs against the bodies, and, if God in mercy prevent not, against the souls of many in this place.

No wonder that the people did actually believe "that the devils were walking about our streets with lengthened chains, making a dreadful noise in our ears; and brimstone (even without a metaphor) was making a horrid and a hellish stench in our nostrils."

To stop these terrible inroads of Satan a special court was created, before which those previously examined were tried. Those found guilty were hanged on a conspicuous eminence which thus acquired the ominous title of Witch-Hill; and how awful was the spectacle there presented to the panic-stricken people may be gathered from the pious ejaculation of the Reverend Mr. Noyes, "What a sad thing it is to see eight firebrands of hell hanging there!" The cruelty engendered by this feeling of insecurity is well indicated by the treatment of Giles Corey, who, refusing to plead either guilty or not guilty, was subjected to the *peine dure et forte,* as the tale is related in Longfellow's *New England Tragedy;* but Longfellow does not relate what we are told in a ballad of the period, that when from the oppression of the stone on his chest Corey's tongue protruded it was rudely thrust back by the staff of a bystander.

In due time this "hellish molestation," as one of the persecuted called it, came to a sudden end; but not before twenty victims had suffered death, many had died in jail, hundreds had endured imprisonment in its worst forms, whole families had been impoverished, and a moral impression had been made upon the community which nothing could efface. The modern historian of the delusion tells us that a sort of curse still rests on the immediate scene of these tragic events and that neglect and desertion still brood on the accursed spot.

Were we to go no further than this episode of Salem history we should find it easy to explain by inheritance that mystic brooding over the dark and intricate effects of sin which the descendant of old John Hathorne has made the substance of his romance, or to account for the realism that underlies the wild fantasies of Poe. And we need only to dip into Cotton Mather's voluminous record of the dealings of Providence in America to see how intensely the mind of the Puritans was occupied with unearthly matters and what a legacy of emotions approaching the weird was left by them to posterity. When the faith of these militant saints was untroubled it often assumed a sweetness and fullness of spiritual content that might even pass into rapturous delight. But always this intoxicating joy bordered on the region of awe—the awe of a soul in the presence of the great and ineffable mysteries of holiness; and the life of Thomas Shepard, which Mather calls *"a trembling walk with God,"* may not unfitly be taken to illustrate the peculiar temper of their religion. And if in the wisest and sanest of the Puritan Fathers this trembling solicitude was never far away, there were others in whom the fear of the Lord became a mania of terror. Consider what the impression on the minds of children must have been when in the midst of their innocent sport the awful apparition of the Rev. James Noyes stood before them and rebuked them into silence with these solemn words: "Cousins, I wonder you can be so merry, unless you are sure of your salvation!" Consider the spiritual state of a young man, celebrated for his godliness, who could note down in his diary with curious precision: "I was almost in the *suburbs of hell* all day."

Literature, in the true sense of the word, could not well flourish among a people who saw in the plastic imagination a mere seduction of the senses, and whose intellectual life was thus absorbed in theological speculation. To be sure, a good deal of verse was written and even printed in early Colonial days; but of all the poets of that age only one attained any real celebrity and has in a way lived on into the present. Michael Wigglesworth, the faithful pastor of Malden, where in the odour of sanctity he died in 1705, is described as "a little feeble *shadow* of a *man*"; but his diminutive frame harboured a mighty spirit. His poems breathed the very quintessence of Puritan faith, and as such obtained immediate and extraordinary popularity. Professor Tyler calculates that in the first year of publication his *Day of Doom* was purchased by at least one in every thirty-five persons of New England; printed as a common ballad it was hawked everywhere about the country, and its lugubrious stanzas were even taught to children along with the catechism. As late as the year 1828 an essayist declared that many an aged person of his acquaintance could still repeat the poem, though they might not have seen a copy of it since they were in leading strings; and in his own time Cotton Mather had thought it might "perhaps find our children till the day itself arrives"—which God forbid.

The strength of Master Wigglesworth's genius, in this picture of the *Day of Doom*, is, as we should expect, devoted to those who

> void of tears, but fill'd with fears,
>   and dreadful expectation
> Of endless pains and scalding flames,
>   stand waiting for Damnation.

One after another the various kinds of sinners are arraigned at the bar and receive their due reward. Most hideous and most famous of all are the stanzas that describe the pleading and condemnation of unbaptised infants. As an expression of the grotesque in literature they are not without a kind of crude power; as the voice of a real and tremendously earnest faith they elude the grasp of a modern mind, one can only shudder and avert his eyes. We contrast with some curiosity and no little bewilderment the unflinching frankness of this earlier Calvinist with the shifting creed of a recent Calvinistic convention which has attempted to explain away the catechism's abandonment of non-elect infants. Yet Wigglesworth, like the Presbyterians of to-day, had his moment of compunction for the poor souls who

> from the womb unto the tomb
>   Were straightway carrièd;—

he at least allowed to them "the easiest room in hell"! Those simple words have of recent years acquired a certain notoriety through literary hand books; indeed, for naked and appalling realism of horror, when all is considered, it would not be easy to find a verse to surpass them.

Wigglesworth's rhymes were, as I said, the intellectual food of the young, and some such strong meat would seem necessary to prepare them for the sermons that nourished their manhood. And at least one of these sermons, Jonathan Edwards's famous Enfield discourse of *Sinners in the Hands of an Angry God*, has gained the unenviable reputation of being perhaps the most tremendous and uncompromising enunciation ever made of the gloomier side of Calvinism. His picture of worldly men hanging over the pit of hell "by a slender thread, with the flames of divine wrath flashing about it, and ready every moment to singe it and burn it asunder," has become classical in its own way.

After the death of Edwards, in 1758, the heart of the country became more and more absorbed in the impending conflict of the Revolution. For a while, at least, religion and the terrors of damnation must give place to the more imminent peril of political subjugation. In New England that other phase of Puritanism, the spirit that had led Cromwell and his Ironsides to victory, and had established the liberties of the English constitution, came to the foreground, and for a time the political pamphlet usurped the place of the sermon. But even then literature did not entirely vanish; and at intervals through the rasping cries of revolution one may catch a note of that pensiveness or gloom, that habitual dwelling on the supernatural significance of life, which had come to be the dominant intellectual tone of the country. Indeed, it was this violent wrenching of the national consciousness into new fields which brought about the change from the old supernaturalism of religion to the shadowy symbolism of literature as exemplified in Hawthorne and Poe. We seem to see the beginning of this new spirit in the haunting pathos that throbs through the anonymous ballad of *Nathan Hale:*

> The breezes went steadily through the tall pines,
>   A saying, "Oh! hu-ush!" a saying, "Oh! hu-ush!"
> As stilly stole by a bold legion of horse,
>   For Hale in the bush, for Hale in the bush.

> "Keep still," said the thrush as she nestled her
>   young,
>   In a nest by the road; in a nest by the road;
> "For the tyrants are near and with them appear
>   What bodes us no good; what bodes us no good."

Of all the gentlemen—and women, too—who wrote verse in those stirring times only one can lay claim to any genuine poetic inspiration. Philip Freneau, of New Jersey, has even yet a slight hold on the memory of the reading public, and would be more read and better known were his works subjected to proper selection and editing. Like all the other versifiers of the period Freneau was caught in the wild vortex of political affairs, and, against the protests of his truer nature as he himself avows, gave up the gentler muses for the raucous voice of satire. But here and there through his works we find a suggestion of what he might have accomplished had he fallen on better times. In him we catch perhaps the first note of the weird as it appears in our later literature, of that transition of overwhelming superstition into shadowy haunting symbolism. Not unseldom a stanza, or a single line it may be, wakes an echo in the mind curiously like Poe. Such, for instance, is the spectral beauty of that stanza of *The Indian Burying Ground*, whose last line, as Poe once pointed out, was borrowed intact, and never acknowledged, by Campbell:

> By midnight moons, o'er moistening dews,
>   In vestments for the chase arrayed,
> The hunter still the deer pursues,
>   The hunter and the deer—a shade.

A glance at the titles of Freneau's poems would show how persistently, when relieved from the immediate pressure of politics, his mind reverted to subjects of decay and quiet dissolution. In one of his longer poems, *The House of Death*, he has just failed of achieving a work which might have come from the brain of Poe himself. At the hour of midnight the poet dreams that he wanders over a desolate country:

Dark was the sky, and not one friendly star
   Shone from the zenith or horizon, clear,
Mist sate upon the woods, and darkness rode
   In her black chariot, with a wild career.

And from the woods the late resounding note
   Issued of the loquacious whip-poor-will,
Hoarse, howling dogs, and nightly roving wolves
   Clamour'd from far off cliffs invisible.

At last he finds himself in the presence of "a noble dome raised fair and high," standing in the midst of "a mournful garden of autumnal hue":

The poppy there, companion to repose,
   Displayed her blossoms that began to fall,
And here the purple amaranthus rose
   With mint strong scented, for the funeral.

In this strange spot, which has something of the unearthly qualities of Rappaccini's garden or Poe's spectral landscapes, stands the desolate home of a young man whose beloved consort Death has recently snatched away, and who now harbours as a guest the grisly person of Death himself. Death, stretched on the couch and surrounded by ghoulish phantoms, lies dying. Over the conversation that ensues and the blasphemies of the ghastly sufferer we may pass without delaying. At last after Death has composed his own epitaph and described the tomb he is to occupy, in

A burying-yard of sinners dead, unblest,

the poet flees terror-smitten out of that house into the tempestuous night.

Nor looked I back, till to a far off wood
   Trembling with fear, my weary feet had sped—
Dark was the night, but at the enchanted dome
   I saw the infernal windows flaming red.

At last the hour of dissolution arrives:

Dim burnt the lamp, and now the phantom Death
    Gave his last groans in horror and despair—
"All hell demands me hence"—he cried, and threw
    The red lamp hissing through the midnight air.

Trembling, across the plain my course I held,
    And found the grave-yard, loitering through the
        gloom,
And, in the midst, a hell-red wandering light,
    Walking in fiery circles round the tomb.

Whereupon with a gruesome picture of Death's interment and a few stanzas of proper exhortation from the author, this remarkable poem comes to an end.

Between the period of the Revolution and the period that may be called the New England renaissance not much was written which has the distinct mark of the American temperament. Yet it is a significant fact that Charles Brockden Brown's *Wieland*, published in 1798, the first novel of the first American novelist, should be built upon a theme as weird and as steeped in "thrilling melancholy," to use Brown's own words, as anything in the later work of Hawthorne or Poe; and in the proper place it would not be uninteresting to show how far, in his imperfect way, Brown anticipates the very methods and tricks of his greater followers. His immediate inspiration comes no doubt from the mystery-mongering novels then so popular in England, but despite the crudeness of a provincial style there does run through the strange unreality of Brown's pages a note of sincerity, the tongue and accents of a man to whom such themes are a native inheritance, lending to his work a sustained interest which I for my part fail to find in the *Castle of Otranto* or the *Mysteries of Udolpho*. Nor is it without significance that even in New York, where if anywhere this world claims her own, Irving in his genial way could fall so easily into brooding on the dead who sleep in Westminster Abbey or relate with such gusto the wild legends of the Hudson. Bryant, too, has kept his fame chiefly on account of his youthful musings on death and the grandiose pomp of those lines that tell how the rock-ribbed hills, the pensive vales, the venerable rivers, brooks,

and, poured around them all,
Old Ocean's grey and melancholy waste,—
Are but the solemn decorations all
Of the great tomb of man.

Necessarily this age-long contemplation of things unearthly, this divorcing of the imagination from the fair and blithe harmonies of life to fasten upon the sombre effects of guilt and reprobation, this constant meditation on earth and decay—necessarily all these exerted a powerful influence on literature when the renaissance appeared in New England and as a sort of reflection in the rest of the country. So, I think, it happened that out of that famous group of men who really created American literature the only two to attain perfection of form in the higher field of the imagination were writers whose minds were absorbed by the weirder phenomena of life. But it must not be inferred thence that the spirit of Hawthorne and Poe was identical with that of Michael Wigglesworth and Jonathan Edwards. With the passage of time the unquestioning, unflinching faith and vision of those heroic men dissolved away. Already in Freneau, himself born of a Huguenot family, a change is noticeable; that which to the earlier Fathers was a matter of infinite concern, that which to them was more real and urgent than the breath of life, becomes now chiefly an intoxicant of the imagination, and in another generation the transition is complete.

It is this precisely that we understand by the term "weird"— not the veritable vision of unearthly things, but the peculiar half vision inherited by the soul when faith has waned and the imagination prolongs the old sensations in a shadowy involuntary life of its own; and herein too lies the field of true and effective symbolism. If Hawthorne and Poe, as we think, possess an element of force and realism such as Tieck and the German school utterly lack, it is because they write from the depths of this profound moral experience of their people.

A Note on Poe's Method

In the Authors Club of New York there hangs a life-size portrait of Poe which engages my attention as often as I visit those chambers. It is a face that might well haunt the dreams of a man for its pathos. On it is stamped the mark of defeat; the very lines of the mouth, the pronounced asymmetry of the two sides, tell only too clearly the secret of broken self-control and the long unsuccessful struggle with insidious habits. In this it is typical, unfortunately, of a whole class of supersensitive, physically unbalanced artists, who have given some basis to the plausible, but I think now rather discredited, theory that would explain all the phenomena of genius by a morbid psychology. But in one thing the face is unlike the type to which it otherwise belongs: there is not the least sign here of that mental relaxation, that loosening of the mind's grasp and determination, which often goes with what must be called—though the phrase should not be wrongly interpreted in Poe's case—the breakdown of character. On the contrary, the eyes retain the look of intense concentration and logical grip.

And in these features the portrait is true to the original. For one of the distinguishing marks of Poe's work is just the combination of nervous irritability, running even into the morbid, with rigorous intellectual analysis. It is a combination not unknown in other writers of the ultra-romantic group; but it is the exception, and it is carried in Poe to an extreme for which it would be hard to find a parallel. Of his reasoning powers and his delight in the exercise of logical argument, no proof is required; it is sufficient merely to mention his story of *The Gold Bug*, his ingenious detective tales, his uncanny skill in predicting the development of one of Dickens' novels while running as a serial, his uncovering of the automatic

From *The Demon of the Absolute*, New Shelburne Essays, Vol. I (Princeton, Princeton University Press, 1928), pp. 77–87.

chess-player, his *Eureka*. But you will observe that his mind is not directed to ethical abstractions and does not work upon ideas, after the fashion of his great contemporaries in the North; it is rather analytical, and interested in the detection of facts and the dissection of sensations. The difference may be illustrated by two stories in which Hawthorne and Poe have treated a similar theme. One of these is *Ethan Brand*, the most extraordinary and characteristic, in my judgement, of all Hawthorne's shorter works. It is the tale, you will remember, of a lime-burner who, in the long solitary watches by his furnace in the hills, meditates on the secret nature of the Unpardonable Sin, until his mind becomes possessed with this one idea, and he is driven to go down into the world and search among men for the key to the mystery. And he discovers it —discovers it in his own breast—and returns with this hideous knowledge to the lime-kiln. Yet he has committed no crime in the ordinary sense of the word; his wickedness lies in the mere search for the idea, and of his victims we hear only vaguely of a girl, "whom," as the account runs, "with such cold and remorseless purpose, [he] made the subject of a psychological experiment, and wasted, absorbed, and perhaps annihilated her soul, in the process." The effect of the story is ghostly, where Poe would have been ghastly. From *Ethan Brand* turn now to the tale of *The Man of the Crowd*, whom Poe pretends to see passing in the mob of a London street, and, fascinated by the singular countenance of the wretch, follows through the night and the day in his restless hurry from one thronged region of the city to another. "This old man," he exclaims at last, "is the type and the genius of deep crime. He refuses to be alone. *He is the man of the crowd*. It will be in vain to follow; for I shall learn no more of him, nor of his deeds. The worst heart of the world is a grosser book than the *Hortulus Animæ*, and perhaps it is but one of the great mercies of God that 'es lässt sich nicht lesen.'" Poe's is a grim and unforgettable story, as original as Hawthorne's but different. Its power over our imagination depends on the analysis of the sensations connected with crime, whereas in *Ethan Brand* the interest is centred upon the search for the idea of evil in itself.

But if Poe differs from the ethical writers by avoiding what may be called the ideal use of the intellect, he differs also from the great mass of the romantic writers, with whom he is otherwise akin, by insistent use of the intellect in his own way. And this distinction comes out even more sharply in his criticism than in his practice. In three of his essays he has developed his critical theory elaborately and consistently, in *The Poetic Principle, The Rationale of Verse*, and *The Philosophy of Composition*, which together form one of the few æsthetic treatises in English of real value. In the first of these, a lecture which was read, it will be remembered, in Boston, he lays down his definition of poetry "as *The Rhythmical Creation of Beauty*. Its sole arbiter is taste. With the intellect or with Conscience, it has only collateral relations. Unless incidentally, it has no concern whatever with Duty or with Truth." Some allowance must be made in this definition for the fact that Poe was flaunting his flag resolutely in the face of the ethical folk of Boston, and we shall see in a moment that his "collateral relations" of the intellect, as he expresses it, need a pretty wide interpretation. The next step in his theory brings us to these significant words: "It is in Music, perhaps, that the soul most nearly attains the great end for which, when inspired by the Poetic Sentiment, it struggles—the creation of Supernal Beauty."

This position he maintains in *The Rationale of Verse*, where he declares that verse "cannot be better designated than as an inferior or less capable Music." So far, of course, he is merely adopting one of the familiar commonplaces of the age. The conception of poetry as reaching its normal goal in music was constantly held forth by the early German theorists of the *Romantische Schule*. It is implied in Schleiermacher's declaration that the religious feeling should "accompany all the doings of a man as if it were a holy music; he should do all *with* religion, nothing *through* religion;" it is carried to its dogmatic extreme by Novalis, who sees the consummation of art in "poems which sound melodiously and are full of beautiful words, but without any sense or connexion." The theory may appear absurd, in fact is absurd, when stated in this bald manner; but it is held nevertheless in scarcely less extravagant terms by some of the radical critics of the present day. Now in their practice the poets of this school ordinarily have sought to attain the effect of musical evocation by throwing the thinking part of us under a kind of hypnotic spell which leaves the emotional part of

101

us free to float off in a state of vague revery. Thus, *Kubla Khan*, the typical poem of the *genre*, was actually composed by Coleridge in his sleep, and its charm upon us is that of a dreamlike magic, beginning anywhere and ending anywhere, lifting us up on luxurious waves of indolent music. No doubt there is verse of this pure evocative quality in our Poe, notably in *The Valley of Unrest* and *The City in the Sea*, and in these lulling cadences of *The Sleeper*:

> At midnight in the month of June,
> I stand beneath the mystic moon.
> An opiate vapour, dewy, dim,
> Exhales from out her golden rim,
> And, softly dripping, drop by drop,
> Upon the quiet mountain top,
> Steals drowsily and musically
> Into the universal valley.

There is, I maintain, an opiate magic in such lines as these equal in potency to anything ever produced by the rhapsodist of Highgate; but it is not, in my opinion, the most characteristic note of Poe. He is even more himself, not when he surrenders his genius to these flowing waves of revery, but when his mind is concentrated and works with a logical precision, with a logical hardness one might almost say, which is the opposite of the ordinary romantic manner. Consider, for instance, the logical structure and completeness of *The Bells*: there, if anywhere in the English tongue, poetry does become pure music and pure beauty, almost to the exclusion of ideas, yet the thing is worked out and its effects calculated with the mathematical finish of a Bach or any other master of counterpoint who composed before spontaneity became identified with genius.

And Poe not only practised this logical concentration, but raised it to a principle of art. We come thus to the third of his æsthetical treatises, that on *The Philosophy of Composition*, in which he sets forth with ruthless frankness the whole method employed by him in composing *The Raven*. According to this extraordinary exhibition of genius at work, having determined to produce a great poem, he first considered what effect he should aim to produce. As beauty in his view was "the sole legitimate province of the poem," his choice was so far decided for him. The "next question referred to the *tone* of its highest manifestation"; and here again his choice was fixed for him by his belief that "all experience has shown this" tone to be one "of sadness. Beauty of whatever kind, in its supreme development, invariably excites the sensitive soul to tears." To evoke this effect, or any poetical effect, he saw that the refrain is the most universally employed and the most cogent instrument; he would therefore make a refrain the keynote of his poem, selecting for this purpose a word capable of protracted emphasis, melodious in itself, and in the fullest possible keeping with the tone of melancholy. These conditions led him immediately to the word "Nevermore" (suggested, probably, by Byron's famous use of it in *Don Juan*). The next step is the most curious of all. He felt the difficulty that "lay in the reconciliation of this monotony with the exercise of reason on the part of the creature repeating the word." It occurred to him that this difficulty might be obviated by putting the refrain into the mouth of a parrot, but he changed to a raven, "as equally capable of speech, and infinitely more in keeping with the intended *tone*." He had now to consider what topic, "according to the *universal* understanding of mankind, is the *most* melancholy." Obviously this would be beauty associated with death, "the death, then, of a beautiful woman." This being determined, his task was to bring together his theme and the instrument of his refrain; but we need not pursue him through all the windings of his ingenious plot.

Now what shall be said of this cold-blooded piece of analysis? To many critics it has seemed to be a grand hoax or a bit of unparalleled effrontery. Or at least the whole thing must be taken as an *ex post facto* account, so to speak; for it is impossible that any poem deeply emotional and effective, or any true product of inspiration, should be thus put together like a piece of calculated machinery. And from the ordinary theory and practice of art such an opinion is right. But I am inclined to believe that *The Raven* was actually composed very much as the author explains, and that his essay is not only essentially true to facts but throws a remarkable light on one phase of his genius. I do not mean to say that in all details the reflection on the method to be adopted would precede by an appreciable moment of time the actual invention; the two processes may have gone on together in his mind. The point is that this *conscious* logical analysis was present with him throughout the whole work of composition to an abnormal degree, now preceding, now accompanying, now following the more inscrutable suggestions of the creative faculty. This, I take it, is Poe's original note, a quality which distinguishes his art from that of the other masters of unearthly revery. Here, too, lies the principal sphere of his influence on Baudelaire and the whole line of foreign poets who have imitated him without reaching his supremacy—they could borrow his method, they could not steal his brains.

Judged thus by the achievement in accordance with his own canon of art, Poe must rank high, if not first, among our American poets, and measured by the extent of his influence he would take a prominent place among the poets of Europe. But when we consider the character of his canon in itself, I fear that certain deductions must be made to his fame. We are forced then to question the very validity of his doctrine of truth and beauty. There is no uncertainty as to the nature of his principles, nor, as is often the case with others, is there any discrepancy in him between theory and practice. To go back to the beginning, let me recall a few words from his criticism of Hawthorne, in which he gives precision to his theory by contrasting the provinces of the tale and the poem. "The tale," he there says, "has a point of superiority over the poem. In fact, while the *rhythm* of this latter is an essential aid in the development of the poem's highest idea—the idea of the Beautiful—the artificialities of this rhythm are an insuperable bar to the development of all points of thought and expression which have their basis in *Truth*." We have here merely the insistent application of the doctrine promulgated in the essay on *The Poetic Principle*, that poetry is "the rhythmical creation of beauty," and that "the demands of truth are severe; she has no sympathy with the myrtle; all *that* which is indispensable in Song, is precisely all *that* with which *she* has nothing to do."

Now just what did Poe mean by this distinction, amounting to an opposition, between truth and beauty, and how did he carry it out in execution? In one sense it is manifest that no poet ever was truer than Poe; all that intense concentration of his mind, that logical grip of his theme, was directed in a way to the attainment of truth—to the perfectly and relentlessly true attainment of the effect which he had chosen to produce. Wherein lies the contrast between truth and beauty to which he was always returning in theory? It lies not in any failure to deal truthfully with his material, but in the restriction of his material to a certain range of emotions and in the exclusion of what he brands as "the heresy of *The Didactic.*" This he declares explicitly is the ground of his hostility to the contrary assumption that "the object of all Poetry is Truth." Had he confined his attack to didacticism as a mode of expression, it would have been well; but his unfortunate identification of didacticism with truth cut him off from a whole range of material, the highest and finest emotions of the human breast, which need not be didactical at all in form, but are connected with the intuition of moral truth. I mean that kind of emotion, to take an extreme case, which is stirred in Emerson's ethical epigrams. It is a question of values. Beautiful as is much of Poe's work, true as it is, I think an honest criticism must add that it leaves almost untouched the richest source of human feeling. Only perhaps one should except from this limitation the stanzas *To Helen*, in which Poe's distinctive sense of unearthly beauty lies close to the Platonic vision of the Ideal. If these stanzas were written, as tradition has it, when Poe was a mere boy (and they were certainly composed before he had reached his majority), they are one of the most astounding pieces of precocity in literary history—and that even though the two noblest lines stood originally in this comparatively flat form:

> To the beauty of fair Greece
> And the grandeur of old Rome.

And there is this also to be said. Taking truth and beauty as Poe did and as Keats did, Poe, I hold, was the more honest and the less mischievous theorizer than Keats. For taking truth and beauty as they did, Poe was manly and clear-headed in opposing them one to the other; whereas Keats delivered a doctrine as dangerous as it was misleading when he threw out those memorable words,

> Beauty is truth, truth beauty,—that is all
> Ye know on earth, and all ye need to know.

So much by way of extenuation. But we cannot forget, Poe himself never lets us forget, that he was a man to whom life in its outer circumstances was a long experience of unmerciful disaster, and that he had also to contend with an enemy in his own breast, the terrible physical taint whose ravages we see in his countenance. It is natural, but it is none the less unfortunate, that such a man should have developed an æsthetic theory which rejected from the province of poetry any claim of truth beyond that of fidelity to a chosen sensation, and which emphasized so strongly the element of melancholy inherent in the perception of physical beauty. His theory thus, instead of correcting the inevitable trend of a nature like his, rather confirmed him in his temperamental weakness. And so we see him often looking for beauty, and indeed finding it, in the ravages of disease and the ghastly secrets of the tomb. In this field of the abnormal Poe has wrought miracles, reaching his climax in that appalling song of madness which strikes the keynote of *The Fall of the House of Usher*. But we are merely darkening counsel if we set him in competition with those normal poets who deal with the larger and more universal aspects of nature and create loveliness out of the more wholesome emotions of our common humanity. Health is above disease in art as it is in life. Poe remains chiefly the poet of unripe boys and unsound men.

So much must be granted. Yet it is to the honour of Poe that in all his works you will come upon no single spot where the abnormal sinks to the unclean, or where there is an effort to intensify the effect of what is morbid emotionally by an appeal to what is morbid morally. The soul of this man was never tainted. How much that means, how great and near was the danger, can be known by turning to certain of his Continental disciples. The line between them is narrow, but it separates two worlds. Poe does not hesitate to descend for his effects into the very grave where beauty and decay come together; but if you wish to understand the perils he escaped, read after *The Sleeper* one of the poems in which Baudelaire, Poe's avowed imitator and sponsor to Europe, gropes with filthy hands among the mysteries of death.

106

The Solitude
of Nathaniel Hawthorne

In a notable passage, Hawthorne has said of his own *Twice-Told Tales* that "they have the pale tint of flowers that blossomed in too retired a shade. . . . Instead of passion there is sentiment. . . . Whether from lack of power or an unconquerable reserve, the author's touches have often an effect of tameness; the merriest man can hardly contrive to laugh at his broadest humour; the tenderest woman, one would suppose, will hardly shed warm tears at his deepest pathos." And a little further on he adds, "The sketches are not, it is hardly necessary to say, profound." Rarely has a writer shown greater skill in self-criticism than Hawthorne, except where modesty caused him to lower the truth, and in ascribing this lack of passion to his works he has struck what will seem to many the keynote of their character. When he says, however, that they are wanting in depth, he certainly errs through modesty. Many authors, great and small, display a lack of passion, but perhaps no other in all the hierarchy of poets who deal with moral problems has treated these problems, on one side at least, so profoundly as our New England romancer; and it is just this peculiarity of Hawthorne, so apparently paradoxical, which gives him his unique place among writers.

Consider for a moment *The Scarlet Letter*: the pathos of the subject, and the tragic scenes portrayed. All the world agrees that here is a masterpiece of mortal error and remorse; we are lost in admiration of the author's insight into the suffering human heart; yet has any one ever shed a tear over that inimitable romance? I think not. The book does not move us to tears; it awakens no sense of shuddering awe such as follows the perusal of the great tragedies of literature; it is not emotional, in the ordinary acceptance of the word, yet shallow or cold it certainly is not.

From *Shelburne Essays*, First Series (Boston and New York, Houghton Mifflin Company, 1904), pp. 22–50.

In the *English Note-Books* Hawthorne makes this interesting comparison of himself with Thackeray:

> *Mr. S—— is a friend of Thackeray [he writes], and, speaking of the last number of* The Newcomes,—*so touching that nobody can read it aloud without breaking down,—he mentioned that Thackeray himself had read it to James Russell Lowell and William Story in a cider cellar! . . . I cannot but wonder at his coolness in respect to his own pathos, and compare it with my emotions when I read the last scene of* The Scarlet Letter *to my wife, just after writing it,—tried to read it, rather, for my voice swelled and heaved, as if I were tossed up and down on an ocean as it subsides after a storm.*

Why, then, we ask, should we have tears ready for *The Newcomes*, and none for *The Scarlet Letter*, although the pathos of the latter tale can so stir the depths of our nature as it did the author's? What curious trait in his writing, what strange attitude of the man toward the moral struggles and agony of human nature, is this that sets him apart from other novelists? I purpose to show how this is due to one dominant motive running through all his tales, —a thought to a certain extent peculiar to himself, and so persistent in its repetition that, to one who reads Hawthorne carefully, his works seem to fall together like the movements of a great symphony built upon one imposing theme.

I remember, some time ago, when walking among the Alps, that I happened on a Sunday morning to stray into the little English church at Interlaken. The room was pretty well filled with a chance audience, most of whom no doubt were, like myself, refugees from civilisation for the sake of pleasure or rest or health. The minister was a young sandy-haired Scotsman, with nothing notable in his aspect save a certain unusual look of earnestness about the eyes; and I wonder how many of my fellow listeners still remember that quiet Sabbath morn, and the sunlight streaming over all, as white and pure as if poured down from the snowy peak of the Jungfrau; and how many of them still at times see that plain little church, and the simple man standing at the pulpit, and hear the tones of his vibrating voice. Opening the Bible he paused a moment, and then read, in accents that faltered a little as if with emotion, the words, "Eloi, Eloi, lama sabachthani?" and then paused again without adding the translation. I do not know what induced him to choose such a text, and to preach such a sermon before an audience of summer idlers; it even seemed to me that a look of surprise and perturbation stole over their faces as, in tones tremulous from the start with restrained passion, he poured forth his singular discourse. I cannot repeat his words. He told of the inevitable loneliness that follows man from the cradle to the grave; he spoke of the loneliness that lends the depth of yearning to a mother's eyes as she bends over her newborn child, for the soul of the infant has been rent from her own, and she can never again be united to what she cherished. It is this sense of individual loneliness and isolation, he said, that gives pathos to lovers' eyes when love has brought them closest together; it is this that lends austerity to the patriot's look when saluted by the acclaiming multitude. And you, he cried, who for a little while have come forth from the world into these solitudes of God, what hope ye to find? Some respite, no doubt, from the anxiety that oppressed you in the busy town, in the midst of your loved ones about the hearth, in the crowded market place; for you believe that these solitudes of nature will speak to your hearts and comfort you, and that in the peace of nature you will find the true communion of soul that the busy world could not give you. Yet are you deceived; for the sympathy and power of communion between you and this fair creation have been ruined and utterly cast away by sin; and this was typified in the beginning by the banishing of Adam from the terrestrial paradise. No, the murmur of these pleasant brooks and the whispering of these happy leaves shall not speak to the deafened ear of your soul; nor shall the verdure of these sunny fields and the glory of these snowy peaks appeal to the darkened eye of your soul: and this you shall learn to your utter sorrow. Go back to your homes, to your toil, to the populous deserts where your duty lies. Go back and bear bravely the solitude that God hath given you to bear; for this, I declare unto you, is the burden and the penalty laid upon us by the eternal decrees for the sin we have done, and for the sin of our fathers before us. Think not, while evil abides in you, ye shall be aught but alone; for evil is the seeking of self

109

and the turning away from the commonalty of the world. Your life shall indeed be solitary until death, the great solitude, absorbs it at last. Go back and learn righteousness and meekness; and it may be, when the end cometh, you shall attain unto communion with him who alone can speak to the recluse that dwells within your breast. And he shall comfort you for the evil of this solitude you bear; for he himself hath borne it, and his last cry was the cry of desolation, of one forsaken and made lonely by his God.

I hope I may be pardoned for introducing memories of so personal a nature into an article of literary criticism, but there seemed no better way of indicating the predominant trait of Hawthorne's work. Other poets of the past have excelled him in giving expression to certain problems of our inner life, and in stirring the depths of our emotional nature; but not in the tragedies of Greece, or the epics of Italy, or the drama of Shakespeare will you find any presentation of this one truth of the penalty of solitude laid upon the human soul so fully and profoundly worked out as in the romances of Hawthorne. It would be tedious to take up each of his novels and tales and show how this theme runs like a sombre thread through them all, yet it may be worth while to touch on a few prominent examples.

Shortly after leaving college, Hawthorne published a novel which his maturer taste, with propriety, condemned. Despite the felicity of style which seems to have come to Hawthorne by natural right, *Fanshawe* is but a crude and conventional story. Yet the book is interesting if only to show how at the very outset the author struck the keynote of his life's work. The hero of the tale is the conventional student that figures in romance, wasted by study, and isolated from mankind by his intellectual ideals. "He had seemed, to others and to himself, a solitary being, upon whom the hopes and fears of ordinary men were ineffectual." The whole conception of the story is a commonplace, yet a commonplace relieved by a peculiar quality in the language which even in this early attempt predicts the stronger treatment of his chosen theme when the artist shall have mastered his craft. There is, too, something memorable in the parting scene between the hero and heroine, where Fanshawe, having earned Ellen's love, deliberately surrenders her to one more closely associated with the world, and himself goes back to his studies and his death.

From this youthful essay let us turn at once to his latest work —the novel begun when the shadow of coming dissolution had already fallen upon him, though still not old in years; to that "tale of the deathless man" interrupted by the intrusion of Death, as if in mockery of the artist's theme—

> Ah, who shall lift that wand of magic power,
> And the lost clue regain!
> The unfinished window in Aladdin's tower
> Unfinished must remain!

In the fragment of *The Dolliver Romance* we have, wrought out with all the charm of Hawthorne's maturest style, a picture of isolation caused, not by the exclusive ambitions of youth, but by old age and the frailty of human nature. No extract or comment can convey the effect of these chapters of minute analysis, with their portrait of the old apothecary dwelling in the time-eaten mansion, whose windows look down on the graves of children and grandchildren he had outlived and laid to rest. With his usual sense of artistic contrast, Hawthorne sets a picture of golden-haired youth by the side of withered eld:

The Doctor's only child, poor Bessie's offspring, had died the better part of a hundred years before, and his grandchildren, a numerous and dimly remembered brood, had vanished along his weary track in their youth, maturity, or incipient age, till, hardly knowing how it had all happened, he found himself tottering onward with an infant's small fingers in his nerveless grasp.

Again, in describing the loneliness that separates old age from the busy current of life, Hawthorne has recourse to a picture which he employed a number of times, and which seems to have been drawn from his own experience and to have haunted his dreams. It is the picture of a bewildered man walking the populous streets, and feeling utterly lost and estranged in the crowd. So the old doctor "felt a dreary impulse to elude the people's observation, as if with a sense that he had gone irrevocably out of fashion; . . .

or else it was that nightmare feeling which we sometimes have in dreams, when we seem to find ourselves wandering through a crowded avenue, with the noonday sun upon us, in some wild extravagance of dress or nudity." We are reminded by the words of Hawthorne's own habit, during his early Salem years, of choosing to walk abroad at night when no one could observe him, and of his trick in later life of hiding in the Concord woods rather than face a passer-by on the road.

Between *Fanshawe*, with its story of the seclusion caused by youthful ambition, and *The Dolliver Romance*, with its picture of isolated old age, there may be found in the author's successive works every form of solitude incident to human existence. I believe no single tale, however short or insignificant, can be named in which, under one guise or another, this recurrent idea does not appear. It is as if the poet's heart were burdened with an emotion that unconsciously dominated every faculty of his mind; he walked through life like a man possessed. Often while reading his novels I have of a sudden found myself back in the little chapel at Interlaken, listening to that strange discourse on the penalty of sin; and the cry of the text once more goes surging through my ears, "Why hast thou forsaken me?" Truly a curse is upon us; our life is rounded with impassable emptiness; the stress of youth, the feebleness of age, all the passions and desires of manhood, lead but to this inevitable solitude and isolation of spirit.

Perhaps the first work to awaken any considerable interest in Hawthorne was the story—not one of his best—of *The Gentle Boy*. The pathos of the poor child severed by religious fanaticism from the fellowship of the world stirred a sympathetic chord in the New England heart: and it may even be that tears were shed over the homeless lad clinging to his father's grave; for his "father was of the people whom all men hate."

But far more characteristic in its weird intensity and philosophic symbolism is the story of *The Minister's Black Veil*. No one who has read them has ever forgotten the dying man's fateful words:

Why do you tremble at me alone? Tremble also at each other! Have men avoided me, and women shown no pity, and children screamed and fled, only for my black veil? What, but the mystery which it obscurely typifies, has made this piece of crape so awful? When the friend shows his inmost heart to his friend, the lover to his best beloved; when man does not vainly shrink from the eye of his Creator, loathsomely treasuring up the secret of his sin; then deem me a monster, for the symbol beneath which I have lived, and die! I look around me, and, lo! on every visage a Black Veil!

In another of the *Twice-Told Tales* the same thought is presented in a form as ghastly as anything to be found in the pages of Poe or Hoffman. The Lady Eleanore has come to these shores in the early colonial days, bringing with her a heart filled with aristocratic pride. She has, moreover, all the arrogance of queenly beauty, and her first entrance into the governor's mansion is over the prostrate body of a despised lover. Her insolence is symbolised throughout by a mantle which she wears, of strange and fascinating splendour, embroidered for her by the fingers of a dying woman,—a woman dying, it proves, of the smallpox, so that the infested robe becomes the cause of a pestilence that sweeps the province. It happens now and then that Hawthorne falls into a revolting realism, and the last scene, where Lady Eleanore, perishing of the disease that has flowed from her own arrogance, is confronted by her old lover, produces a feeling in the reader almost of loathing. Yet the lady's last words are significant enough to be quoted: "The curse of Heaven hath stricken me, because I would not call man my brother, nor woman sister. I wrapped myself in PRIDE as in a MANTLE, and scorned the sympathies of nature; and therefore has nature made this wretched body the medium of a dreadful sympathy." Alas for the poor broken creature of pride! She but suffered for electing freely a loneliness which, in one form or another, whether voluntary or involuntary, haunts all the chief persons of her creator's world. It is, indeed, characteristic of this solitude of spirit that it presents itself now as the original sin awakening Heaven's wrath, and again as itself the penalty imposed upon the guilty soul: which is but Hawthorne's way of portraying evil and its retribution as simultaneous—nay, as one and the same thing.

113

But we linger too long on these minor works of our author. Much has been written about *The Scarlet Letter*, and it has been often studied as an essay in the effects of crime on the human heart. In truth, one cannot easily find, outside of Æschylus, words of brooding so profound and single-hearted on this solemn subject; their meaning, too, should seem to be written large, yet I am not aware that the real originality and issue of the book have hitherto been clearly discussed. Other poets have laid bare the workings of a diseased conscience, the perturbations of a soul that has gone astray; others have shown the confusion and horror wrought by crime in the family or the state, and something of these, too, may be found in the effects of Dimmesdale's sin in the provincial community; but the true moral of the tale lies in another direction. It is a story of intertangled love and hatred working out in four human beings the same primal curse,—love and hatred so woven together that in the end the author asks whether the two passions be not, after all, the same, since each renders one individual dependent upon another for his spiritual food, and each is in a way an attempt to break through the boundary that separates soul from soul. From the opening scene at the prison door, which, "like all that pertains to crime, seemed never to have known a youthful era," to the final scene on the scaffold, where the tragic imagination of the author speaks with a power barely surpassed in the books of the world, the whole plot of the romance moves about this one conception of our human isolation as the penalty of transgression.

Upon Arthur Dimmesdale the punishment falls most painfully. From the cold and lonely heights of his spiritual life he has stepped down, in a vain endeavour against God's law, to seek the warmth of companionship in illicit love. He sins, and the very purity and fineness of his nature make the act of confession before the world almost an impossibility. The result is a strange contradiction of effects that only Hawthorne could have reconciled. By his sin Dimmesdale is more than ever cut off from communion with the world, and is driven to an asceticism and aloofness so complete that it becomes difficult for him to look any man in the eye; on the other hand, the brooding secret of his passion gives him new and powerful sympathies with life's burden of sorrow, and fills his sermons with a wonderful eloquence to stir the hearts of men. This, too, is the paradox running like a double thread through all the author's works. Out of our isolation grow the passions which but illuminate and render more visible the void from which they sprang; while, on the other hand, he is impressed by that truth which led him to say: "We are but shadows, and all that seems most real about us is but the thinnest substance of a dream,—till the heart be touched. That touch creates us,— then we begin to be,—thereby we are beings of reality and inheritors of eternity."

Opposed to the erring minister stands Roger Chillingworth, upon whom the curse acts more hideously, if not more painfully. The incommunicative student, misshapen from his birth hour, who has buried his life in books and starved his emotions to feed his brain, would draw the fair maiden Hester into his heart, to warm that innermost chamber left lonely and chill and without a household fire. Out of this false and illicit desire springs all the tragedy of the tale. Dimmesdale suffers for his love; but the desire of Chillingworth, because it is base, and because his character is essentially selfish, is changed into rancorous hatred. And here again the effect of the man's passion is twofold: it endows him with a malignant sympathy toward the object of his hate, enabling him to play on the victim's heart as a musician gropes among the strings of an instrument, and at the same time it severs him more absolutely from the common weal, blotting out his life, "as completely as if he indeed lay at the bottom of the ocean."

And what shall we say of the fair and piteous Hester Prynne? Upon her the author has lavished all his art: he has evoked a figure of womanhood whose memory haunts the mind like that of another Helen. Like Helen's, her passive beauty has been the cause of strange trials and perturbations of which she must herself partake; she is more human than Beatrice, nobler and larger than Marguerite,—a creation altogether fair and wonderful. Yet she too must be caught in this embroilment of evil and retribution. The Scarlet Letter upon her breast is compared by the author to the brand on the brow of Cain,—a mark that symbolises her utter separation from the mutual joys and sorrows of the world. She walks about the provincial streets like some lonely bearer of a monstrous fate. Yet because her guilt lies open to the eyes of mankind, and because she accepts the law of our nature, striving to aid and uplift the faltering hearts about her without seeking release from the curse in closer human attachments, following unconsciously the doctrine of the ancient Hindu book,—

> Therefore apply thyself unto work as thy duty bids,
> yet without attachment;
> Even for the profiting of the people apply thyself
> unto work,—

because she renounces herself and the cravings of self, we see her gradually glorified in our presence, until the blessings of all the poor and afflicted follow her goings about, and the Scarlet Letter, ceasing to be a stigma of scorn, becomes "a type of something to be sorrowed over, and looked upon with awe, yet with reverence too."

As a visible outcome of the guilty passion little Pearl stands before us, an elfin child that "lacked reference and adaptation to the world into which she was born," and that lived with her mother in a "circle of seclusion from human society." But the suffering of the parents is efficient finally to set their child free from the curse; and at the last, when the stricken father proclaims his guilt in public and acknowledges his violation of the law, we see Pearl kissing him and weeping, and her tears are a pledge that she is to grow up amid common joys and griefs, nor forever do battle with the world.

And in the end what of the love between Arthur and Hester? Was it redeemed of shame, and made prophetic of a perfect union beyond the grave? Alas, there is something pitiless and awful in the last words of the two, as the man lies on the scaffold, dying in her arms:

"Shall we not meet again?" whispered she, bending her face down close to his. "Shall we not spend our immortal life together? Surely, surely, we have ransomed one another, with all this woe! Thou lookest far into eternity, with those bright dying eyes! Then tell me what thou seest?"

"Hush, Hester, hush!" said he, with tremulous solemnity. "The

law we broke!—the sin here so awfully revealed!—let these alone be in thy thoughts! I fear! I fear! It may be that, when we forgot our God,—when we violated our reverence each for the other's soul,—it was thenceforth vain to hope that we could meet hereafter, in an everlasting and pure reunion."

With his next novel Hawthorne enters upon a new phase of his art. Henceforth he seems to have brooded not so much on the immediate effect of evil as on its influence when handed down in a family from generation to generation, and symbolised (for his mind must inevitably speak through symbols) by the ancestral fatality of gurgling blood in the throat or by the print of a bloody footstep. But whatever the symbol employed, the moral outcome of the ancient wrong is always the same: in *Septimius Felton*, in *The Dolliver Romance*, and most of all in *The House of the Seven Gables*, the infection of evil works itself out in the loneliness of the last sufferers, and their isolation from the world.

It is not my intention to analyse in detail Hawthorne's remaining novels. As for *The House of the Seven Gables*, we know what unwearied care the author bestowed on the description of Miss Hepzibah Pyncheon, alone in the desolate family mansion, and on her grotesque terrors when forced to creep from her seclusion; and how finely he has painted the dim twilight of alienation from himself and from the world into which the wretched Clifford was thrust! And Judge Pyncheon, the portly, thick-necked, scheming man of action,—who, in imagination, does not perceive him, at last, sitting in the great oaken chair, fallen asleep with wide-staring eyes while the watch ticks noisily in his hand? Asleep, but none shall arouse him from that slumber, and warn him that the hour of his many appointments is slipping by. What immutable mask of indifference has fallen upon his face? "The features are all gone: there is only the paleness of them left. And how looks it now? There is no window! There is no face! An infinite, inscrutable blackness has annihilated sight! Where is our universe? All crumbled away from us; and we, adrift in chaos, may hearken to the gusts of homeless wind, that go sighing and murmuring about, in quest of what was once a world. Is there no other sound? One other, and a fearful one. It is the ticking of the Judge's watch, which, ever since Hepzibah left the room in search of Clifford, he has been holding in his hand. Be the cause what it may, this little, quiet, never ceasing throb of Time's pulse, repeating its small strokes with such busy regularity, in Judge Pyncheon's motionless hand, has an effect of terror, which we do not find in any other accompaniment of the scene."

Many times, while reading this story and the others that involve an ancestral curse, I have been struck by something of similarity and contrast at once between our New England novelist and Æschylus, the tragic poet of Athens. It should seem at first as if the vast gap between the civilisations that surrounded the two writers and the utterly different forms of their art would preclude any real kinship; and yet I know not where, unless in these late romances, any companion can be found in modern literature to the Orestean conception of satiety begetting insolence, and insolence calling down upon a family the inherited curse of Atë. It may be reckoned the highest praise of Hawthorne that his work can suggest any such comparison with the masterpiece of Æschylus, and not be entirely emptied of value by the juxtaposition. But if Æschylus and Hawthorne are alike poets of Destiny and of the fateful inheritance of woe, their methods of portraying the power and handiwork of Atë are perfectly distinct. The Athenian too represents Orestes, the last inheritor of the curse, as cut off from the fellowship of mankind; but to recall the Orestean tale, with all its tragic action of murder and matricide and frenzy, is to see in a clearer light the originality of Hawthorne's conception of moral retribution in the disease of inner solitude. There is in the difference something, of course, of the constant distinction between classic and modern art; but added to this is the creative idealism of Hawthorne's rare and elusive genius.

I have dwelt at some length on *The Scarlet Letter* and *The House of the Seven Gables*, because they are undoubtedly the greatest of Hawthorne's romances and the most thoroughly permeated with his peculiar ideas,—works so nearly perfect, withal, in artistic execution that the mind of the reader is overwhelmed by a sense of the power and self-restraint possible to human genius.

Over the other two long novels we must pass lightly, although they are not without bearing on the subject in hand. *The Blithe-*

dale Romance, being in every way the slightest and most colour-less of the novels, would perhaps add little to the discussion. But in *The Marble Faun* it would be interesting to study the awaken-ing of Donatello's half-animal nature to the fullness of human sympathies by his love for Miriam; and to follow Miriam herself, moving, with the dusky veil of secrecy about her, amidst the crumbling ruins and living realities of Rome like some phantom of the city's long-buried tragedies. Hawthorne never made known the nature of the shadow that hovered over this exotic creature, and it may be that he has here indulged in a piece of pure mystifi-cation; but for my own part I could never resist the conviction that she suffers for the same cause as Shelley's Beatrice Cenci. Grant-ing such a conjecture to be well founded, it would throw light on our thesis to compare the two innocent victims of the same hideous crime: to observe the frenzy aroused in Beatrice by her wrong, and the passion of her acts, and then to look upon the silent, unearthly Miriam, snatched from the hopes of humanity, and wrapped in the shadows of impenetrable isolation. Powerful as is the story of the Cenci, to me, at least, the fate of Miriam is replete with deeper woe and more transcendent meaning.

It is natural that the reader of these strange stories and stranger confessions should ask, almost with a shudder, what manner of man was the author. We do not wonder that his family, in their printed memoirs, should have endeavoured in every way to set forth the social and sunny side of his character, and should have published the *Note-Books* with the avowed purpose of dispelling the "often-expressed opinion that Mr. Hawthorne was gloomy and morbid." Let us admit with them that he had but the "inevi-table pensiveness and gravity" of one to whom has been given "the awful power of insight." No one supposes for a moment that Hawthorne's own mind was clouded with the remorseful con-sciousness of secret guilt; and we are ready to accept his statement that he had "no love of secrecy and darkness," and that his ex-treme reserve had only made his writings more objective.

Morbid in any proper sense of the word Hawthorne cannot be called, except in so far as throughout his life he cherished one dominant idea, and that a peculiar state of mental isolation which destroys the illusions leading to action, and so tends at last to weaken the will; and there are, it must be confessed, signs in the maturer age of Hawthorne that his will actually succumbed to the attacks of this subtle disillusionment. But beyond this there is in his work no taint of unwholesomeness, unless it be in itself unwholesome to be possessed by one absorbing thought. We have no reason to discredit his own statement: "When I write anything that I know or suspect is morbid, I feel as though I had told a lie." Nor was he even a mystery-monger: the mysterious element in his stories, which affects some prosaic minds as a taint of morbidness, is due to the intense symbolism of his thought, to the intrinsic and unconscious mingling of the real and the ideal. Like one of his own characters, he could "never separate the idea from the symbol in which it manifests itself." Yet the idea is always there. He is strong both in analysis and generalisation; there is no weakening of the intellectual faculties. Furthermore, his pages are pervaded with a subtle ironical humour hardly compatible with morbidness,—not a boisterous humour that awakens laughter, but the mood, half quizzical and half pensive, of a man who stands apart and smiles at the foibles and pretensions of the world. Now and then there is something rare and unexpected in his wit, as, for example, in his comment on the Italian mosquitoes: "They are bigger than American mosquitoes; and if you crush them, after one of their feasts, it makes a terrific blood spot. It is a sort of suicide to kill them." And if there is to be found in his tales a fair share of disagreeable themes, yet he never confounds things of good and evil report, nor things fair and foul; the moral sense is intact. Above all, there is no undue appeal to the sensations or emotions.

Rather it is true, as we remarked in the beginning, that the lack of outward emotion, together with their poignancy of silent appeal, is a distinguishing mark of Hawthorne's writings. The thought underlying all his work is one to trouble the depths of our nature, and to stir in us the sombrest chords of brooding, but it does not move us to tears or passionate emotion: those affections are dependent on our social faculties, and are starved in the rarefied air of his genius. Hawthorne indeed relates that the closing chapters of *The Scarlet Letter*, when read aloud to his wife, sent her to bed with a sick headache. And yet, as a judicious critic has observed, this may have been in part just because the book seals up the fountain of tears.

It needs but a slight acquaintance with his own letters and *Note-Books,* and with the anecdotes current about him, to be assured that never lived a man to whom ordinary contact with his fellows was more impossible, and that the mysterious solitude in which his fictitious characters move is a mere shadow of his own imperial loneliness of soul. "I have made a captive of myself," he writes in a letter of condolence to Longfellow, "and put me into a dungeon, and now I cannot find the key to let myself out; and if the door were open, I should be almost afraid to come out. You tell me that you have met with troubles and changes. I know not what these may have been, but I can assure you that trouble is the next best thing to enjoyment, and that there is no fate in this world so horrible as to have no share in its joys or sorrows." Was ever a stranger letter of condolence penned?

Even the wider sympathies of the race seem to have been wanting in the man as they are wanting in his books. It is he who said of himself, "Destiny itself has often been worsted in the attempt to get me out to dinner." Though he lived in the feverish ante-bellum days, he was singularly lacking in the political sense, and could look with indifference on the slave question. When at last the war broke out, and he was forced into sympathies foreign to his nature, it seemed as if something gave way within him beneath the unaccustomed stress. It is said, and with probable truth, that the trouble of his heart actually caused his death. His novels are full of brooding over the past, but of real historic sympathy he had none. He has mentioned the old Concord fight almost with contempt, and in his travels the homes of great men and the scenes of famous deeds rarely touched him with enthusiasm. Strangest of all, in a writer of such moral depth, is his coldness toward questions of religion. So marked was this apathy that George Ripley is reported to have said on the subject of Hawthorne's religious tendencies, "There were none, no reverence in his nature." He was not sceptical, to judge from his occasional utterances, but simply indifferent; the matter did not interest him. He was by right of inheritance a Puritan; all the intensity of the

Puritan nature remained in him, and all the overwhelming sense of the heinousness of human depravity, but these, cut off from the old faith, took on a new form of their own. Where the Puritan teachers had fulminated the vengeance of an outraged God, Hawthorne saw only the infinite isolation of the errant soul. In one of his stories, in many ways the most important of his shorter works, he has chosen for his theme the Unpardonable Sin, and it is interesting to read the tale side by side with some of the denunciatory sermons of the older divines.

It is not necessary to repeat the story of *Ethan Brand*, the lime burner, who, in the wilderness of the mountains, in the silences of the night while he fed the glowing furnace, conceived the idea of producing in himself the Unpardonable Sin. Every one must remember how at last he found his quest in his own wretched heart that had refused to beat in human sympathy, and had regarded the men about him as so many problems to be studied. In the end, he who had denied the brotherhood of man, and spurned the guidance of the stars, and who now refuses to surrender his body back to the bosom of Mother Earth,—in the end he must call on the deadly element of fire as his only friend, and so, with blasphemy on his lips, flings himself into the flaming oven. It is a sombre and weird catastrophe, but the tragic power of the scene lies in the picture of utter loneliness in the guilty breast. And would you hear by its side the denunciations of our greatest theologian against sin? Read but a paragraph from the sermons of Jonathan Edwards:

The God that holds you over the pit of hell, much as one holds a spider or some loathsome insect over the fire, abhors you, and is dreadfully provoked. . . . If you cry to God to pity you, he will be so far from pitying you in your doleful case, or showing you the least regard or favour, that, instead of that, he will only tread you underfoot. . . . And though he will know that you cannot bear the weight of omnipotence treading upon you, yet he will not regard that; but he will crush you under his feet without mercy; he will crush out your blood and make it fly, and it shall be sprinkled on his garments, so as to stain all his raiment.

Is it a wonder that strong men were moved to tears and women

122

fainted beneath such words? Yet in the still hours of meditation there is to us, at least, something more appalling in the gloomy imaginations of Hawthorne, because they are founded more certainly on everlasting truth.

I have spoken as if the mental attitude of Hawthorne was one common to the race, however it may be exaggerated in form by his own inner vision; and to us of the western world, over whom have passed centuries of Christian brooding, and who find ourselves suddenly cut loose from the consolation of Christian faith, his voice may well seem the utterance of universal experience, and we may be even justified in assuming that his words have at last expressed what has long slumbered in human consciousness. His was not the bitterness, the fierce indignation of loneliness, that devoured the heart of Swift; nor yet the terror of a soul like Cowper's, that believed itself guilty of the unpardonable sin, and therefore condemned to everlasting exile and torment; nor Byron's personal rancour and hatred of society; nor the ecstasy of Thomas à Kempis, whose spirit was rapt away out of the turmoil of existence; but rather an intensification of the solitude that invests the modern world, and by right found its deepest expression in the New England heart. Not with impunity had the human race for ages dwelt on the eternal welfare of the soul; for from such meditation the sense of personal importance had become exacerbated to an extraordinary degree. What could result from such teaching as that of Jonathan Edwards but an extravagant sense of individual existence, as if the moral governance of the world revolved about the action of each mortal soul? And when the alluring faith attendant on this form of introspection paled, as it did during the so-called transcendental movement into which Hawthorne was born, there resulted necessarily a feeling of anguish and bereavement more tragic than any previous moral stage through which the world had passed. The loneliness of the individual, which had been vaguely felt and lamented by poets and philosophers of the past, took on a poignancy altogether unexampled. It needed but an artist with the vision of Hawthorne to represent this feeling as the one tragic calamity of mortal life, as the great primeval curse of sin. What lay dormant in the teaching of Christianity became the universal protest of the human heart.

123

In no way can we better estimate the universality, and at the same time the modern note, of Hawthorne's solitude than by turning for a moment to the literature of the far-off Ganges. There, too, on the banks of the holy river, men used much to ponder on the life of the human soul in its restless wandering from birth to birth; and in their books we may read of a loneliness as profound as Hawthorne's, though quite distinct in character. To them, also, we are born alone, we die alone, and alone we reap the fruits of our good and evil deeds. The dearest ties of our earthly existence are as meaningless and transient as the meeting of spar with drifting spar on the ocean waves. Yet in all this it is the isolation of the soul from the source of universal life that troubles human thought; there is no cry of personal anguish here, such as arises from Christianity, for the loss of individuality is ever craved by the Hindu as the highest good. And besides this distinction between the Western and Eastern forms of what may be called secular solitude, the Hindu carried the idea into abstract realms whither no Occidental can penetrate.

> HE, in that solitude before
> The world was, looked the wide void o'er
> And nothing saw, and said, Lo, I
> Alone!—and still we echo the lone cry.

> Thereat He feared, and still we fear
> In solitude when naught is near:
> And, Lo, He said, myself alone!
> What cause of dread when second is not known!

But into this dim region of Oriental mysticism we have no reason to intrude. We may at least count it among the honours of our literature that it was left for a denizen of this far Western land, living in the midst of a late-born and confused civilisation, to give artistic form to a thought that, in fluctuating form, has troubled the minds of philosophers from the beginning. Other authors may be greater in so far as they touch our passions more profoundly, but to the solitude of Nathaniel Hawthorne we owe the most perfect utterance of a feeling that must seem to us now as old and as deep as life itself.

It would be easy to explain Hawthorne's peculiar temperament, after the modern fashion, by reference to heredity and environment. No doubt there was a strain of eccentricity in the family. He himself tells of a cousin who made a spittoon out of the skull of his enemy; and it is natural that a descendant of the old Puritan witch judge should portray the weird and grotesque aspects of life. Probably this native tendency was increased by the circumstances that surrounded his youth: the seclusion of his mother's life; his boyhood on Lake Sebago, where, as he says, he first got his "cursed habit of solitude"; and the long years during which he lived as a hermit in Salem. But, after all, these external matters, and even the effect of heredity so far as we can fathom it, explain little or nothing. A thousand other men might have written his books if their source lay in such antecedents. Behind it all was the dæmonic force of the man himself, the everlasting mystery of genius habiting in his brain, and choosing him to be an exemplar and interpreter of the inviolable individuality in which lie the pain and glory of our human estate.

Hawthorne: Looking
Before and After

Nathaniel Hawthorne was born just one hundred years ago, and, by a happy coincidence, the one artist who worked in materials thoroughly American and who is worthy to take a place among the great craftsmen of the world celebrates his nativity on the birthday of the nation.[1] By something more than a mere coincidence he lived and wrote at the only period in the history of the country which could have fostered worthily his peculiar genius; he came just when the moral ideas of New England were passing from the conscience to the imagination and just before the slow, withering process of decay set in. As I read his novels and tales to-day, with the thought of this centenary in my mind, the inevitable comparison arises with what preceded and what exists now; he stands as a connecting link between old Cotton Mather and—*magna cum parvis*—Mary Wilkins Freeman,* and only by looking thus before and after can one get a clear idea of his work.

It seldom happens, in fact, that the history of a country shows so logical a development as that represented by these three names. To look backward, almost all of Hawthorne may be found in germ in the group of ecclesiastical writers among whom Cotton Mather rises pre-eminent, and he in turn is but a spokesman of that half-civilisation which migrated across the Atlantic under the pressure of the Laudian persecutions. I say half-civilisation, for the begin-

---

From *Shelburne Essays*, Second Series (Boston and New York, Houghton Mifflin Company, 1905), pp. 173–87.

[1] On the Fourth of July, 1904, the centenary of Hawthorne's birth was celebrated at Salem, Mass., at Bowdoin College and elsewhere. I was asked to write something in commemoration of the season for the *Independent*, and it seemed appropriate to consider Hawthorne's work historically, as the central point of a long development in New England literature.

* [Mary E. Wilkins Freeman (1852–1930), author of tales of rural New England life.]

nings of New England took place when the mother country was split, as no people in the world ever before was divided, not by sectional but by moral differences into two hostile parties; nor do we always remember how largely the brilliant flowering and quick decay of New England depend on this incompleteness of her origins. Especially is this true in literature. Read through the critical essays that were written in the Elizabethan and Jacobean ages and you will be struck by the fact that the most serious debate was whether poetry had any right to exist at all. That discussion, of course, is as old as Plato and was taken up by the Italians of the Renaissance as part of their classical inheritance. But in England the question was not academic, but vital; it came to the actual test of battle. As early as 1579, in the very first bloom of that "perpetual spring of ever-growing invention," Stephen Gosson dedicated to Sir Philip Sidney his *School of Abuse*, which he aptly describes as "an invective against poets, pipers, players, jesters, and such-like caterpillars of a Commonwealth." "The fathers of lies, pipes of vanity, and schools of abuse," to use another of the crabbed Gosson's phrases, remained snugly in the mother country, along with those who thought it possible to worship God with the homage of the imagination, who made of religion, in fact, a fine sense of decorum in the ordering of the world. The wonder might seem to be that any literature at all ever sprang from the half-civilisation that came to New England, or that any sense of art found root among a people who contemned the imagination as evil and restricted the outpouring of emotion to the needs of a fervid but barren worship. The root was indeed long in coming to flower, yet there are passages in the *Magnalia* of Cotton Mather both magnificent in themselves and indispensable for a right understanding of what was to follow. There is, for example, that famous account of the death of John Cotton, worthy of repeated quotation:

After this in that study, *which had been* perfumed *with many such* days *before, he now spent a* day *in secret* humiliations *and* supplications *before the Lord; seeking the special assistances of the Holy Spirit, for the great work of dying, that was now before him. What glorious* transactions *might one have heard passing between the Lord Jesus Christ, and an excellent servant of his, now coming*

127

unto him, if he could have had an hearing place *behind the* hangings *of the chamber, in such a day! But having finished the duties of the day, he took his leave of his beloved* study, *saying to his consort,* I shall go into that room no more!

That is the positive side of the ideal, and it is a dull heart to-day that can read this story of rapt holiness without a thrill of wonder and admiration. But the negative side is close at hand. The same annalist records of another of his family, Nathaniel Mather, a little incident that shows how inveterate was the suppression of the easy enjoyments and emotions of life. The quotation is from Nathaniel's diary:

When very young *I went astray from God, and my mind was altogether taken with* vanities *and follies; such as the remembrance of them doth greatly abase my soul within me. Of the manifold sins which then I was guilty of, none so sticks upon me, as that being very young, I was* whittling on the Sabbath-day; *and for fear of being seen, I did it behind the door. A great reproach of God! a specimen of that* atheism *that I brought into the world with me!*

One may be inclined to smile, perhaps, at this early intrusion into sacred literature of the Yankee's proverbial trick of whittling, but he will be more apt to marvel at the austerity of a discipline which could associate such a childish escapade with life-long remorse. It is not strange that melancholy hovered over that chosen land. To quote from the *Magnalia* once again:

There are many men, who in the very constitution of their bodies, *do afford a bed, wherein busy and bloody devils, have a sort of lodging provided for them. . . . 'T is well if* self-murder *be not the sad end, into which these hurried people are thus precipitated.* New England, *a country where* splenetic *maladies are prevailing and pernicious, perhaps above any other, hath afforded numberless instances, of even* pious people, *who have contracted those* melancholy indispositions, *which have unhinged them from all service or comfort; yea not a few persons have been hurried thereby to lay* violent hands *upon themselves at the last. These are among the* unsearchable judgments *of God!*

It is not fanciful, I think, to find in these three passages from the greatest of the early New England divines the ideas that were in due time to blossom into a true and peculiar literature. That isolation from the world and absorption in an ideal that signalised the death of John Cotton were to leave an echo in many lives through the following years. Nor did the inability to surrender to the common expansive emotions of human nature and the dark brooding on damnation utterly die out when the real cause ceased to act. They changed, but did not pass away. When, with the coming of the nineteenth century, the fierce democracy of those Northern States asserted itself against priestly control and at the same time shook off the bondage of orthodoxy, it only moved the burden from one shoulder to the other, and the inner tyranny of conscience became as exacting as the authority of the Church had been. But this shifting of the centre of authority from without to within was at least fruitful in one important respect: it brought about that further transition from the conscience to the imagination which made possible the only serious literature this country has yet produced. In that shift from the conscience to the imagination lies the very source of Hawthorne's art. The awful voice of the old faith still reverberates in his stories of New England life and gives them their depth of consciousness; the dissolution of the commands of a sectarian conscience into the forms of a subtle symbolism lifts them from provincial importance merely to the sphere of universal art.

Nor is it at all difficult to follow the religion of the seventeenth into the art of the nineteenth century. In an earlier essay on *The Solitude of Nathaniel Hawthorne* I pointed out—what must be plain to every reader of that author—the central significance of his *Ethan Brand* in the circle of his works. So manifestly do the doctrines of Cotton Mather stalk through that tale under the transparent mask of fiction that it might almost seem as if Hawthorne had taken the passages just quoted from the *Magnalia* as a text for his fancy. For the first quotation, in place of the rigid theologian "perfuming" the bleak atmosphere of his study with meditations on the great work of dying orthodoxly, we have Ethan Brand, the lime-burner, dwelling in the fragrant solitude of the mountains, watching his kiln through the long revolutions of the sun and the stars, perplexing his mind with no problem of predestination and free-will, but with the meaning of life itself, with its tangle of motives and restraining intelligence. For the second quotation, in place of remorse over one act of surrender to impulse against the arbitrary dictates of religion, we have a strange reversal of Puritan faith through the lens of the imagination. Ethan Brand returns to his long-abandoned lime-kiln after wandering over the world, bringing with him the sense that he has sought and found at last in his own heart the Unpardonable Sin, the sin of banishing from the breast all those natural, spontaneous emotions in the pursuit of an idea. He bears the mark, not of an artificial atheism, like that which abased the soul of the young divine, but of that ananthropism (if I may use the word) which was the real sin of New England, symbolised by the strange nature of his successful search. "He had lost his hold of the magnetic chain of humanity. He was no longer a brotherman, opening the chambers or the dungeons of our common nature by the key of holy sympathy, which gave him a right to share in all its secrets; he was now a cold observer, looking on mankind as the subject of his experiment." There lies the tragedy not of Ethan Brand alone, but of the later New England. The dogmas of faith had passed away and left this loneliness of an unmeaning idealism; the enthusiasm which had trampled on the kindly emotions of the day has succumbed, and the contempt of the human heart has given place to this intolerable loneliness.

And last of all there is the "splenetic malady," the melancholy that pursues this thwarting of nature and drives the wanderer to lay violent hands on himself. The burning of Ethan Brand in the lime-kiln, within the circle of whose crimson light he had pondered the Unpardonable Sin, is not, in the sense of Cotton Mather, one of the unsearchable judgments of God, but a cunningly devised symbol of literary art.

This is the second act of the New England drama, and the third proceeds from it as naturally as the second proceeded from the first. From the religious intolerance of Cotton Mather to the imaginative isolation of Hawthorne and from that to the nervous impotence of Mrs. Freeman's men and women, is a regular progress. The great preacher sought to suppress all worldly emotions;

the artist made of the solitude which follows this suppression one of the tragic symbols of human destiny; the living novelist portrays a people in whom some native spring of action has been dried up, and who suffer in a dumb, unreasoning inability to express any outreaching passion of the heart or to surrender to any common impulse of the body. It is true, of course, that Mrs. Freeman describes only a single phase of New England character, just as Hawthorne did before her; but the very genealogy of her genius shows that she has laid hold of an essential trait of that character, and, indeed, it needs but little acquaintance with the stagnant towns of coast and mountains to have met more than one of the people of her books actual in the flesh. Her stories are not tragic in the ordinary sense of the word; they have no universal meaning and contain no problem of the struggle between human desires and the human will, or between the will and the burden of circumstances. They are, as it were, the echo of a tragedy long ago enacted; they touch the heart with the faint pathos of flowers pressed and withered in a book, which, found by chance, awaken the vague recollection of outlived emotions. They are very beautiful in their own way, but they are thoroughly provincial, just as the treatises of Cotton Mather were provincial; they have passed from the imagination to the nerves.

Already in Hawthorne we find the beginnings of this strangely repressed life. Hepzibah Pyncheon, struggling in an agony of shame and impotence to submit to the rude contact of the world, is the true parent of all those stiffened, lonely women that haunt the scenes of Mrs. Freeman's little stage. Only there is this signal difference: poor, blighted Hepzibah is part of a great drama of the conscience which in its brooding over the curse of ancestral sin can only be compared with the Atë of the Æschylean theatre. All the characters that move within the shadow of that *House of the Seven Gables* are involved in one tragic idea assimilated by the author's imagination from the religious inheritance of the society about him—the idea that pride, whether worldly or unworldly, works out its penalty in the separation of the possessor from the common heart of humanity. But in Mrs. Freeman's tales this moral has utterly vanished; they have no significance beyond the pathos of the lonely desolation depicted. Her first book, *A Humble Ro-*

mance, is made up of these frustrate lives, which are withheld by some incomprehensible paralysis of the heart from accepting the ordinary joys of humanity, and her latest book, *The Givers*, appeals to our sympathy by the same shadow of a foregone tragedy.

Very characteristic in the first book is the story of the *Two Old Lovers*. There was nothing to keep them apart, none of the well-used obstacles of romance in the shape of poverty or tyrannous parents or religious differences or an existing alliance—nothing save the ingrown inability of the man to yield to the simple call of his own bosom. For many years he visits the girl and, as time passes, the aged woman, as an accepted but curiously undemonstrative lover. There is, to me at least, a pathos like the nightly memory of tears in the watchfulness of the waiting woman over her diffident wooer:

She saw him growing an old man, and the lonely, uncared-for life that he led filled her heart with tender pity and sorrow for him. She did not confine her kind offices to the Saturday baking. Every week his little house was tidied and set to rights, and his mending looked after. Once, on a Sunday night, when she spied a rip in his coat, that had grown long from the want of womanly fingers constantly at hand, she had a good cry after he had left and she had gone to her room. There was something more pitiful to her, something that touched her heart more deeply, in that rip in her lover's Sunday coat, than in all her long years of waiting. As the years went on, it was sometimes with a sad heart that Maria stood and watched the poor lonely old figure moving slower than ever down the street to his lonely home; but the heart was sad for him always, and never for herself.

Only in the end, when he lies dying in his solitary house and she is summoned to his bedside, does the approach of the great silence of death unlock the dumbness of his breast:

He looked up at her with a strange wonder in his glazing eyes. "Maria"—a thin, husky voice, that was more like a wind through dry cornstalks, said—"Maria, I'm dyin', an'—I allers meant to—have asked you—to—marry me."

Is it fanciful to say that this story has the shadowy pathos of emotions long ago fought against and overcome? The tragedy of New England came when Hawthorne wrought the self-denial of the ancient religion into a symbol of man's universal isolation, when out of the deliberate contemning of common affections he created the search for the Unpardonable Sin. In the pages of Mrs. Freeman we hear only an echo, we revive a fading memory, of that sombre tragedy. *Ethan Brand* was a problem of the will, a question of morality; the tale of the *Two Old Lovers* is a sad picture of palsied nerves.

The latest volume of Mrs. Freeman's sketches treats the same theme, with this difference, however, that here it is the woman who abandons her lover for many years, returning to him only when both are grown old and past the age of spontaneous pleasures. There is perhaps some softening of tone, a kindlier feeling that into this strange desolation of the heart some consolation of the spirit may descend with chastened joy. Hardly in the earlier books, I think, will one find any picture of the possible mellowing effect of solitude comparable to this description of the waiting lover:

> *He was a happy man, in spite of the unfulfilled natural depths of his life. His great sweetness of nature had made even of the legitimate hunger of humanity a blessing for the promoting of spiritual growth. It had fostered within him that grand acquiescence which is the essence of perfect freedom.*

But beautiful as this *grand acquiescence* may be, it is not in that direction lies the real freedom of New England life or literature. Rather shall the deliverance come in the way hinted at in that other phrase, the *hunger of humanity*. The whole progress from Cotton Mather to Mrs. Freeman was determined by the original attempt to stamp out that legitimate hunger for the sake of an all-absorbing pride of the spirit. And now, when the spirit, after having been victorious in the long warfare, has itself starved away and left the barrenness of a dreary stagnation, the natural reversal may well be looked for, and we may expect the hunger of humanity to grow up out of the waste, untempered by spiritual ideals. Already in the New England of Hawthorne, in the exaggerated sentimentalism of the abolitionists and a thousand other reforming sects, this movement had begun. Hawthorne himself, despite his humorous insight and his aloofness from the currents of life about him, did not wholly escape its influence. Through the dark pages of *The House of the Seven Gables* moves the hopeful figure of young Holgrave, the daguerreotypist. To him, says Hawthorne, thinking no doubt of the burden that weighed on his own imagination, it seemed "that in this age, more than ever before, the moss-grown and rotten Past is to be torn down, and lifeless institutions to be thrust out of the way, and their dead corpses buried, and everything to begin anew." There is a world of significance in the analysis which follows of Holgrave's restless and ardent nature, of his generous impulses, that might solidify him into the champion of some practical cause. He is the type of a whole race of men who were to take revenge on the despotism of the spirit by casting it out altogether for the idealised demands of the hunger of humanity.

But what was foreshadowed in Hawthorne becomes the one dominant human note of Mrs. Freeman's stories, heard through the desert silence that otherwise encompasses her characters. This vision of a growing humanitarianism that shall awaken new motives for healthy, active life and feed the hunger of the heart is the real theme of the best of her novels, *Jerome*. There is a scene in that book where the hero, beaten and marred by hard circumstance, suddenly gives vent in his awkward, unschooled manner to the late-born recalcitrance against the tyranny of Providence:

What was it to the moon and all those shining swarms of stars, and that far star-dust in the Milky Way, whether he, Jerome Edwards, had shoes to close or not? Whether he and his mother starved or not, they would shine just the same. . . . He was maddened at the sting and despite of his own littleness in the face of that greatness. Suddenly a wild impulse of rebellion that was almost blasphemy seized him. He clinched a puny fist at a great star. "Wish I could make you stop shinin'," he cried out, in a loud, fierce voice; "wish I could do somethin'!"

And then, later, comes the companion scene, again under the cold eyes of the heavens, when the final determination takes shape be-

134

fore him and he sees at last the work which the world holds for him:

A great passion of love and sympathy for the needy and oppressed of his kind, and an ardent defence of them, came upon Jerome Edwards, poor young shoemaker, going home with his sack of meal over his shoulder. Like a bird, which in the spring views every little straw and twig as toward his nest and purpose of love, Jerome would henceforth regard all powers and instrumentalities that came in his way only in their bearing upon his great end of life.

We have followed the development of that half-civilisation which moulded New England from the religious enthusiasm of Cotton Mather, through the tragic art of Hawthorne, down to the pathetic paralysis portrayed in these stories of a living writer. We have seen a morbid spirituality, spurning the common nourishment of mankind, slowly starve itself into impotence. Now, as the hunger of humanity begins to assert itself unhampered by any vision beyond its own importunate needs, are we to behold a new ideal create in turn another half-civilisation, blindly materialistic as its predecessor was harshly spiritual? That question may not be lightly answered. Only it is clear that, for the present, the way of growth for the literature of New England lies through the opening of this door of strictly human sympathies.

The Centenary of Longfellow

The position of Longfellow is somewhat curious. He was, and I suppose still is, the most beloved poet of the past century, and this not only among the ignorant and half-educated, but among people of the finest culture. Men as different in temperament as Kipling and J. H. Shorthouse give credit to his wonderful knowledge of the sea, and to Shorthouse, at least, he was always "very dear." He was also one of the favourite poets of so cunning a magician in words as Lafcadio Hearn; and to such names one might add indefinitely. Yet it remains true that Longfellow has never been quite accepted by the professed critics, that they have spoken of him commonly with reservation, sometimes even with contempt. Not many, indeed, have adopted just the insolent tone of Mr. Francis Gribble, to whom Longfellow was merely a "prig," with no characteristic habit except that of "decorating his person," a "poet of the obvious and the hum-drum," a man "equally devoid of humour and of passion," whose "intellectual outfit consists of a 'store suit' from a theological emporium." We have a right to be incensed at the tone of such writing, but, waiving this, we must still acknowledge that there has been a distinct undercurrent of protest against the poet's easy popularity. Not his the felicity he attributed to a greater name, thinking, no doubt, of the cavilling he himself endured even during his life: "O happy poet, by no critic vext!"

And this contrast between the love of so many readers for Longfellow and the hesitation of his critics is perfectly comprehensible. The critics are mainly right. Let us not blunt or pervert our taste by ignoring distinctions. In the first place, no one who has stored his mind with the work of the great poets can read Longfellow without stumbling continually over reminiscences that do not fall exactly under the head of plagiarism, but that have the effect of

From *Shelburne Essays*, Fifth Series (Boston and New York, Houghton Mifflin Company, 1908), pp. 132–57.

reducing what has been nobly and individually written to a kind of smooth commonplace. I might from my own recollection fill pages with these dulled echoes of a finer music. Let me illustrate by a few examples. Longfellow, we are told by his biographer, wrote but a single love poem (and I, for one, am ready to honour him for this reserve), that sonnet to "My morning and my evening star of love! My best and gentlest lady!" 'Tis a pretty, and, among poets, rare compliment to his wife; but somehow the taste of it grows flat, and that *best and gentlest lady* drops to something resembling the merely respectable, when we recall the most perfect of Greek epigrams, Plato's Ἀστὴρ πρὶν μὲν ἔλαμπες,* which came to Longfellow, no doubt, through Shelley's version:

> Thou wert the morning star among the living,
> Ere thy fair light had fled;—
> Now, having died, thou art as Hesperus, giving
> New splendour to the dead.

It is not, observe, that our Longfellow has taken the precise thought of the original; there is here no charge of stealing. It is rather that his image suggests the same image used differently and more poetically by another. In the same way his complaint beginning, "Half of my life is gone, and I have let The years slip from me," inevitably forces a comparison with Milton's more resonant note: "When I consider how my light is spent Ere half my days."
Again Longfellow writes:

> God sent his Singers upon earth
> With songs of sadness and of mirth,
> That they might touch the hearts of men,
> And bring them back to heaven again—

and we remember Keats:

> Bards of Passion and of Mirth,
> Ye have left your souls on earth!

* The translation of the complete epigram runs: "Morning Star, that once didst shine among the living, now deceased thou showest the Evening Star among the dead." (Trans. by J. W. Mackail.)

> Have ye souls in heaven, too,
> Double-lived in regions new?

Longfellow writes of the unseen dwellers in *Haunted Houses*:

> We meet them at the doorway, on the stair,
>   Along the passages they come and go,
> Impalpable impressions on the air,
>   A sense of something moving to and fro—

and the memory goes back to Thomas Hood's lines in the most ghostly of English poems:

> Those dreary stairs, where with the sounding stress
>   Of ev'ry step so many echoes blended,
> The mind, with dark misgivings, fear'd to guess
>   How many feet ascended.
>
>   ～ ～ ～
>
> O'er all there hung the shadow of a fear,
>   A sense of mystery the spirit daunted,
> And said, as plain as whisper in the ear,
>   The place is Haunted!

But it would be tedious to multiply examples. The point, as I have said, is not that Longfellow was a plagiarist or lacked originality—greater poets than he have taken their own where they found it with a more royally predatory hand—but that these rather vague resemblances of language and metaphor so often draw our attention to the lower plane upon which his imagination moves. And here I would beg for a little indulgence. This distinction between the higher and lower planes of the imagination goes so near to the very roots of taste and criticism, it is a matter so elusive withal, that I would run the risk of an insistence which may seem like the proverbial breaking of a butterfly upon a wheel. The question turns upon that dualism, or duplicity, in human nature, often misunderstood and to-day more often ignored, the perception of which does yet in some way mark the degree of a poet's or a philosopher's initiation into the mysteries of experience. To make the point clearer, let me compare two poems which are known by heart to

138

all, and whose effect can be tested by the impressions of memory. One is Longfellow's *Weariness*, of which I will quote the first and last stanzas:

> O little feet! that such long years
> Must wander on through hopes and fears,
>   Must ache and bleed beneath your load;
> I, nearer to the wayside inn
> Where toil shall cease and rest begin,
>   Am weary, thinking of your road!

∿ ∿ ∿

> O little souls! as pure and white
> And crystalline as rays of light
>   Direct from heaven, their source divine;
> Refracted through the mist of years,
> How red my setting sun appears,
>   How lurid looks this soul of mine!

The other is Heine's even more familiar lyric on a somewhat similar theme: *Du bist wie eine Blume*, which in my translation will at least be less trite, however much of its charm may have evaporated:

> So fair and fresh and pure
>   Even as a flower thou art;
> I look on thee, and sadness
>   Glideth into my heart.

> 'T is as tho' my hands were resting
>   Upon thy head in prayer,
> Asking that God might keep thee
>   So pure and fresh and fair.

Now, both of these poems have the power of touching the heart, and both have attained the noble distinction of living in the mouths of men; yet it would be uncritical to say that the impression from them is quite the same, or that their reputation is quite equal. I would not seem to be insensible to the tenderness of Longfellow's lines, but something, one feels, is still lacking to give them that penetrating, clinging appeal which belongs to Heine's even

139

simpler song. And I think that, if we look into this difference, it will appear to depend most of all upon the greater and lesser depth of that sense of dualism which the two poets have felt and put into language. There is in Longfellow's poem the contrast of innocent childhood and old age wearied of the world; but this contrast springs from the cumulative effect, so to speak, of time, the refracting mist of years, and beyond this the idea scarcely goes. The emotion conveyed is barely, if at all, distinguished from the sentimental pathos of daily, commonplace life. Whereas in Heine something different and, it must be said, higher, enters. It is not easy, as it never is in the case of true poetry, to define precisely where this added touch comes in—whether in the imagery of the prayer, the lingering cadence of the repeated epithets, or in some haunting vagueness of romantic irony—but one instinctively thinks more of the symbolical power of the poem than of any personal incident or emotion; and this contrast between the loveliness of youth and the satiety of age becomes a sign of a conflict inherent in the poet's own heart, nay, if you will, of the enigmatical dualism, the pathetic or terrible sense of transiency, that runs through the heart of the world.

Well, let us accept this lower position for the greater part—but not for all, as I shall attempt to show—of Longfellow's poetry. Let us admit that his peculiar popularity is due to the fact that he does not require of us any violent readjustment of our ordinary moods, that he sets our own daily thoughts and emotions to music. Is he not to be prized, and praised, for this? Like Whittier, he is the poet of the hearth and the home; yet with a difference. It is in accordance with the well-known tricks of poetic inspiration that the Quaker poet, who was never married and in his earlier years of manhood had no settled abode, should have written lovingly of the peace and protection of the home; whereas Longfellow, who knew all the intimate joys of the family, should have dwelt more on the forebodings and memories of loss. We think of Whittier's *Snow-Bound*, with its snug comforts of the hearth in a New England winter, or of his *Pennsylvania Pilgrim*, that blandest of pastoral poems; even his fancies of the future life took on this ideal of the home, as I have pointed out in another essay. But these are not the notes of Longfellow. He, rather, in a hundred various keys sings of the parting of friends; of resignation for the "one vacant chair"—

> The air is full of farewells to the dying,
>   And mournings for the dead;

of the cry of David in the Chamber over the Gate for Absalom his son. Even in his child poems there often lurks a shadow of anxiety:

> I said unto myself, if I were dead,
>   What would befall these children? what would be
>   Their fate, who now are looking up to me
>   For help and furtherance? Their lives, I said,
> Would be a volume wherein I have read
>   But the first chapters, and no longer see
>   To read the rest of their dear history,
>   So full of beauty and so full of dread.

It is the treatment of these, and other such themes as these, that has made him the one poet whom you will find in almost every household, the poet who is really read and enjoyed by the people; for it is just this sentiment of facile pathos that marks the true popularity. And here, also, we discover his relation to the Teutonising and romanticising—if the word may be passed—of New England culture. From sources of German metaphysics, whether directly or indirectly, from Fichte and Schelling and Schleiermacher, Emerson brought in his transcendental philosophy; from the same romantic school came the impulse that strengthened Hawthorne in his love of the weird and the subterranean, as also his aggravated sense of solitude in the world; there Thoreau got his mystic nature cult—always, it need not be added, with differences caused by other surroundings and traditions. Longfellow brought from Germany the ideal of a world literature which should absorb the best of all lands; but more than that, he imported into Cambridge the sentimental note that runs through German letters. He gave to our poetry the romantic *Empfind-*

141

*samkeit,** refined and qualified indeed by the purity and sweetness and strength of his own nature.

For there is about his muse, I know not what, a certain gracious sweetness, which has the power, as was said when he received his degree at Cambridge, England, "to solace the ills of life and draw men from its low cares *ad excelsiora*"**—an allusion which was caught and applauded by the captious undergraduates. One might analyse the elements of this charm in part, if it were profitable. He had in the first place the rare gift of rhythm; his lines sing themselves inevitably, and there is never, except in some of his hexameters and his blank verse, any doubt about the cadence, or any feeling that the cadence does not fit the thought. Lowell was thinking of this easy rhythmical quality when he wrote of Longfellow on his sixtieth birthday:

> I need not praise the sweetness of his song,
>   Where limpid verse to limpid verse succeeds
> Smooth as our Charles, when, fearing lest he wrong
> The new moon's mirrored skiff, he glides along,
>   Full without noise, and whispers in his reeds.

And then Longfellow has the second, and still rarer, gift of interest, the power of catching the reader's attention with the first word and holding it to the end. Personally I am not particularly fond of *Evangeline* and the other longer poems, with the exception of some of the *Tales of a Wayside Inn* and *The Golden Legend*; I think his virtue lies elsewhere. But all, or nearly all of them have at least the trick of arousing interest. So the fancy is stirred by those first words of *Evangeline*, "This is the forest primeval," and kept awake by the shifting scenes of nature and the sentimental appeal until the very close:

> While from its rocky caverns the deep-voiced neigh-
>   bouring ocean
> Speaks, and in accents disconsolate answers the
>   wail of the forest.

* [Sensitivity.]
** [To higher things.]

(Hexameters, by the way, as sonorous and rhythmical as any in the language.) Not all the great poets have this gift of interest; it is not conspicuous in Milton or Virgil or Wordsworth; it even goes at times with very inferior qualities: but always it is an immense aid in enforcing whatever other powers a writer may possess. It would not be easy to say in just what this faculty of interest resides. In Longfellow it, perhaps, depends mainly on his power of making the reader feel at once that here are his own ideas, almost his own language. Nor are the artifices of rhetoric wanting. Especially, like Lowell, our poet had a wonderful gift of metaphor. You would be surprised if you went through Longfellow and marked the copiousness, the variety, and the ingenuity of these figures. Even from memory one might bring together a long list of metaphors and similes transforming a single group of appearances, such, for example, as the phenomena of night. One might begin with the first words of the poem that follows the prelude of his first volume of collected verse:

> I heard the trailing garments of the Night
> Sweep through her marble halls.

How miraculously that too familiar image expresses the gradual hushing of the earth as twilight descends! Or, to pass from sound to vision, there is the even better stanza:

> . . . and the darkness
> Falls from the wings of Night,
> As a feather is wafted downward
> From an eagle in his flight.

Less subtle and less familiar are a dozen other metaphors of the night that might be quoted, such as the lines in *Hiawatha*:

> Where into the empty spaces
> Sinks the sun, as the flamingo
> Drops into her nest at nightfall
> In the melancholy marshes;—

or this more trivial comparison:

143

> In broad daylight, and at noon,
> Yesterday I saw the moon
> Sailing high, but faint and white,
> As a schoolboy's paper kite;—

or this more aerial fancy:

> As a pale phantom with a lamp
> Ascends some ruin's haunted stair,
> So glides the moon along the damp
> Mysterious chambers of the air.

These are but a few of the metaphors I might from my own memory bring together on a single theme. Most wonderful of all, perhaps, is that comparison whose beauty has grown dim to us through too much repetition:

> And the cares, that infest the day,
> Shall fold their tents, like the Arabs,
> And as silently steal away.

(And here again his art is helped by his delicate rhythmical sense. As an example of the force of little things, let the stanza be read without the word "as" in the last line, and see how flat it seems in comparison.)

Now metaphors, I know, are a dangerous rhetorical weapon, and as a rule they are used with extreme parsimony by the greatest poets; you will find a score of them in Longfellow to one in Milton. Their tendency is to substitute the diversion of fancy for the more tenacious vision of the imagination; they distract the mind ordinarily from its intense preoccupation and so lessen, while diversifying, our intellectual emotion. But they are peculiarly appropriate to such a talent as Longfellow's, as they are to Lowell's, and to them is largely due the continuance and ease of the reader's interest. And apparently they flowed into Longfellow's mind quite unbidden. There is in his published verse nothing better in its way than this simile jotted down in his diary January 29th, 1849:

Another of Emerson's wonderful lectures. The subject Inspiration; *the lecture itself an illustration of the theme. Emerson is*

THE CENTENARY OF LONGFELLOW

*like a beautiful portico, in a lovely scene of nature. We stand
expectant, waiting for the High Priest to come forth; and lo,
there comes a gentle wind from the portal, swelling and sub-
siding; and the blossoms and the vine leaves shake, and far away
down the green fields the grasses bend and wave; and we ask,
"When will the High Priest come forth and reveal to us the
truth?" and the disciples say, "He has already gone forth, and is
yonder in the meadows." "And the truth he was to reveal?" "It
is Nature; nothing more."*

These are the qualities of thought and manner that have at
once made Longfellow the most beloved of poets and kept him
from full acceptance among the critical. But there is still another
aspect of his work, which is sometimes overlooked. The weakness
in his genius, as in that of the New England school generally to
which he belonged, was an absence of resistance. There is a
significant entry in his diary, under the date March 22, 1848:
"He [Lowell] says he means never to write any more poetry—at
least for many years; he 'cannot write slowly enough.'" One feels
this lack of the inward check in much of Longfellow; the lines
flow from him too smoothly and fluently; they have not been
held back long enough to be steeped in the deeper and more
obstinate emotions of the breast—

> Fi, du rhythme commode,
> Comme un soulier trop grand.*

When the proper resistance came to him, it was commonly the
result of some check imposed by the difficulties of form, rather
than of his own artistic inhibition. Thus of all his poems, the
dramas in blank verse are about the flattest, and in general his
power increases with the intricacy of the rhymes employed. The
rule is, of course, not without exceptions. To some readers the
easy flow of the trochees in *Hiawatha* has the charm of a singing
brook that bubbles over its pebbles all a summer's day. And occasionally in those free quatrains, whose secret he learned from
Heine, and which seem so easy, but are really so difficult, he

* ["Fie on the comfortable rhythm,
    Like an oversized shoe."]

145

strikes a note that is rare enough in English. So, one sleepless night, he makes this entry in his diary: "Nahant, September 8, 1880, four o'clock in the morning," and then turns the memorandum into verse:

> Four by the clock! and yet not day;
> But the great world rolls and wheels away,
> With its cities on land and ships at sea,
> Into the dawn that is to be!
>
> Only the lamp in the anchored bark
> Sends its glimmer across the dark,
> And the heavy breathing of the sea
> Is the only sound that comes to me.

When reading these lines, it is easy to understand why Kipling reckoned Longfellow among the few poets who really knew the sea. No one who has spent much of his time on some quiet harbour of our Atlantic coast can fail to be struck by the magic evocation of that second stanza—the nightbound shore, the single light low on the water, the sleepy wash of the waves. Or, take this stanza from the poem of meditations before the flames of a driftwood fire:

> And, as their splendour flashed and failed,
>   We thought of wrecks upon the main,
> *Of ships dismasted, that were hailed*
> *And sent no answer back again.*

Has ever any poet, in a few quiet words, expressed more perfectly the awe and mystery of the sea, the sense of that vastness where so much may happen unseen and unknown of the world?

Such triumphs Longfellow wins now and then in the least resistant metres, but his greater work, that on which his artistic fame will depend, is in the more elaborate forms, particularly in the sonnet. Professor C. E. Norton, who speaks of Longfellow with the authority of a friend and a critic, has just published a sketch of Longfellow's life, with a selection of his autobiographic poems. It is an excellent book for the occasion, but one could wish that he had, instead, brought together all the sonnets, with a study of Longfellow as an artist.[1] For ripeness of style and imagery such a volume would stand easily at the head of American poetry, and it would show an aspect of Longfellow's genius which is obscured by the bulk of his more popular work. It would place him as a peer among the great writers of England. We should have but a slender volume—there are altogether only sixty-three of the original sonnets—but of what richness and variety of scope! Here in brief compass are all the interests of his life. His long acquaintance with books speaks in those six magnificent sonnets prefixed to the translation of *The Divine Comedy*, and in the separate sonnets on Dante, and Milton, and Keats. Was ever poet more happily celebrated than Chaucer in these lines?

> An old man in a lodge within a park;
>> The chamber walls depicted all around
>>> With portraitures of huntsman, hawk, and hound,
>> And the hurt deer. He listeneth to the lark,
> Whose song comes with the sunshine through the
>> dark
>>> Of painted glass in leaden lattice bound;
>> He listeneth and he laugheth at the sound,
>> Then writeth in a book like any clerk.
> He is the poet of the dawn, who wrote
>> The Canterbury Tales, and his old age
>>> Made beautiful with song; and as I read
> I hear the crowing cock, I hear the note
>> Of lark and linnet, and from every page
>>> Rise odours of ploughed field or flowery mead.

And then by the side of this set the contrasted picture of Shakespeare's stage:

> A vision as of crowded city streets,
>> With human life in endless overflow;
>> Thunder of thoroughfares; trumpets that blow
>> To battle; clamour, in obscure retreats,
> Of sailors landed from their anchored fleets;

[1] Since this was written the sonnets have been edited by Ferris Greenslet and issued separately. Houghton Mifflin Co., 1907.

147

> Tolling of bells in turrets, and below
> Voices of children, and bright flowers that throw
> O'er garden walls their intermingled sweets!

To write like this is to combine at once the function of the critic and the poet. Wordsworth may have surpassed him, but no other, I think, in this use of the sonnet.

But the literary flavour in this little book of ours would be no stronger than the other interests we associate with him. Here in the sonnets to Agassiz and Felton and Sumner, the friendships that made so large a part of his life would find expression; his tender solicitude for children speaks in A Shadow and To-Morrow; his love of nature and the sea finds here its full utterance; his reserved, yet earnest, part in the Abolition movement and the war gives pathetic dignity to A Nameless Grave, which Mr. Howells has signalised for its perfect grace and ease; his reminiscences of travel, which did so much to overcome American provincialism, give colour to Venice, The River Rhone, and half a dozen others; the sad fortitude of his old age, as all old age is sad, breathes in this last sonnet he was to write, his farewell inscribed to My Books:

> Sadly, as some old mediæval knight
>   Gazed at the arms he could no longer wield,
>   The sword two-handed and the shining shield
> Suspended in the hall, and full in sight,
> While secret longings for the lost delight
>   Of tourney or adventure in the field
>   Came over him, and tears but half-concealed
> Trembled and fell upon his beard of white,
> So I behold these books upon their shelf,
>   My ornaments and arms of other days;
>   Not wholly useless, though no longer used,
> For they remind me of my former self,
>   Younger and stronger, and the pleasant ways
>   In which I walked, now clouded and confused.

These are but glimpses of the riches in little room that a book of Longfellow's sonnets would offer. They would set forth to unbelievers an artist of rare tact and power, and they would be the best commemoration of the sweetest character that ever revealed itself in rhymes. I know that some have professed to find a certain solemn self-complacency in Longfellow. They turn to the selections from his diary in the Life published by his brother, and point with a kind of patronising smile at such an entry as this:

December 6. [1838. He was then in his thirty-second year.] A beautiful holy morning within me. I was softly excited, I knew not why; and wrote with peace in my heart and not without tears in my eyes, The Reaper and the Flowers, a Psalm of Death.

This man takes himself too seriously, they say: he has no humour. And what then? Why, most of the great poets of the world were without humour, and have they been any the less accepted for that? Humour is well in its place, but there is no reason why we should make a fetich of it, as most of us do in these days. And as for taking his moods and inspiration overseriously, there is nothing in Longfellow's diary that in any way approaches the stupendous solemnity of Wordsworth's introductory notes to his own poems. But the best refutation of such churlish criticism is in the poems of Longfellow, especially those in the sonnet form, which from the time of Petrarch, and of Shakespeare in English, has been the chosen vehicle for poetic confession.

Turn again to that desired book of sonnets if you wish to see the mellow sweetness and the strength of Longfellow's character. I have already referred to his single love-poem, the sonnet to "My morning and my evening star," which, like most of such effusions to a man's wife, rings rather flat; but not so that other sonnet of commemoration. The story of the second Mrs. Longfellow's terrible death by fire and of her husband's efforts to save her is too well known to bear repeating, as may seem also the lines which he wrote eighteen years afterwards, and which were found in his portfolio, unpublished, after his own death:

In the long, sleepless watches of the night,
    A gentle face—the face of one long dead—

149

> Looks at me from the wall, where round its head
> The night-lamp casts a halo of pale light.
> Here in this room she died; and soul more white
> Never through martyrdom of fire was led
> To its repose; nor can in books be read
> The legend of a life more benedight.
> There is a mountain in the distant West
> That, sun-defying, in its deep ravines
> Displays a cross of snow upon its side.
> Such is the cross I wear upon my breast
> These eighteen years, through all the changing
> scenes
> And seasons, changeless since the day she died.

I think we need have no fear of the slurs of shallowness and foppery cast upon a man who carried his suffering so deep in his heart that the world was unaware of its existence. And it is pleasant to hear that the woman so honoured was worthy to be a poet's wife. She is described as having "great beauty, and a presence of dignity and distinction, the true image of a beautiful nature." Everybody knows the home over which she presided, the Craigie House, in Cambridge, that looks out from Brattle Street over which is now a park, named after the poet, to the river Charles, celebrated by him in so many songs. It had been Washington's headquarters when he was in command of the army about Boston, and Longfellow felt the ghostly presence of his great predecessor:

> Once, ah, once, within these walls,
> One whom memory oft recalls,
> The Father of his Country, dwelt,
> And yonder meadows broad and damp
> The fires of the besieging camp
> Encircled with a burning belt.
> Up and down these echoing stairs,
> Sounded his majestic tread;
> Yes, within this very room
> Sat he in those hours of gloom,
> Weary both in heart and head.

But there were other memories attached to the old mansion, which Longfellow did not put into verse. The lady who owned the house and with whom Longfellow lodged before it came into his own possession, was a personage that caused a good deal of wonder and some consternation among the pious folk of Cambridge. There are probably people still living who can recall her figure as she sat at the window reading—reading that archmocker, Voltaire, in the original French, it was believed. One of the legends about her is to the effect that she sturdily refused to allow the caterpillars on her elm-trees to be burned. "Leave them alone!" she would cry; "what are we ourselves but miserable worms!"—which would seem to be as much scriptural as Voltairian.

Here Longfellow lived a large and bountiful life, befitting one to whom fame and honour and prosperity came hand in hand, neither reluctantly nor singly. It is mainly in recognition of his character as a man and poet that his centenary has been turned all over the country into a kind of *agape*; but it is partly also because, even better than Lowell, he represents a beautiful society now passed away and almost forgotten. I was interested the other day in looking through a pamphlet just published, which contains the proceedings of the Cambridge Historical Society— an association of gentlemen and ladies formed a couple of years ago to gather and preserve local traditions. The papers are filled with memories of the little college town to which Longfellow came as a young teacher, steeped in the literatures of Europe. It would be pleasant to quote at length from the recollections of Colonel Higginson and Professor Norton; they give almost a better picture of the quaint life of the day than Lowell's essay on *Cambridge Thirty Years Ago.* Says Professor Norton in his opening address:

So great are the changes in the town since my childhood that the aspects and conditions of those days seem more than a lifetime away. I have the happiness of passing my old age in the house in which I was born. It has always been my home; but when I was a boy, it was in the country—now it is suburban and in the heart of a city. Kirkland Street was a country road with not a single house on its southern side, but with a wide stretch quite over to Harvard Street of marsh land and huckleberry pasture, with channels running through the thick growth of shrubs, often frozen

151

in the winter, and on which we boys used to skate over the very site of the building in which we have met to-night. Down as far as to Inman Square, the region was solitary, while beyond Inman Square, toward Boston, was an extensive wood of pines with a dense underbrush, the haunt, as we boys used to believe, of gamblers and other bad characters from the neighbouring city, and to be swiftly hurried by if nightfall caught us near it. The whole region round my father's house was, indeed, so thinly settled that it preserved its original rural character. It was rich in wild growth, and well known to botanists as the habitat of many rare flowers; the marshes were fragrant in spring with azalea and the clethra; and through spring, summer, and autumn there was a profuse procession of the familiar flowers of New England. It was a favourite resort of birds, but there is now little left of it fit for their homes, though many of them still revisit in their migrations the noisy locality where their predecessors enjoyed a peaceful and retired abode.

But even a greater change than that from country village to surburban town has taken place here in Old Cambridge in the last seventy years. The people have changed. In my boyhood the population was practically all of New England origin, and in large proportion Cambridge-born, and inheritors of Old Cambridge traditions. The fruitful invasion of barbarians had not begun. The foreign-born people could be counted upon the fingers. There was Rule, the excellent Scotch gardener, who was not without points of resemblance to Andrew Fairservice; there was Sweetman, the one Irish day labourer, faithful and intelligent, trained as a boy in one of the "hedge-schools" of his native Ireland, and ready to lean on his spade and put the troublesome schoolboy to a test on the Odes of Horace, or even on the Arma virumque cano; and at the heart of the village was the hair-cutter, Marcus Reamie, from some unknown foreign land, with his shop full, in a boy's eyes, of treasures, some of his own collecting, some of them brought from distant romantic parts of the world by his sailor son. There were doubtless other foreigners, but I do not recall them, except a few teachers of languages in the College, of whom three filled in these and later years an important place in the life of the town—

Dr. Beck, Dr. Follen, and Mr. Sales. But the intermixture of foreign elements was so small as not to affect the character of the town; in fact, everybody knew not only everybody else in person, but also much of everybody's tradition, connections, and mode of life. It has been a pathetic experience for me to live all my life in one community and to find myself gradually becoming a stranger to it.

And what society was gathered together in this village among the fields and fens! Read the poems written by Longfellow on the death of his friends—on Hawthorne, Dana, Sumner, Agassiz, Felton, and I know not how many others. Or, which of our cities to-day can show any gathering of men equal to the weekly meetings of Longfellow and Lowell and Professor Norton to discuss the translation of Dante? We may, if we choose, look back upon that life as in many ways provincial; but how much of the strain and inconsequence of our would-be cosmopolitan society it lacked. One need not be a New Englander, or a Harvard man, to join heartily in honouring the poet who represents the highest and most homogeneous culture this country has yet produced.

And it is wholesome for us to read and praise Longfellow. It is not necessary to place his work as a whole beside that of the greatest poet, or to overlook his shortcomings; but I think even those shortcomings have their special value at the present hour. We are apt to take our poets rather solemnly, when we read them at all, to search for deep and complex meanings; and in the process we often lose the inward serenity and unvexed faith which it is the mission of the poet to bestow. Not the stress of our emotion or our intellectual perturbation is the measure of our understanding, but rather the depth of our response to that word of the exiled Dante, when, in the convent court, he was questioned as to what he sought—*La pace*, peace. And Longfellow knew the meaning of that word as Dante used it. In the sorrow that fell upon him after his tragic bereavement, he found solace, or at least strength, in the daily translation of *The Divine Comedy*. Every lover of poetry knows the first and finest of the sonnets he prefixed to that work:

153

Oft have I seen at some cathedral door
   A labourer, pausing in the dust and heat,
   Lay down his burden, and with reverent feet
Enter, and cross himself, and on the floor
   Kneel to repeat his paternoster o'er;
   Far off the noises of the world retreat:
The loud vociferations of the street
   Become an undistinguishable roar.
So, as I enter here from day to day,
   And leave my burden at this minster gate,
Kneeling in prayer, and not ashamed to pray,
   The tumult of the time disconsolate
To inarticulate murmurs dies away,
   While the eternal ages watch and wait.

We need have no fear of paying homage to a poet who wrote such lines as those. And he himself, if he did not, like Dante and his peers, build at the great cathedral of song, did at least add to it a fair and homely chapel, where also, to one who comes humbly and reverently, the eternal ages watch and wait.

Whittier the Poet

Last month we took the new edition of Cowper's Letters as an occasion to consider the life of the poet, who brought the quiet affections of the home into English literature, and that may be our excuse for waiving the immediate pressure of the book-market and turning to the American poet whose inspiration springs largely from the same source. Different as the two writers are in so many respects, different above all in their education and surroundings, yet it would not be difficult to find points of resemblance to justify such a sequence. In both the spirit of religion was bound up with the cult of seclusion; to both the home was a refuge from the world; to both this comfort was sweetened by the care of a beloved companion, though neither of them ever married. But, after all, no apology is needed, I trust, for writing about a poet who is very dear to me as to many others, and who has suffered more than most at the hands of his biographers and critics.

It should seem that no one could go through Whittier's poems even casually without remarking the peculiar beauty of the idyl called *The Pennsylvania Pilgrim*. It is one of the longest and, all things considered, quite the most characteristic of his works. Yet Mr. Pickard in his official biography brings the poem into no relief; Professor Carpenter names it in passing without a word of comment; and Colonel Higginson in his volume in the English Men of Letters Series does not mention it at all—but then he has a habit of omitting the essential. Among those who have written critically of American literature the poem is not even named, so far as I am aware, by Mr. Stedman or by Professors Richardson, Lawton, Wendell, and Trent. I confess that this conspiracy of silence, as I hunted through one historian and critic after an-

---

From *Shelburne Essays*, Third Series (Boston and New York, Houghton Mifflin Company, 1906), pp. 28–53.

other, grew disconcerting, and I began to distrust my own judgment until I chanced upon a confirmation in two passages of
Whittier's letters. Writing of *The Pennsylvania Pilgrim* to his
publisher in May, 1872, he said: "I think honestly it is as good
as (if not better than) any long poem I have written"; and a
little later to Celia Thaxter: "It is as long as *Snow-Bound*, and
better, but nobody will find it out." One suspects that all these
gentlemen in treating of Whittier have merely followed the line
of least resistance, without taking much care to form an independent opinion; and the line of least resistance has a miserable
trick of leading us astray. In the first place, Whittier's share in
the Abolition and other reforming movements bulks so large
in the historians' eyes that sometimes they seem almost to forget
Whittier the poet. And the critics have taken the same cue.
"Whittier," says one of them, "will be remembered even more
as the trumpet-voice of Emancipation than as the peaceful singer
of rural New England."

The error, if it may be said with reverence, can be traced even
higher, and in Whittier we meet only one more witness to the
unconcern of Nature over the marring of her finer products.
The wonder is not that he turned out so much that is faulty,
but that now and then he attained such exquisite grace. Whittier
was born, December 17, 1807, in East Haverhill, in the old
homestead which still stands, a museum now, hidden among
the hills from any other human habitation. It is a country not
without quiet charm, though the familiar lines of *Snow-Bound*
make us think of it first as beaten by storm and locked in by
frost. And, notwithstanding the solace of an affectionate home,
life on the farm was unnecessarily hard. The habits of the grim
pioneers had persisted and weighed heavily on their dwindled
descendants. Thus the Whittiers, who used to drive regularly
to the Quaker meeting at Amesbury, eight miles distant, are said
to have taken no pains to protect themselves from the bleakest
weather. The poet suffered in body all his life from the rigour
of this discipline; nor did he suffer less from insufficiency of
mental training. Not only was the family poor, but it even appears that the sober tradition of his people looked askance at
the limited means of education at hand. Only at the earnest

solicitation of outsiders was the boy allowed to attend the academy at Haverhill. Meanwhile, he was a little of everything: farm worker, shoemaker, teacher—he seems to have shifted about as chance or necessity directed. There were few—he has told us how few—books in the house, and little time for reading those he could borrow. But if he read little, he wrote prodigiously. The story of his first printed poem in the *Free Press* of Newburyport and of the encouragement given him by the far-sighted editor, William Lloyd Garrison, is one of the best known and most picturesque incidents in American letters. The young poet— he was then nineteen—was launched; from that time he became an assiduous writer for the press, and was at intervals editor of various country or propagandist newspapers.

The great currents of literary tradition reached him vaguely from afar and troubled his dreams. Burns fell early into his hands, and the ambition was soon formed of transferring the braes and byres of Scotland to the hills and folds of New England. The rhythms of Thomas Moore rang seductively in his ears. Byron, too, by a spirit of contrast, appealed to the Quaker lad, and one may read in Mr. Pickard's capital little book, *Whittier-Land*, verses and fragments of letters which show how deeply that poison of the age had bitten into his heart. But the influence of those sons of fire was more than counteracted by the gentle spirit of Mrs. Hemans—indeed, the worst to be said of Whittier is that never, to the day of his death, did he quite throw off allegiance to the facile and innocent muse of that lady. It is only right to add that in his later years, especially in the calm that followed the civil war, he became a pretty widely read man, a man of far more culture than he is commonly supposed to have been.

Such was the boy, then—thirsting for fame, scantily educated, totally without critical guidance or environment, looking this way and that—who was thrust under the two dominant influences of his time and place. To one of these, transcendentalism, we owe nearly all that is highest, and unfortunately much also that is most inchoate, in New England literature. Its spirit of complacent self-dependence was dangerous at the best, although in Whittier I cannot see that it did more than confirm his habit of uncritical prolixity; it could offer no spiritual seduction to one who held liberally the easy doctrine of the Friends. But to the other influence he fell a natural prey. The whole tradition of the Quakers—the memory of Pastorius, whom he was to sing as the Pennsylvania Pilgrim; the inheritance of saintly John Woolman, whose Journal he was to edit—prepared him to take part in the great battle of the Abolitionists. From that memorable hour when he met Garrison face to face on his Haverhill farm to the ending of the war in 1865, he was no longer free to develop intellectually, but was a servant of reform and politics. I am not, of course, criticising that movement or its achievement; I regret only that one whose temper and genius called for fostering in quiet fields should have been dragged into that stormy arena. As he says in lines that are true if not elegant:

> Hater of din and riot,
> He lived in days unquiet;
> And, lover of all beauty,
> Trod the hard ways of duty.

It is not merely that political interests absorbed the energy which would otherwise have gone to letters; the knowledge of life acquired might have compensated and more than compensated for less writing, and, indeed, he wrote too much as it was. The difficulty is rather that "the pledged philanthropy of earth" somehow militates against art, as Whittier himself felt. Not only the poems actually written to forward the propaganda are for the most part dismal reading, but something of their tone has crept into other poems, with an effect to-day not far from cant. Twice the cry of the liberator in Whittier rose to noble writing. But in both cases it is not the mere pleading of reform but a very human and personal indignation that speaks. In *Massachusetts to Virginia* this feeling of outrage calls forth one of the most stirring pieces of personification ever written, nor can I imagine a day when a man of Massachusetts shall be able to read it without a tingling of the blood, or a Virginian born hear it without a sense of unacknowledged shame; in *Ichabod* he uttered a word of individual scorn that will rise up for quotation whenever any strong leader

158

misuses, or is thought to misuse, his powers. Every one knows the
lines in which Webster is pilloried for his defection:

> Of all we loved and honoured, naught
>   Save power remains;
> A fallen angel's pride of thought,
>   Still strong in chains.

> All else is gone; from those great eyes
>   The soul has fled;
> When faith is lost, when honour dies,
>   The man is dead!

> Then pay the reverence of old days
>   To his dead fame;
> Walk backward, with averted gaze,
>   And hide the shame!

It is instructive that only when his note is thus pierced by
individual emotion does the reformer attain to universality of
appeal. Unfortunately most of Whittier's slave songs sink down
to a dreary level—down to the almost humorous bathos of the
lines suggested by *Uncle Tom's Cabin:*

> Dry the tears for holy Eva,
> With the blessed angels leave her. . . .

What he needed above everything else, what his surroundings
were least of all able to give him, was a canon of taste, which
would have driven him to stiffen his work, to purge away the
flaccid and set the genuinely poetical in stronger relief—a purely
literary canon which would have offset the moralist and reformer
in him, and made it impossible for him (and his essays show that
the critical vein was not absent by nature) to write of Longfellow's
Psalm of Life: "These nine simple verses are worth more than
all the dreams of Shelley, and Keats, and Wordsworth. They are
alive and vigorous with the spirit of the day in which we live—
the moral steam enginery of an age of action." While Tennyson
and Matthew Arnold were writing in England, the earlier tra-

dition had not entirely died out in America that the first proof
of genius is an abandonment of one's mind to temperament and
"inspiration." Byron had written verse as vacillating and formless
as any of Whittier's; Shelley had poured forth page after page
of effusive vapourings; Keats learned the lesson of self-restraint
almost too late; Wordsworth indulged in platitudes as simpering
as "holy Eva"; but none of these poets suffered so deplorably
from the lack of criticism as the finest of our New England spirits.
The very magnificence of their rebellion, the depth and originality
of their emotion, were a compensation for their licence, were perhaps inevitably involved in it. The humbler theme of Whittier's
muse can offer no such apology; he who sings the commonplace
joys and cares of the heart needs above all to attain that *simplex
munditiis* which is the last refinement of taste; lacking that, he
becomes himself commonplace. And Whittier knew this. In
the Proem to the first general collection of his poems, he wrote:

> Of mystic beauty, dreamy grace,
> No rounded art the lack supplies;
> Unskilled the subtle line to trace,
> Or softer shades of Nature's face,
> I viewed her common forms with unanointed eyes.
>
> Nor mine the seer-like power to show
> The secrets of the heart and mind;
> *To drop the plummet line below*
> *Our common world of joy and woe,*
> *A more intense despair or brighter hope to find.*

But at this point we must part company with his confession.
His reward is not that he showed "a hate of tyranny intense" or
laid his gifts on the shrine of Freedom, but that more completely
than any other poet he developed the peculiarly English *ideal of
the home* which Cowper first brought intimately into letters, and
added to it those *homely comforts of the spirit* which Cowper
never felt. With Longfellow he was destined to throw the glamour
of the imagination over "our common world of joy and woe."

Perhaps something in his American surroundings fitted him
peculiarly for this humbler rôle. The fact that the men who had

made the new colony belonged to the middle class of society tended to raise the idea of home into undisputed honour, and the isolation and perils of their situation in the earlier years had enhanced this feeling into something akin to a cult. America is still the land of homes. That may be a lowly theme for a poet; to admire such poetry may, indeed it does, seem to many to smack of a bourgeois taste. And yet there is an implication here that carries a grave injustice. For myself, I admit that Whittier is one of the authors of my choice, and that I read him with ever fresh delight; I even think there must be something spurious in that man's culture whose appreciation of Milton or Shelley dulls his ear to the paler but very refined charm of Whittier. If truth be told, there is sometimes a kind of exquisite content in turning from the pretentious poets who exact so much of the reader to the more immediate appeal of our sweet Quaker. In comparison with those more exalted muses his nymph is like the nut-brown lass of the old song—

> But when we come where comfort is,
> She never will say No.

And often, after fatiguing the brain with the searchings and inquisitive flight of the Masters, we are ready to say with Whittier:

> I break my pilgrim staff, I lay
> Aside the toiling oar;
> The angel sought so far away
> I welcome at my door.

There, to me at least, and not in the ballads which are more generally praised, lies the rare excellence of Whittier. True enough, some of these narrative poems are spirited and admirably composed. Now and then, as in *Cassandra Southwick*, they strike a note which reminds one singularly of the real ballads of the people; in fact, it would not be fanciful to discover a certain resemblance between the manner of their production and of the old popular songs. Their publication in obscure newspapers, from which they were copied and gradually sent the rounds of the country, is not essentially different from the way in which many

161

of the ballads were probably spread abroad. The very atmosphere that surrounded the boy in a land where the traditions of border warfare and miraculous events still ran from mouth to mouth prepared him for such balladry. Take, for example, this account of his youth from the Introduction to *Snow-Bound*:

> *Under such circumstances story-telling was a necessary resource in the long winter evenings. My father when a young man had traversed the wilderness to Canada, and could tell us of his adventures with Indians and wild beasts, and of his sojourn in the French villages. My uncle was ready with his record of hunting and fishing, and, it must be confessed, with stories, which he at least half-believed, of witchcraft and apparitions. My mother, who was born in the Indian-haunted region of Somersworth, New Hampshire, between Dover and Portsmouth, told us of the inroads of the savages, and the narrow escape of her ancestors.*

No doubt this legendary training helped to give more life to Whittier's ballads and border tales than ordinarily enters into that rather factitious form of composition; and for a while he made a deliberate attempt to create out of it a native literature. But the effect was still deeper, by a kind of contrast, on his poetry of the home. After several incursions into the world as editor and agitator, he was compelled by ill health to settle down finally in the Amesbury house, which he had bought in 1836; and there with little interruption he lived from his thirty-third to his eighty-fifth year, the year of his death. In *Snow-Bound* his memory called up a picture of the old Haverhill homestead, unsurpassed in its kind for sincerity and picturesqueness; in poem after poem he celebrated directly or indirectly "the river hemmed with leaning trees," the hills and ponds, the very roads and bridges of the land about these sheltered towns. On the one hand, the recollection of the wilder life through which his parents had come added to the snugness and intimacy of these peaceful scenes, and, on the other hand, the encroachment of trade and factories into their midst lent a poignancy of regret for a grace that was passing away. Mr. Pickard's little guidebook, to which I have already referred, brings together happily the innumerable allusions of local

interest; there is no spot in America, not even Concord, where
the light of fancy lies so entrancingly:

> A tender glow, exceeding fair,
> A dream of day without its glare.

For it must be seen that the crudeness of Whittier's education,
and the thorny ways into which he was drawn, marred a large
part, but by no means all, of his work. There are a few poems
in his collection of an admirable craftsmanship in that genre
which is none the less difficult—which I sometimes think is
almost more difficult—because it lies so perilously near the trivial
and mean. There are others which need only a little pruning,
perhaps a little heightening here and there, to approach the
same perfection of charm. Especially they have that harmony
of tone which arises from the unspoiled sincerity of the writer
and ends by subduing the reader to a restful sympathy with
their mood. No one can read much in Whittier without feeling
that these hills and valleys about the Merrimac have become
one of the inalienable domiciles of the spirit—a familiar place
where the imagination dwells with untroubled delight. Even the
little things, the flowers and birds of the country, are made to
contribute to the sense of homely content. There is one poem in
particular which has always seemed to me significant of Whittier's
manner, and a comparison of it with the famous flower poems of
Wordsworth will show the difference between what I call the
poetry of the hearth and the poetry of intimate nature. It was
written to celebrate a gift of *Pressed Gentian* that hung at the
poet's window, presenting to wayside travellers only a "grey disk
of clouded glass":

> They cannot from their outlook see
> The perfect grace it hath for me;
> For there the flower, whose fringes through
> The frosty breath of autumn blew,
> Turns from without its face of bloom
> To the warm tropic of my room,
> As fair as when beside its brook
> The hue of bending skies it took.

163

> So from the trodden ways of earth
> Seem some sweet souls who veil their worth,
> And offer to the careless glance
> The clouding grey of circumstance. . . .

There is not a little of self-portraiture in this image of the flower, and it may be that some who have written of Whittier patronisingly are like the hasty passer-by—they see only the *grey disk of clouded glass.*

And the emotion that furnishes the loudest note to most poets is subdued in Whittier to the same gentle tone. To be sure, there is evidence enough that his heart in youth was touched almost to a Byronic melancholy, and he himself somewhere remarks that "Few guessed beneath his aspect grave, What passions strove in chains." But was there not a remnant of self-deception here? Do not the calmest and wisest of us like to believe we are calm and wise by virtue of vigorous self-repression? Wordsworth, we remember, explained the absence of love from his poetry on the ground that his passions were too violent to allow any safe expression of them. Possibly they were. Certainly, in Whittier's verse we have no reflection of those tropic heats, but only "the Indian summer of the heart." The very title, *Memories,* of his best-known love poem (based on a real experience, the details of which have recently been revealed) suggests the mood in which he approaches this subject. It is not the quest of desire he sings, but the home-coming after the frustrate search and the dreaming recollection by the hearth of an ancient loss. In the same way, his ballad *Maud Muller,* which is supposed to appeal only to the unsophisticated, is attuned to that shamelessly provincial rhyme,

> For of all sad words of tongue or pen,
> The saddest are these: "It might have been!"

It is a little so with us all, perhaps, as it was with the judge and the maiden; only, as we learn the lesson of years, the disillusion is likely to be mingled strangely with relief, and the sadness to take on a most comfortable and flattering Quaker drab—as it did with our "hermit of Amesbury."

164

If love was a memory, religion was for Whittier a hope and an ever-present consolation—peculiarly a consolation, because he brought into it the same thought of home-coming that marks his treatment of nature and the passions. Partly, this was due to his inherited creed, which was tolerant enough to soften theological dispute: "Quakerism," he once wrote to Lucy Larcom, "has no Church of its own—it belongs to the Church Universal and Invisible." In great part the spirit of his faith was private to him; it even called for a note of apology to the sterner of his brethren:

> O friends! with whom my feet have trod
>   The quiet aisles of prayer,
> Glad witness to your zeal for God
>   And love of man I bear.
>
> I trace your lines of argument;
>   Your logic linked and strong
> I weigh as one who dreads dissent,
>   And fears a doubt as wrong.
>
> But still my human hands are weak
>   To hold your iron creeds:
> Against the words ye bid me speak
>   My heart within me pleads. . . .

And the inimitably tender conclusion:

> And so beside the Silent Sea
>   I wait the muffled oar;
> No harm from Him can come to me
>   On ocean or on shore.
>
> I know not where His islands lift
>   Their fronded palms in air;
> I only know I cannot drift
>   Beyond His love and care.
>
> O brothers! if my faith is vain,
>   If hopes like these betray,
> Pray for me that my feet may gain
>   The sure and safer way.

165

> And Thou, O Lord! by whom are seen
>> Thy creatures as they be,
> Forgive me if too close I lean
>> My human heart on Thee!

Not a strenuous mood it may be, or very exalted—not the mood of the battling saints, but one familiar to many a troubled man in his hours of simpler trust. We have been led to Whittier through the familiar poetry of Cowper; consider what it would have been to that tormented soul if for one day he could have forgotten the awe of his divinity and *leaned his human heart* on God. It is not good for any but the strongest to dwell too much with abstractions of the mind. And, after all, change the phrasing a little, substitute if you choose some other intuitive belief for the poet's childlike faith, and you will be surprised to find how many of the world's philosophers would accept the response of Whittier:

> We search the world for truth; we cull
> The good, the pure, the beautiful,
> From graven stone and written scroll,
> From all old flower-fields of the soul;
> And, weary seekers of the best,
> We come back laden from our quest,
> To find that all the sages said
> Is in the Book our mothers read.

Such a rout of the intellect may seem ignominious, but is it any more so than the petulance of Renan because all his learning had only brought him to the same state of skepticism as that of the gamin in the streets of Paris? Our tether is short enough, whichever way we seek escape. It is worth noting that in his essay on Baxter (he who conceived of the saints' rest in a very different spirit) Whittier blames that worthy just for the exaltation of his character. "In our view," he says, "this was its radical defect. He had too little of humanity, he felt too little of the attraction of this world, and lived too exclusively in the spiritual and the unearthly."

And if Whittier's faith was simple and human, his vision of the other world was strangely like the remembrance of a home that we have left in youth. There is a striking expression of this in one of

his prose tales, now almost forgotten despite their elements of pale
but very genuine humour and pathos, as if written by an attenu-
ated Hawthorne. The good physician, Dr. Singletary, and his
friends are discussing the future life, and says one of them:

*Have you not felt at times that our ordinary conceptions of
heaven itself, derived from the vague hints and Oriental imagery
of the Scriptures, are sadly inadequate to our human wants and
hopes? How gladly would we forego the golden streets and gates
of pearl, the thrones, temples, and harps, for the sunset lights of
our native valleys; the woodpaths, where moss carpets are woven
with violets and wild flowers; the songs of birds, the low of cattle,
the hum of bees in the apple-blossoms—the sweet, familiar voices
of human life and nature! In the place of strange splendours and
unknown music, should we not welcome rather whatever reminded
us of the common sights and sounds of our old home?*

It was eminently proper that, as the poet lay awaiting death,
with his kinsfolk gathered about him, one of them should have
recited the stanzas of his psalm *At Last:*

> When on my day of life the night is falling,
>   And, in the winds from unsunned spaces blown,
> I hear far voices out of darkness calling
>   My feet to paths unknown,
>
> Thou who hast made my home of life so pleasant,
>   Leave not its tenant when its walls decay;
> O Love Divine, O Helper ever present,
>   Be Thou my strength and stay!
>   ∽   ∽   ∽
> I have but Thee, my Father! let Thy spirit
>   Be with me then to comfort and uphold;
> No gate of pearl, no branch of palm I merit,
>   Nor street of shining gold.
>
> Suffice it if—my good and ill unreckoned,
>   And both forgiven through Thy abounding
>   grace—
> I find myself by hands familiar beckoned
>   Unto my fitting place.

I would not call this the highest religious poetry, pure and sweet as it may be. Something still is lacking, but to see that want fulfilled one must travel out of Whittier's age, back through all the eighteenth century, back into the seventeenth. There you will find it in Vaughan and Herbert and sometimes in Marvell—poets whom Whittier read and admired. Take two poems from these two ages, place them side by side, and the one thing needed fairly strikes the eyes. The first poem Whittier wrote after the death of his sister Elizabeth (who had been to him what Mrs. Unwin had been to Cowper) was *The Vanishers*, founded on a pretty superstition he had read in Schoolcraft:

> Sweetest of all childlike dreams
>   In the simple Indian lore
> Still to me the legend seems
>   Of the shapes who flit before.
>
> Flitting, passing, seen, and gone,
>   Never reached nor found at rest,
> Baffling search, but beckoning on
>   To the Sunset of the Blest.
>
> From the clefts of mountain rocks,
>   Through the dark of lowland firs,
> Flash the eyes and flow the locks
>   Of the mystic Vanishers!

Now Vaughan, too, wrote a poem on those gone from him:

> They are all gone into the world of light,
>   And I alone sit lingering here;
> Their very memory is fair and bright,
>   And my sad thoughts doth clear.
>
> It glows and glitters in my cloudy breast,
>   Like stars upon some gloomy grove,
> Or those faint beams in which this hill is dress'd,
>   After the sun's remove.

> I see them walking in an air of glory,
>   Whose light doth trample on my days:
> My days, which are at best but dull and hoary,
>   Mere glimmering and decays.

It is not fair comparison to set one of Whittier's inferior productions beside this superbest hymn of an eloquent age; but would any religious poem of the nineteenth century, even the best of them, fare much better? There is indeed one thing lacking, and that is *ecstasy*. But ecstasy demands a different kind of faith from that of Whittier's day or ours, and, missing that, I do not see why we should begrudge our praise to a genius of pure and quiet charm.

I have already intimated that too complete a preoccupation with the reforming and political side of Whittier's life has kept the biographers from recognising that charm in what he himself regarded as his best poem. In 1872, in the full maturity of his powers and when the national peace had allowed him to indulge the peace in his own heart, he wrote his exquisite idyl, *The Pennsylvania Pilgrim*. Perhaps the mere name of the poem may suggest another cause why it has been overlooked. Whittier has always stood preeminently as the exponent of New England life, and for very natural reasons. And yet it would not be difficult to show from passages in his prose works that his heart was never quite at ease in that Puritan land. The recollection of the sufferings which his people had undergone for their faith's sake rankled a little in his breast, and he was never in perfect sympathy with the austerity of New England traditions. We catch a tone of relief as he turns in imagination to the peace that dwelt "within the land of Penn":

> Who knows what goadings in their sterner way
> O'er jagged ice, relieved by granite grey,
> Blew round the men of Massachusetts Bay?

> What hate of heresy the east-wind woke?
> What hints of pitiless power and terror spoke
> In waves that on their iron coast-line broke?

It was no doubt during his early residence in Philadelphia that he learned the story of the good Pastorius, who, in 1683, left the

fatherland and the society of the mystics he loved to lead a colony
of Friends to Germantown. The Pilgrim's life in that bountiful
valley between the Schuylkill and the Delaware—

> Where, forest-walled, the scattered hamlets lay
> Along the wedded rivers—

offered to Whittier a subject admirably adapted to his powers.
Here the faults of taste that elsewhere so often offend us are sunk
in the harmony of the whole and in the singular unity of impression; and the lack of elevation that so often stints our praise becomes a suave and mellow beauty. All the better elements of his
genius are displayed here in opulent freedom. The affections of the
heart unfold in unembittered serenity. The sense of home seclusion is heightened by the presence of the enveloping wilderness,
but not disturbed by any harsher contrast. Within is familiar joy
and retirement unassailed—not without a touch of humour, as
when in the evening, "while his wife put on her look of love's
endurance," Pastorius took down his tremendous manuscript—

> And read, in half the languages of man,
> His *Rusca Apium*, which with bees began,
> And through the gamut of creation ran.

(The manuscript still exists; pray heaven it be never published!)
Now and then the winter evenings were broken by the coming of
some welcome guest—some traveller from the Old World bringing
news of fair Von Merlau and the other beloved mystics; some
magistrate from the young city,

> Lovely even then
> With its fair women and its stately men
> Gracing the forest court of William Penn;

or some neighbour of the country, the learned Swedish pastor who,
like Pastorius, "could baffle Babel's lingual curse,"

> Or painful Kelpius, from his forest den
> By Wissahickon, maddest of good men.

170

Such was the life within, and out of doors were the labours of the gardener and botanist, while

> the seasons went
> Their rounds, and somewhat to his spirit lent
> Of their own calm and measureless content.

The scene calls forth some of Whittier's most perfect lines of description. Could anything be more harmonious than this, with its economy of simple grace,

> Slow, overhead, the dusky night-birds sailed?

No poem would be thoroughly characteristic of Whittier without some echo of the slavery dispute, and our first introduction to Pastorius is, indeed, as to a baffled forerunner of John Woolman. But the question here takes on its most human and least political form; it lets in just enough of the outside world of action to save the idyl from unreality. Nor could religion well be absent; rather, the whole poem may be called an illustration through the Pilgrim's life of that Inner Guide, speaking to him not with loud and controversial tones, as it spoke to George Fox, but with the still, small voice of comfortable persuasion:

> A Voice spake in his ear,
> And lo! all other voices far and near
> Died at that whisper, full of meanings clear.
> The Light of Life shone round him; one by one
> The wandering lights, that all misleading run,
> Went out like candles paling in the sun.

The account of the grave Friends, unsummoned by bells, walking meeting-ward, and of the gathered stillness of the room into which only the songs of the birds penetrated from without, is one of the happiest passages of the poem. How dear those hours of common worship were to Whittier may be understood from another poem, addressed to a visitor who asked him why he did not seek rather the grander temple of nature:

171

But nature is not solitude;
She crowds us with her thronging wood;
Her many hands reach out to us,
Her many tongues are garrulous;
Perpetual riddles of surprise
She offers to our ears and eyes.

~   ~   ~

And so I find it well to come
For deeper rest to this still room,
For here the habit of the soul
Feels less the outer world's control;
The strength of mutual purpose pleads
More earnestly our common needs;
And from the silence multiplied
By these still forms on every side,
The world that time and sense have known
Falls off and leaves us God alone.

For the dinner given to Whittier on his seventieth birthday
Longfellow wrote a sonnet on *The Three Silences of Molinos*—
the silence of speech, of desire, and of thought, through which are
heard "mysterious sounds from realms beyond our reach." Perhaps
only one who at some time in his life has caught, or seemed to
catch, those voices and melodies is quite able to appreciate the
charm of Whittier through the absence of so much that calls to us
in other poets.

Emerson

It becomes more and more apparent that Emerson, judged by an international or even by a true national standard, is the outstanding figure of American letters. As a steady force in the transmutation of life into ideas and as an authority in the direction of life itself he has obtained a recognition such as no other of his countrymen can claim. And he owes this pre-eminence not only to his personal endowment of genius, but to the fact also that, as the most complete exponent of a transient experiment in civilization, he stands for something that the world is not likely to let die.

Ralph Waldo Emerson, born in Boston, May 25, 1803, gathered into himself the very quintessence of what has been called the Brahminism of New England, as transmitted through the Bulkeleys, the Blisses, the Moodys, and the direct paternal line. Peter Bulkeley, preferring the wilderness of Satan to Laudian conformity, came to this country and, in 1636, founded Concord. William Emerson, his descendant in the fifth generation, was builder of the Old Manse in the same town, and a sturdy preacher to the minute-men at the beginning of the Revolution; and of many other ministerial ancestors stories abound which show how deeply implanted in this stock was the pride of rebellion against traditional forms and institutions, united with a determination to force all mankind to worship God in the spirit. With William, son of him of Concord and father of our poet, the fires of zeal began to wane. Though the faithful pastor of the First Church (Unitarian) of Boston, it is recorded of him that he entered the ministry against his will. Yet he too had his unfulfilled dream of "coming out" by establishing a church in Washington which

From A New England Group and Others, Shelburne Essays, Eleventh Series (Boston and New York, Houghton Mifflin Company, 1921), pp. 69–94.

should require no sort of profession of faith. He died when the future philosopher was a boy of ten, leaving the family to shift for itself as best it could. Mrs. Emerson cared for the material welfare of the household by taking in boarders. The chief intellectual guidance fell to the aunt, Mary Moody Emerson, of whom her nephew drew a portrait in his *Lectures and Biographies*. "She gave high counsels," he says. Indubitably she did; but a perusal of her letters and the extracts from her journals leaves the impression that the pure but erratic enthusiasms of her mind served rather to push Emerson in the direction of his weaker inclination than to fortify him against himself. When a balloon is tugging at its moorings there is need of low counsels.

In 1817, Emerson entered Harvard College, and in due course of time graduated. Then, after teaching for a while in his brother's school in Boston, he returned to Cambridge to study for the ministry, and was in the autumn of 1826 licensed to preach. Three years later he was called to the Second Church of Boston, as assistant to Henry Ware, whom he soon succeeded. His ministration there was quietly successful, but brief. In 1832, he gave up his charge on the ground that he could not conscientiously celebrate the Communion, even in the symbolic form customary among the Unitarians. He was for the moment much adrift, his occupation gone, his health broken, his wife lost after a short period of happiness. In this state he went abroad to travel in Italy, France, and England. One memorable incident of the journey must be recorded, his visit to Carlyle at Craigenputtock, with all that it entailed of friendship and influence; but beyond that he returned with little more baggage than he took with him. He now made his residence in Concord, and married a second wife, who was to be a true helpmeet until the end. Thenceforth there was to be no radical change in his life, but only the gradual widening of the circle. The house that he bought, he continued to inhabit until it was burned down in 1872; and then his friends, in a manner showing exemplary tact, subscribed money for rebuilding it on the same lines. For a number of years he preached in various pulpits, and once even considered the call to a settled charge in New Bedford, but could not overcome his aversion to the ritual of the Lord's Supper and to regular prayers.

Meanwhile, by the medium of lectures delivered here and there and by printed essays, he was making of himself a kind of lay preacher to the world. His method of working out the more characteristic of these discourses has long been known. He would select a theme, and then ransack his note-books for pertinent passages which could be strung together with the addition of such developing and connecting material as was necessary. But since the publication of his *Journals* it has been possible to follow him more precisely in this procedure and to see more clearly how it conforms with the inmost structure of his mind. These remarkable records were begun in early youth and continued, though at the close in the form of brief memoranda, to the end of his life. The first entry preserved (not the first written, for it is from *Blotting Book*, No. XVII) dates from his junior year at college and contains notes for a prize dissertation on the Character of Socrates. Among the sentences is this:

What is God? said the disciples, and Plato replied, It is hard to learn and impossible to divulge.

And the last page of the record, in the twelfth volume, repeats what is really the same thought:

The best part of truth is certainly that which hovers in gleams and suggestions unpossessed before man. His recorded knowledge is dead and cold. But this chorus of thoughts and hopes, these dawning truths, like great stars just lifting themselves into his horizon, they are his future, and console him for the ridiculous brevity and meanness of his civic life.

There is of course much variety of matter in the *Journals*— shrewd observations on men and books, chronicles of the day's events, etc.—but through it all runs this thread of self-communion, the poetry, it might be called, of the New England conscience deprived of its concrete deity and buoying itself on gleams and suggestions of eternal beauty and holiness. Of the same stuff, not seldom indeed in the same words, are those essays of his that have deeply counted; they are but a repetition to the world of fragments of this long inner conversation. Where they fail to reach the reader's heart, it is not so much because they are fundamentally disjointed, as if made up of sentences jostled together like so many mutually repellent particles; as because from the manner of his composition Emerson often missed what is the essence of good rhetoric, that is to say the consciousness of his hearer's mind as well as of his own. We hear him as it were talking to himself, with no attempt to convince by argument or to enlighten by analysis. If our dormant intuition answers to his, we are profoundly kindled and confirmed; otherwise his sentences may rattle ineffectually about our ears.

Emerson's first published work was *Nature* (1836), which contains the gist of his transcendental attitude towards the phenomenal world, as a kind of beautiful symbol of the inner spiritual life floating dreamlike before the eye, yet, it is to be noted, having discipline as one of its lessons for the attentive soul. The most characteristic and influential of his books are the two volumes of *Essays*, issued respectively in 1841 and 1844. In the former of these are those great discourses on Self-Reliance, Compensation, and the Over-Soul, into which was distilled the very quintessence of the volatile and heady liquid known as Emersonianism. Other volumes followed in due course. The later publications, however, beginning with *Letters and Social Aims* (1875), are made up mainly of gleanings from the field already harvested, and were even gathered by hands not his own.

Two of his addresses (now both included in the volume with *Nature*) deserve special notice for the attention they attracted at the time. The first of these is the oration before the Phi Beta Kappa Society of Harvard, in 1837, a high but scarcely practical appeal to the American Scholar to raise himself above the dust of pedantries, even out of the routine of what is "decent, indolent, complaisant," and to reach after the inspiration of "the Divine Soul which also inspires all men." The other lecture was delivered the next year before the senior class in Divinity College, Cambridge, and held up to the prospective preacher about the same ideal as was presented to the scholar. Historical Christianity is condemned because "it is not the doctrine of the soul, but an exaggeration of the personal, the positive, the ritual. It has dwelt, it dwells, with noxious exaggeration about the *person* of Jesus." The founder of Christianity saw, indeed, "with open eye the mystery of the soul," but what as a man he saw and knew of man's divinity cannot be given to man to-day by instruction, but only on the terms of a like intuition. The Unitarians of Massachusetts had travelled far from the Calvinistic creed of the Pilgrim Fathers, but Emerson's suave displacement of the person of Jesus for the "chorus of thought and hopes" in any human soul, perhaps even more his implicit rejection of all rites and institutions, raised a good deal of protest among the worshippers of the day. For the most part he answered the criticism by silence, but in a letter replying to one of the more courteous of his opponents he used these significant words: "I could not give an account of myself, if challenged. I could not possibly give you one of the 'arguments' you cruelly hint at, on which any doctrine of mine stands; for I do not know what arguments are in reference to any expression of a thought." There may be some guile in this pretence to complete intellectual innocence, but it is nevertheless a fair statement of a literary method which seeks, and obtains, its effect by throwing a direct light into the soul of the hearer and bidding him look there and acknowledge what he sees.

Of the events of these years there is not much to relate. A journey to Europe, in 1847, resulted in the only two of his books that may be said to have been composed as units: *Representative Men* (published in 1850, from a series of lectures delivered in London), which displays Emerson's great powers as an ethical critic, and *English Traits* (1856), which proves that his eyes were observing the world about him with Yankee shrewdness all the while that he seemed to be gazing into transcendental clouds. Into the question of slavery and disunion which was now agitating the country, he entered slowly. It was natural that one to whom the power and meaning of institutions had little appeal and to whom liberty was the all-including virtue, should have been drawn to the side of the Abolitionists, but at first there was a philosophical aloofness in his attitude. Only after the passing of the Fugitive Slave Law and Webster's defection were his passions deeply engaged. Then he spoke ringing words:

There is infamy in the air. I have a new experience. I awake in the morning with a painful sensation, which I carry about all day, and which, when traced home, is the odious remembrance of that

177

ignominy which has fallen on Massachusetts, which robs the landscape of beauty, and takes the sunshine out of every hour.

And the war came to him as a welcome relief from a situation which had grown intolerable.

A third trip to Europe was made in 1872, when his central will was already relaxing and his faculties were losing their edge. It was at this time that Charles Eliot Norton talked with Carlyle, and heard the old man, eight years older than Emerson, expatiate on the fundamental difference in their tempers. Norton records the conversation in his *Journal*:

As we were sitting together just after my coming in this afternoon, Carlyle spoke of Emerson. "There's a great contrast between Emerson and myself. He seems verra content with life, and takes much satisfaction in the world, especially in your country. One would suppose to hear him that ye had no troubles there, and no share in the darkness that hangs over these old lands. It's a verra strikin' and curious spectacle to behold a man so confidently cheerful as Emerson in these days.

"Well, it may be as you say. I'm not such a verra bloody-minded old villain after all," (here a cordial laugh,) "not quite so horrid an ogre as some good people imagine. But the warld is verra black to me; and I see nothin' to be content with in this brand new, patent society of ours."

For some time there had been a gradual loosening of Emerson's hold on life. Though always an approachable man and fond of conversation, there was in him a certain lack of human warmth, of "bottom," to use his own word, which he recognized and deplored. Commenting in his *Journal* (May 24, 1864) on the burial of Hawthorne, he notes the statement of James Freeman Clarke that the novelist had "shown a sympathy with the crime in our nature," and adds: "I thought there was a tragic element in the event, that might be more fully rendered,—in the painful solitude of the man, which, I suppose, could not longer be endured, and he died of it." A touch of this romantic isolation, though never morose or "painful," there was in himself, a failure to knit himself strongly into the bonds of society. "I have felt sure of him," he says of Hawthorne in the same passage, "in his neighbourhood, and in his necessities of sympathy and intelligence,—that I could well wait his time,—his unwillingness and caprice,—and might one day conquer a friendship. . . . Now it appears that I waited too long." Eighteen years later, standing by the body of Longfellow, he was heard to say: "That gentleman was a sweet, beautiful soul, but I have entirely forgotten his name." Such forgetfulness, like a serene and hazy cloud, hovered over Emerson's brain in his closing years. A month afterwards, on the 27th of April, 1882, he himself faded away peacefully. He lies buried under the shadow of a tall pine-tree in Sleepy Hollow.

To one who examines the events of Emerson's quiet life with a view to their spiritual bearing it will appear that his most decisive act was the surrender of his pulpit in 1832. Nearly a century earlier, in 1750, the greatest of American theologians had suffered what now befell the purest of American seers; and though the manner of their parting was different (Jonathan Edwards had been unwillingly ejected, whereas Emerson left with good will on both sides), yet there is significance in the fact that the cause of separation in both cases was the administration of the Lord's Supper. Nor is there less significance in the altered attitude of the later man towards this vital question. Both in a way turned from the ritualistic and traditional use of the Communion, and in this showed themselves leaders of the spirit which had carried the New England Fathers across the ocean as rebels against the Laudian tyranny of institutions. Edwards had revolted against the practice of Communion as a mere act of acquiescence in the authority of religion; he was determined that only those should approach the Table who could give evidence of a true conversion, by conversion meaning a complete emotional realization of the dogma of divine Grace and election. The eucharist was not a rite by conforming with which in humility men were to be made participators in the larger religious experience of the race, but a jealously guarded privilege of the few who already knew themselves set apart from the world. He was attempting to push to its logical issue the Puritan notion of religion as a matter of individual and inward experience; and if he failed it was because life can never be rigidly logical and because the worshippers of his day were already beginning to lose their intellectual grasp on the Calvinistic creed. By

179

Emerson's time, among the Unitarians of Boston, there could be no question of ritualistic grace or absolute conversion, but his act, nevertheless, like that of Edwards, was the intrusion of un-yielding consistency among those who were content to rest in habit and compromise.

Emerson had come to the inevitable conclusion of New England individualism; he had, in a word, "come out." Edwards had denied the communal efficacy, so to speak, of rites, but had insisted on inner conformity with an established creed. Emerson disavowed even a conformity in faith, demanding in its stead the entire liberty of each soul to rise on its own spiritual impulse. He was perspicacious and honest enough to acknowledge to himself the danger of such a stand. "I know very well," he wrote in his journal at the time of his decision, "that it is a bad sign in a man to be too conscientious, and stick at gnats. The most desperate scoundrels have been the over-refiners. Without accommodation society is inpracticable." But, he adds, he could "not go habitually to an institution which they esteem holiest with indifference and dis-like"; and again, looking deeper into his heart, "This is the end of my opposition, that I am not interested in it."

Emerson's act of renunciation was not only important as deter-mining the nature of his career, but significant also of the transi-tion of New England from theological dogmatism to romantic liberty. Much has been written about the influences that shaped his thoughts and about the relation of his transcendentalism to German metaphysics. In his later years it is clear that the specula-tions of Kant and Schelling and Fichte were known to him and oc-casionally coloured his language, but his *Journals* prove conclu-sively enough that the whole stamp of his mind was taken before these sources were open to him. Indirectly, no doubt, something of the German spirit came to him pretty early through Carlyle, and a passage in his *Journal* for December 13, 1829, shows that he was at that time already deeply engaged in the Teutonized rhapsodies of Coleridge. But it would be easy to lay too much stress even on this indirect affiliation. Long before that date, as early as his senior year in college, he is yearning "to separate the soul for sublime con-templation till it has lost the sense of circumstances," and other-wise giving implicit expression to the full circle of transcendental faith. He was in fact the product of a great movement that was sweeping over the world as it listed; his early reading went back mainly to the Greek philosophers and the poets and preachers of seventeenth-century England, but they were interpreted by him under the light of the new emancipation of the emotions. When he declared, in *Nature*, that "the vision of genius comes by renouncing the too officious activity of the understanding, and giving leave and amplest privilege to the spontaneous sentiment," he was merely stating in precise terms an idea familiar to Blake and to the romanticists of every land—the elevation of enthusiasm above judgment, of emotion above reason, of spontaneity above discipline, and of unlimited expansion above centripetal control. But there was another element as strongly formative of Emerson's disposition as was the broadening current of rebellion against the reason, and that was his ancestral inheritance. Romantic spontaneity moved in various directions in accordance with the field in which it worked; in an Emerson, with all the divinity of Massachusetts in his veins, it might move to repudiate theological dogma and deny Jehovah, but it could not get out of hearing of the question "What is God?" It could not fall into the too common confusion of spiritual aspiration with the sicklier lusts of the flesh; it could never, for all its centrifugal wandering, overstep the bounds of character. There, I think, we touch the quick of the matter. The course of Puritan emancipation led in the end to an individualism and a trust in sheer unrestrained spontaneity which are in many ways akin to the temper of the European revolt. You will find the marks of this affiliation as far back as in the reveries in which Jonathan Edwards records his isolation from mankind and absorption in inanimate nature; and when German literature reached this land it found in Emerson and Longfellow and others a material ready to its hand. But with all the similarity between the two movements and despite the influence of German literature, when it came, upon Concord and Cambridge, there remained this striking and fundamental distinction: the spontaneity and individualism of the romantic movement on the Continent went with a dissolution of character against which the Puritan mind, so long as it held true to its origin, was impregnably fortified. Emersonianism may be defined as romanticism rooted in Puritan divinity.

It is scarcely necessary to illustrate this union of religious individualism and stability of character by quotations from Emerson's verse; yet, for the light they throw on his literary method, if for no other reason, I will quote one or two of his familiar pieces. The best known expression of the idea of the deity sitting in the breast of each man, yet embracing the world, is found in those stanzas entitled *Brahma*, which, it is hard to know why, caused such a stir when they first appeared. Even clearer in purport, as showing how this faith in the inner power grew out of the Puritan distrust of traditional rites and institutions, are the opening lines of *The Problem:*

> I like a church; I like a cowl;
> I love a prophet of the soul;
> And on my heart monastic aisles
> Fall like sweet strains, or pensive smiles:
> Yet not for all his faith can see
> Would I that cowlèd churchman be.
>
> Why should the vest on him allure,
> Which I could not on me endure?
> Not from a vein of shallow thought
> His awful Jove young Phidias brought;
> Never from lips of cunning fell
> The thrilling Delphic oracle;
> Out from the heart of nature rolled
> The burdens of the Bible old;
> The litanies of nations came,
> Like the volcano's tongue of flame,
> Up from the burning core below,—
> The canticles of love and woe:
> The hand that rounded Peter's dome
> And groined the aisles of Christian Rome
> Wrought in a sad sincerity;
> Himself from God he could not free;
> He builded better than he knew;—
> The conscious stone to beauty grew.

It is significant of this confidence in individual inspiration that generally in Emerson, as in other poets, it tends to looseness and

182

formless spontaneity of style. When, on the contrary, he turns to the note of character, his language becomes instantly terse and restrained, and falls naturally into symmetrical form. Matthew Arnold has cited for approval the two quatrains in which this note is heard most clearly:

> So nigh is grandeur to our dust,
>   So near is God to man,
> When Duty whispers low, *Thou must,*
>   The youth replies, *I can*—

and this other,

> Though love repine and reason chafe,
> There came a voice without reply,—
> "'T is man's perdition to be safe,
> When for the truth he ought to die."

(It may be interesting to observe that the two last lines, as we learn from Emerson's *Journal*, were taken bodily from the sermon of a Puritan divine preached in 1642. That by the way.) Of the two quatrains as a whole Matthew Arnold remarks that they are "exceptional" in our poet. They are that, and something more: they are exceptional in literature. One would have to search far in English to discover anything equal to them in their own kind. They have the cleanness and radiance of the couplets of the Greek Simonides. They may look easy, but as a matter of fact the ethical epigram is an extremely difficult *genre*, and to attain this union of gravity and simplicity is one of the supreme accomplishments of art. Along with absolute sureness of touch there is required an entire balance and control of the faculties, a deep respect for the springs of human nature—in a word, character.

While speaking of these traits I ought not to pass by the little poem entitled *Days*, in which the feeling for beauty in itself, superadded to insight and the note of character, produces a work of exquisite finish and haunting charm:

> Daughters of Time, the hypocritic Days,
> Muffled and dumb like barefoot dervishes,

And marching single in an endless file,
Bring diadems and fagots in their hands.
To each they offer gifts after his will,
Bread, kingdoms, stars, and sky that holds them all.
I, in my pleachèd garden, watched the pomp,
Forgot my morning wishes, hastily
Took a few herbs and apples, and the Day
Turned and departed silent. I, too late,
Under her solemn fillet saw the scorn.

These, it must be admitted, are rare occurrences in Emerson, the event of what Plato would call a divine chance; if they had come oftener, or had been at his command, he would have been, despite the limitations of his subject-matter, one of the very great poets of the world. But this was not to be. On the contrary, by the side of these poems which are marked by masterly form and restraint you will find others, and these the more numerous, in which he surrenders himself to the shifting breath of inspiration like a rudderless boat, to such a degree, indeed, that over much of his work his own word "whim" might be set as a superscription.

The philosophy of his prose essays—so far as he can be said to have systematized his thoughts at all—shows this same light-hearted legerdemain. Nor is this philosophy hard to discover; the whole circle of his ideas is likely to be present, explicit or implicit, in any one of his great passages:—the clear call to self-reliance, announcing that "a man should learn to detect and watch that gleam of light which flashes across his mind from within"; the firm assurance that, through all the balanced play of circumstance, "there is a deeper fact in the soul than compensation, to wit, its own nature"; the intuition, despite all the mists of illusion, of the Over-Soul which is above us and still ourselves: "We live in succession, in division, in parts, in particles; meanwhile within man is the soul of the whole; the wise silence; the universal beauty . . . ; the eternal One."

Emerson's philosophy is thus a kind of vanishing dualism, and a man's attitude towards it in the end will be determined by his sense of its sufficiency or insufficiency to meet the facts of experience. One of Emerson's latest biographers has attempted to set forth this philosophy as "a synthesis and an anticipation," in that we find in it, as Emerson had already found in Plato and Plotinus, a reconciliation which all men are seeking of "the many and the one," the everlasting flux and the motionless calm at the heart of things:

An ample and generous recognition of this transiency and slipperiness both in the nature of things and in man's soul seems more and more a necessary ingredient in any estimate of the universe which shall satisfy the intellect of the coming man. But it seems equally true that the coming man who shall resolve our problems will never content himself with a universe a-tilt, a universe in cascade, so to speak; the craving for permanence in some form cannot be jauntily evaded. Is there any known mind which foreshadows the desired combination so clearly as Emerson's? Who has felt more profoundly the evanescence and evasiveness of things? . . . Yet Emerson was quite as firm in his insistence on a single unalterable reality as in his refusal to believe that any aspect or estimate of that reality could be final.[1]

The necessity of the dualism that underlies Emerson's philosophy could scarcely be put more neatly, and the kind of synthesis, or reconciliation, in which Emerson floated is admirably expressed. But I am not so sure that this synthesis anticipates the solution of the troublesome problems of life, or that it will afford the kind of spiritual consolation which hitherto mankind has found in religion. There will be those who will ask whether the power of religion for mature minds does not depend after all on its feeling for evil as a tremendous reality. How otherwise, in fact, shall religion meet those harder questions of experience when its aid is most needed? And in like manner they will say that the power of philosophy as the *dux vitæ* depends on its acquaintance with the scope and difficulties of scepticism. Both religion and philosophy would seem, in such a view, to rest not only on a statement of the dualism of good and evil, knowledge and ignorance, but on a realization of the full meaning and gravity, practical and intellectual, of this dualism. Now Emerson certainly recognizes the double nature of experience, but it is a fair question whether he realizes

[1] O. W. Firkins, *Ralph Waldo Emerson*, p. 364.

its full meaning and fateful seriousness. He accepts it a trifle too jauntily; is sometimes too ready to wave aside its consequences, as if a statement of the fact were an escape from its terrible perplexities. To be reconciled so cheerfully to this dark dilemma is not a reconciliation of the dilemma itself, but argues rather some deep-lying limitation of spiritual experience. Carlyle meant something of the sort when he worried over Emerson's inability to see the hand of the devil in human affairs—a strange paradoxical charge to bring against the purest inheritor of the old faith of New England, yet essentially true.

A good way to learn what this denial of evil led to in practice is to turn from Emerson to some of his weaker-minded followers or friends. For example, Bronson Alcott, one of the Concord illuminati, chanced to be in England in the year 1842, and there, in concert with one or two Englishmen who had imbibed his vaporous ideas, concocted a plan to found in the vicinity of Boston and Concord "a New Eden," where man might live in primitive simplicity and forget the wretched illusion of the existence of sin. So came about the experiment of "Fruitlands," the communal farm of philosophers at the village of Harvard, one of the funniest and, for some of those involved, one of the saddest attempts to disregard the facts of life and human nature.

Of the group of "consecrated cranks," as a rebel afterwards styled them, one, a mild lunatic named Samuel Brown, believed in salvation by the grace of nakedness. The poor fellow soon became discontented because, in deference to the ladies of the community, they forced him to restrict his practice of salvation to the hours of night, and even then to mitigate its purity by wearing a single garment. In that garb he used to wander over the hills like a white ghost, until rumours of the unearthly apparition got about among the farming folk and caused a prosaic search for the visitant with a *posse comitatis*. Meanwhile, as he was confined to his chamber by day, he did not contribute much to the physical well-being of the settlement. Another of the genial come-outers was a cooper by trade, described in a letter as "an excellent assistant here, very faithful to every work he undertakes, very serious." That sounds promising. But unfortunately there were drawbacks to his full acceptance by the leaders of the band. He "has had rather deep experience," continues the writer of the letter, "having been imprisoned in a mad house by his relatives because he had a little property, but still he is not a spiritual being, at least not consciously and wishfully so." Really that is one of the most delicious sentences on record from the pen of a saint—imprisoned in a mad house, but still (note the conjunction) not a spiritual being.

These good people had a double purpose: one, sufficiently humble, to support themselves, that is, their unmentionable bodies, on the pure fruits of the earth; the other, more elevated, to plant "a love colony," as their Eden was called, where the brotherhood of man should reign unpolluted by the lust of property, and by their illustrious example to aid "entire human regeneration." It cannot be said that they succeeded very well in feeding themselves, and when food was bad they took it out, like other mortals, in grumbling at the cooks. The men of the colony were so absorbed in the contemplation of the mystery of holiness that the fruits of the field rather languished. As Alcott's daughter said, they "were so busy discussing and defining great duties that they forgot to perform the small ones." The barley crops somehow would not harvest themselves, so they were got in by the women while the masculine sages were wandering off in the amiable desire of "aiding entire human regeneration." Things grew worse and worse, until it came to a question of leaving or starving. It is very pretty to declare that the body is "all sham"; but you can't feed it by shamming work.

And as for the spirit, by some unaccountable means the serpent seems to have crept into this Eden, as he did into the original experiment. The "love colony" soon developed into a circle of disappointed, jealous, fault-finding men and women, who found it to their advantage to seek shelter from one another by scattering in the wicked world. This is one of Father Hecker's memoranda: "Somebody once described 'Fruitlands' as a place where Mr. Alcott looked benign and talked philosophy, while Mrs. Alcott and the children did all the work." It is well to look benign, but another of the colonists wrote in a different vein. "All the persons," he complains, "who have joined us during the summer have from some cause or other quitted, they say in consequence of Mr. Alcott's despotic manner, which he interprets as their not being equal to the Spirit's demands." It looks a little as if these spiritual demands were not unaccompanied with spiritual pride; and pride, we remember, is sometimes said to have been the sin that broke up the original Eden.

Emerson, of course, was too knowing ever to have joined himself in the flesh to these altruistic humbugs; but one cannot forget that he was a patron of Alcott's and for the most part took that dilapidated Platonist with portentous seriousness. For instance, he observes in his *Journal* for 1857:

Last night in the conversation Alcott appeared to great advantage, and I saw again, as often before, his singular superiority. As pure intellect I have never seen his equal. The people with whom he talks do not ever understand him; . . . do not know that all they have in their baby brains is incoherent and spotty; that all he sees and says is like astronomy, lying there real and vast, every part and fact in eternal connection with the whole.

The truth is that Alcott is in a way a caricature of Emerson; but it is just as a caricature that he shows with startling vividness what Emersonianism runs to when divested of the common sense and strong character which were ballast to the master's shining optimism. Emerson saw the good and radiated spiritual light as few other men of his century did; but his blindness to the reality of evil was not of his strength, it was of his weakness. Hence it is that he often loses value for his admirers in proportion to their maturity and experience. He is pre-eminently the poet of religion and philosophy for the young; whereas men as they grow older are inclined to turn from him, in their more serious needs, to those sages who have supplemented insight with a firmer grasp of the whole of human nature.

That is undoubtedly true; nevertheless, as time passes the deficiencies of this brief flowering period of New England, of which Emerson was the perfect spokesman, may well be more and more condoned for its rarity and beauty. One of the wings of the spirit is hope, and nowhere is there to be found a purer hope than in the books of our New England sage; rather, it might be said that he went beyond hope to the assurance of present happiness. The world had never before seen anything quite of this kind, and may not see its like again.

The Influence of Emerson

It is a quality of the human spirit on which Emerson himself was wont to dwell, that it forever seeks and knows no rest save in death. Almost it should seem that one cannot acquaint himself with the history of great religions and philosophies without falling at last into a state of wondering indifference or despair, so many times has the truth appeared to men and been formulated for the uplifting of a generation, only to give way in turn to another glimpse of the same haunting reality. We comfort ourselves with the words of the poet whom Emerson loved to quote,—a modern version of Pandora:

> So strength first made a way:
> Then beautie flow'd, then wisdome, honour, pleas-
> ure:
> When almost all was out, God made a stay,
> Perceiving that alone of all his treasure
> Rest in the bottome lay. . . .
>
> For if I should (said he)
> Bestow this jewell also on my creature,
> He would adore my gifts instead of me,
> And rest in Nature, not the God of Nature.
> So both should losers be.*

When, therefore, we consider how the wisdom of prophets and philosophers in the past has so swiftly solidified into a formalism that holds the weaker in bondage like a strait jacket, and when we remember how our sage of Concord pointed out that Christianity too must needs fall into "the error that corrupts

---

From *Shelburne Essays*, First Series (Boston and New York, Houghton Mifflin Company, 1904), pp. 71–84.

* [From "The Pulley," by George Herbert (1593–1633).]

all attempts to communicate religion," when we reflect on the inevitable course of human thought, those of us who are lovers of Emerson—as I myself am a lover—need feel no grievance to be told that Emersonianism to-day is a sign of limitation, not of strength; of palsy, not of growth. I say Emersonianism, meaning the influence of Emerson as it works on large masses of men; but I would not imply that the individual reader of Emerson may not go to him for ever renewed inspiration and assurance in the things of the spirit. It is always so. The teaching of Plato was as true in the days of the later Academy, is as true now, as it was when Socrates disputed with his disciple in the market-place of Athens; yet almost in the space of a generation Platonism became a snare to those who rest in words and possess no corresponding inner vision of their own. So Emerson cannot escape his own condemnation of the wise: "Though in our lonely hours we draw a new strength out of their memory, yet, pressed on our attention, as they are by the thoughtless and customary, they fatigue and invade."

Only there is a difference to observe. The evil which has sprung from other systems of thought has been due chiefly to the very fact that they were systems and thus attempted to lay restraining hands on the ever fluent human spirit. Out of the pursuit of truth has grown a metaphysic; out of religious faith has developed a theology. But with Emerson the opposite is true; the mischief that now works in his name is owing in large part to his very lack of system. Yet it is but a shallow reader who would go a step further and accept Emerson's quizzical profession of inconsistency without reserve. "I would write on the lintels of the door-post, *Whim*," he said, but added immediately, "I hope it is somewhat better than whim at last." His essays ripple and recoil on the surface, but underneath there is a current setting steadily to one point. Indeed I have never been able to understand the minds of those who, like Richard Garnett, declare that the separate sentences in Emerson are clear, but that his essays as a whole are dark because composed without any central constructive thought and, in fact, filled with contradictions. It should seem that critics who find Emerson self-contradictory are just those who should never have meddled with him, for the reason that the guiding and formative principle in all his work is meaningless to them. Though often capricious in expression and on the surface illogical, Emerson, more than almost any other writer of wide influence, displays that inner logic which springs from the constant insistence on one or two master ideas. The apparent contradictions in his pages need but a moment's reflection and a modicum of understanding to reduce them to essential harmony. Like all teachers of spiritual insight he was profoundly impressed by the ubiquitous dualism of life. "Philosophically considered," he wrote in his first famous manifesto, "the universe is composed of Nature and the Soul." I will not stay to show how this commonplace of thought becomes fruitful of varied wisdom through the sincerity and depth of Emerson's vision. I think, in fact, that anyone who understands with his heart as well as with his head the central ideas of the essay on the Oversoul and of that on Experience will need no such guidance; he possesses a cue that will carry him like Ariadne's thread through all the labyrinth of Emerson's philosophy. Thus of the Oversoul it is written:

Meanwhile within man is the soul of the whole; the wise silence; the universal beauty, to which every part and particle is related; . . . this deep power in which we exist, and whose beatitude is all accessible to us, self-sufficing and perfect in every hour;

and of the Experience of nature it is written:

Dream delivers us to dream, and there is no end to illusion. Life is a train of moods like a string of beads, and, as we pass through them, they prove to be many-coloured lenses which paint the world their own hue, and each shows only what lies in its own focus.

It is characteristic of Emerson's fine integrity that he never sought—as all systematic philosophies and religions hitherto had attempted—to bridge over the gap between these two realms by a scheme of ratiocination or revelation. He was content to let them lie side by side unreconciled, and hence his seeming fluctuations to those of shallow understanding. In conduct, however, he knew well how to draw the desired lesson from this dilemma. Indeed, I am not sure that all the manifold applications of his

191

genius may not be found summed up in this single paragraph from his later essay on Fate:

One key, one solution to the mysteries of human condition, one solution to the old knots of fate, freedom and foreknowledge, exists, the propounding, namely, of the double consciousness. A man must ride alternately on the horses of his private and public nature, as the equestrians in the circus throw themselves nimbly from horse to horse, or plant one foot on the back of one, and the other foot on the back of the other. So when a man is the victim of his fate, has sciatica in his loins, and cramp in his mind; a club-foot, and a club in his wit; a sour face, and a selfish temper; a strut in his gait, and a conceit in his affection; or is ground to powder by the vice of his race; he is to rally on his relation to the Universe, which his ruin benefits. Leaving the dæmon who suffers, he is to take sides with the Deity who secures universal benefit by his pain.

But because Emerson's thought revolves so harmoniously about these two central principles, it does not therefore follow that he has a philosophical system. Not only does he make no attempt to connect them logically, but he is satisfied to apply now one and now the other of them to the solution of a thousand minor questions without much order or method. Hence it is that readers who carry to his essays a sense for ratiocination but no ultimate vision of truth find him both contradictory and obscure. And as he neglected to mould his own thought into a system, so he requires of those who come to him no systematic preparation. The truth that Emerson proclaimed is the old, old commonplace that has arisen before the minds of sages and prophets from the beginning of time; but they have each and all conditioned this truth on some discipline of the reason or the emotions. They have invariably demanded some propædeutic, some adherence to a peculiar belief or submission to a divine personality, before the disciple should be carried into the inner circle of ennobled experiences. With Plato it was dialectics; with Buddha it was the four-fold truth and the eight-fold path and a comprehension of the twelve-fold wheel of causation; with Jesus it was Follow me. And in this system or discipline we seem to discern an authentication of their high claims. Bound up as we are with so many petty concerns, so many demands of the body, blinded by sloth and made callous by the conflict of so many material powers,—it is hard for us to accept with more than lip assent this call to the life of the spirit. These words that the philosophers and prophets utter so glibly—are they not mere words after all, we ask? Do they signify any reality of life that a man should barter houses and land for them? We need assurance that these ecstasies and these long contents of the spiritual man are not idle boasts, and so this discipline of faith we accept readily as a necessary part of the scheme of salvation. We have not ourselves partaken of such blessings, yet we can imagine that by some extraordinary means, some nimble gymnastics of the brain, we might be raised to these incredible heights. But now comes this Yankee prophet, offering the same spiritual exaltations freely and without condition to all. If we may believe him, a man shall walk out under the open sky and breathe the sweet influences of the spirit as cheaply as he inhales the untainted breeze. The preacher stands at the meeting of the ways and cries to all that pass by: Ho, ye who are wrapt in the swaddling clothes of reverence and obedience, cast aside these trammels and walk upright in your own strength. What have we to do with the sacredness of tradition? No law can be sacred to us but that of our own nature. Nay, follow the whim of the hour; consistency is the hobgoblin of little minds. Give me health and a day and I will make the pomp of emperors ridiculous.

> I am the owner of the sphere,
> Of the seven stars and the solar year,
> Of Cæsar's hand, and Plato's brain,
> Of Lord Christ's heart, and Shakespeare's strain.

And the wonder of it is that no man whose hearing is not utterly drowned by the clamour of the world can read a page of these essays without recognising that Emerson speaks with an absolute and undeceived sincerity. We remember his confession, that "when a man lives with God, his voice shall be as sweet as the murmur of the brook and the rustle of the corn," and it is with him as

> When the harmony of heaven
> Soundeth the measures of a lively faith.

Upon the reader, despite himself it may be, there steals something of the pure and noble enthusiasm of the seer, and he knows straightway that the things of the inner life are real.

If this were all it would be well. If his message stood only as a perpetual instigation to the strong and a noble promise to inspired youth, we should have much to say of Emerson and little of Emersonianism. And, in fact, it would be indiscriminating to lay at Emerson's door the whole evil of a faded and vulgarised transcendentalism. He was but one of many; others—some, as Channing, even before his day—had taught the same facility of the spiritual life. Yet in him the movement came to its beautiful flower; we are justified in holding him mainly responsible for the harm that flowed from it, as we honour him for the glory that lay therein. And, alas, even in his own day, the doubtful influence of this fatally easy philosophy began to make itself felt. Hawthorne, the most stalwart observer of all that group, tells us how many bats and owls, which were sometimes mistaken for fowls of angelic feather, were attracted by that beacon light of the spirit. It was moreover impossible, he avows, to dwell in Emerson's vicinity without inhaling more or less the mountain atmosphere of his lofty thought; but in the brains of some people it wrought a singular giddiness. And if Emersonianism was mischievous to weak minds then, what shall we say of its influence in New England to-day—nay, throughout the whole country? For it is rampant in our life; it has wrought in our religion, our politics, and our literature a perilous dizziness of the brain.

There is a mysterious faith abroad in the land, which, however we grudge to say it, is the most serious manifestation of religion discoverable in these days. We call it Christian Science, or faith healing, or what not—the gospel of a certain Mrs. Baker-Eddy; but in reality it does not owe its strength to the teaching of an ignorant woman in New Hampshire. It is a diluted and stale product of Emersonianism, and the parentage, I think, is not difficult to discern. To Emerson, as to Mrs. Baker-Eddy, sin and

194

suffering had no real existence; a man need only open his breast to the random influences of heaven to lead the purely spiritual life. Nor is it correct to say, as some fondly suppose, that Christian Science or Emersonianism has any vital connection with Oriental mysticism. True, both Emerson and the sages of the East taught that spirit was the only reality and that the world of the body and of evil was a deception. "Life itself is a bubble and a scepticism and a sleep within a sleep," said Emerson, and the Hindu summed up the same thought in his name for the creator, Mâyâ, illusion. But there is a radical difference in their attitude to this truth. Though the material world was in one sense illusion and unreality to the Hindu, yet in another sense it was tremendously real. Over the misery and insufficience of mortal existence he brooded in a way that to us is inconceivable; we call him a pessimist, and from our ordinary point of view rightly. He was haunted as with an infinite sadness by the vision of endlessly recurring birth and death, of ceaseless unmeaning mutation. To escape this life of unspeakable sorrow he laboured at vast systems of philosophy, he was ready to undergo, if needs were, a lifetime of crushing asceticism. He could no more have understood the jaunty optimism of Emerson than we can understand what we style his pessimism. There is a story—how authentic I do not know—that when Emerson was visiting Carlyle, the gruff Scotchman, who certainly believed heartily in evil and damnation, carried his guest to the slums of London and pointed out to him one horrible sight after another. "And do you believe in the deil, noo?" he would say; and always Emerson would shake his head in gentle denial. The story is at least *ben trovato*; it sets forth clearly the facile optimism out of which Christian Science was to spring. Such a creed, when professed by one who spoke with the noble accent and from the deep insight of an Emerson, was a radiant possession for seeking humanity forever; it is folly and inner deception when repeated parrot-like by men and women with no mental training and, visibly to all the world, with no warrant of spiritual experience. To suppose that you and I and our neighbour can at our sweet will cast off the impediments of sin and suffering is a monstrous self-deceit. So has the very lack of system

195

in Emerson's message become a snare to mankind more deadly than the hardening systems of other philosophies. These are at least virile.

It is at best an ungrateful office to lay bare the harmful influence of a beloved teacher, and I would hurry over what little remains to be said. In politics the unreflecting optimism of transcendental Boston has given birth to that unformed creature called Anti-imperialism. I do not mean such anti-imperialism as would dispute on the grounds of expediency our policy in the Philippines or elsewhere—this is a question of statesmanship—but that "Saturnalia or excess of Faith" which wantonly closes the eyes to distinctions and would see a Washington in every Aguinaldo. It is a blinking of the eyes to those "unconcerning things, matters of fact," in political fitness as Christian Science was in moral fitness; it is the glorification of untried human nature preached by Channing, made beautiful by Emerson, acted by the Abolitionists, and reduced to the absurd by Mr. Atkinson. And the same optimism has made itself felt in recent New England literature. "The vision of genius comes by renouncing the too officious activity of the understanding and giving leave and amplest privilege to the spontaneous sentiment," wrote Emerson; and again, "The poet must be a rhapsodist, his inspiration a sort of casualty"; and yet again, "The Supreme Mind finds itself related to all its works and will travel a royal road to particular knowledges and powers";—excellent doctrine for a Shakespeare or an Emerson, a noble source of inspiration for all, indeed; but conceive the havoc it might work, has indeed actually wrought, when accepted literally by writers of a single talent. I was impressed recently by a criticism in the London *Times* which held up to ridicule the cheap enthusiasms, the utter want of discrimination between inspiration and twaddle, the flaccid sublimities, of a certain book by Lilian Whiting, which deals with the literary memories of those old Boston Days. It set me to reflecting on the widespread mischief done to New England writing of to-day by this self-abandonment to ecstasy and this easy acceptance of genius wherever it proclaims itself—in New England at least. Pessimism is morbid and stationary, but I sometimes think that the black hopelessness of a Leopardi would be better than this self-deceit of a facile optimism.

But enough. I feel already something of that shame which must have fallen upon the *advocatus diaboli* constrained by his office to utter a protest against the saints. Yet I trust my words will not be taken as directed against the sweet spirit of Emerson, whom I reverence this side idolatry; I have merely written on the ancient text, *Corruptio optimi pessima.**

P.S.—This essay was published in the *Independent* in connection with the centenary of Emerson's birth, May 25, 1903, and immediately drew from Mrs. Eddy a promulgation setting forth to all the world the extent of her education and denouncing the idea that Christian Science owes anything to Emerson, or to Greek or Roman. She and God alone, it appears, are to be accredited with this new faith. In view of the fact that Mrs. Eddy now numbers her disciples by the million—many of them educated and thoughtful people—we regard this promulgation as one of the most extraordinary documents in the history of religion.

"I was early," she says, "the pupil of Miss Sarah J. Bodwell, the principal of Sanbornton Academy of New Hampshire, and finished my course of studies under Prof. Dyer H. Sanborn, author of Sanborn's Grammar. Among my early studies were Comstock's Natural Philosophy, chemistry, Blair's Rhetoric, Whateley's Logic, Watts's *On the Mind and Moral Science.* At sixteen years of age I began writing for leading newspapers, and for many years wrote for the best magazines in the South and North. I have lectured in large and crowded halls in New York City, Chicago, Boston, Portland, and at Waterville College, and have been invited to lecture in London and Edinburgh. In 1883 I started the *Christian Science Journal,* and for several years was the proprietor and sole editor of that journal. In 1893 Judge S. J. Hanna became editor of the *Christian Science Journal,* and for ten subsequent years he knew my ability as an editor. In his recent lecture at Chicago, he said: 'Mrs. Eddy is, from every point of view, a woman of sound education and liberal culture' . . .

"I am the author of the Christian Science text book, *Science and Health with Key to the Scriptures,* and the demand for this book increases, and the book is already in its two hundred and seventy-fourth edition of one thousand copies each. I am rated in the *National Magazine* (1903) as 'standing the eighth in a list of twenty-two of

* [The corruption of the best is the worst.]

the foremost living authors.' "—But withal she is modest. "I claim," she concludes, "no special merit of any kind. All that I am in reality God has made me."

Fatuity has not often gone beyond this. *Tantum religio potuit suadere* ineptiarum.*

* [So much folly could religion suggest.]

A Hermit's Notes on Thoreau

Near the secluded village of Shelburne that lies along the peaceful valley of the Androscoggin, I took upon myself to live two years as a hermit after a mild Epicurean fashion of my own. Three maiden aunts wagged their heads ominously; my nearest friend inquired cautiously whether there was any taint of insanity in the family; an old grey-haired lady, a veritable saint who had not been soured by her many deeds of charity, admonished me on the utter selfishness and godlessness of such a proceeding. But I clung heroically to my resolution. Summer tourists in that pleasant valley may still see the little red house among the pines—empty now, I believe; and I dare say gaudy coaches still draw up at the door, as they used to do, when the gaudier bonnets and hats exchanged wondering remarks on the cabalistic inscription over the lintel, or spoke condescendingly to the great dog lying on the steps. As for the hermit within, having found it impossible to educe any meaning from the tangled habits of mankind while he himself was whirled about in the imbroglio, he had determined to try the efficacy of undisturbed meditation at a distance. So deficient had been his education that he was actually better acquainted with the aspirations and emotions of the old dwellers on the Ganges than with those of the modern toilers by the Hudson or the Potomac. He had been deafened by the "indistinguishable roar" of the streets, and could make no sense of the noisy jargon of the market place. But—shall it be confessed?—although he discovered many things during his contemplative sojourn in the wilderness, and learned that the attempt to criticise and not to create literature was to be his labour in this world, nevertheless he returned to civilisation as ignorant, alas, of its meaning as when he left it.

From *Shelburne Essays*, First Series (Boston and New York, Houghton Mifflin Company, 1904), pp. 1–21.

However, it is not my intention to justify the saintly old lady's charge of egotism by telling the story of my exodus to the desert; that, perhaps, may come later and at a more suitable time. I wish now only to record the memories of one perfect day in June, when woods and mountains were as yet a new delight.

The fresh odours of morning were still swaying in the air when I set out on this particular day; and my steps turned instinctively to the great pine forest, called the Cathedral Woods, that filled the valley and climbed the hill slopes behind my house. There, many long roads that are laid down in no map wind hither and thither among the trees, whose leafless trunks tower into the sky and then meet in evergreen arches overhead. There,

> The tumult of the times disconsolate

never enters, and no noise of the world is heard save now and then, in winter, the ringing strokes of the woodchopper at his cruel task. How many times I have walked those quiet cathedral aisles, while my great dog paced faithfully on before! Underfoot the dry, purple-hued moss was stretched like a royal carpet; and at intervals a glimpse of the deep sky, caught through an aperture in the groined roof, reminded me of the other world, and carried my thoughts still farther from the desolating memories of this life. Nothing but pure odours were there, sweeter than cloistral incense; and murmurous voices of the pines, more harmonious than the chanting of trained choristers; and in the heart of the wanderer nothing but tranquillity and passionless peace.

Often now the recollection of those scenes comes floating back upon his senses when, in the wakeful seasons of a summer night, he hears the wind at work among the trees; even in barren city streets some sound or spectacle can act upon him as a spell, banishing for a moment the hideous contention of commerce, and placing him beneath the restful shadows of the pines. May his understanding cease its function, and his heart forget to feel, when the memory of those days has utterly left him and he walks in the world without this consolation of remembered peace.

Nor can I recollect that my mind, in these walks, was much called away from contemplation by the petty curiosities of the herbalist or bird-lorist, for I am not one zealously addicted to scrutinising into the minuter secrets of Nature. It never seemed to me that a flower was made sweeter by knowing the construction of its ovaries, or assumed a new importance when I learned its trivial or scientific name. The wood thrush and the veery sing as melodiously to the uninformed as to the subtly curious. Indeed, I sometimes think a little ignorance is wholesome in our communion with Nature, until we are ready to part with her altogether. She is feminine in this as in other respects, and loves to shroud herself in illusions, as the Hindus taught in their books. For they called her Mâyâ, the very person and power of deception, whose sway over the beholder must end as soon as her mystery is penetrated.

Dear as the sound of the wood thrush's note still is to my ears, something of charm and allurement has gone from it since I have become intimate with the name and habits of the bird. As a child born and reared in the city, that wild, ringing call was perfectly new and strange to me when, one early dawn, I first heard it during a visit to the Delaware Water Gap. To me, whose ears had grown familiar only with the rumble of paved streets, the sound was like a reiterated unearthly summons inviting me from my narrow prison existence out into a wide and unexplored world of impulse and adventure. Long afterwards I learned the name of the songster whose note had made so strong an impression on my childish senses, but still I associate the song with the grandiose scenery, with the sheer forests and streams and the rapid river of the Water Gap. I was indeed almost a man—though the confession may sound incredible in these days—before I again heard the wood thrush's note, and my second adventure impressed me almost as profoundly as the first. In the outer suburbs of the city where my home had always been, I was walking one day with a brother, when suddenly out of a grove of laurel oaks sounded, clear and triumphant, the note which I remembered so well, but which had come to have to my imagination the unreality and mystery of a dream of long ago. Instantly my heart leapt within me. "It is the fateful summons once more!" I cried; and, with my companion who was equally ignorant of bird-lore, I ran into the grove to discover the wild trumpeter. That was a strange chase in the fading twilight, while the unknown songster led us on from tree to tree, ever deeper into the woods. Many times we saw him on one of the lower boughs, but could not for a long while bring ourselves to believe that so wondrous a melody should proceed from so plain a minstrel. And at last, when we had satisfied ourselves of his identity, and the night had fallen, we came out into the road with a strange solemnity hanging over us. Our ears had been opened to the unceasing harmonies of creation, and our eyes had been made aware of the endless drama of natural life. We had been initiated into the lesser mysteries; and if the sacred pageantry was not then, and never was to be, perfectly clear to our understanding, the imagination was nevertheless awed and purified.

If the knowledge and experience of years have made me a little more callous to these deeper influences, at least I have not deliberately closed the door to them by incautious prying. Perhaps a long course of wayward reading has taught me to look upon the world with eyes quite different from those of the modern exquisite searchers into Nature. I remember the story of Prometheus, and think his punishment is typical of the penalty that falls upon those who grasp at powers and knowledge not intended for mankind,— some nemesis of a more material loneliness and a more barren pride torturing them because they have turned from human knowledge to an alien and forbidden sphere. Like Prometheus, they shall in the end cry out in vain:—

> O air divine, and O swift-wingëd winds!
> Ye river fountains, and thou myriad-twinkling
> Laughter of ocean waves! O mother earth!
> And thou, O all-discerning orb o' the sun!—
> To you, I cry to you; behold what I,
> A god, endure of evil from the gods.

Nor is the tale of Prometheus alone in teaching this lesson of prudence, nor was Greece the only land of antiquity where reverence was deemed more salutary than curiosity. The myth of the veiled Isis passed in those days from people to people, and was everywhere received as a symbol of the veil of illusion about Nature, which no man might lift with impunity. And the same idea was, if anything, intensified in the Middle Ages. The common people, and the Church as well, looked with horror on such scholars as Pope Gerbert, who was thought, for his knowledge of Nature, to have sold himself to the devil; and on such discoverers as Roger Bacon, whose wicked searching into forbidden things cost him fourteen years in prison. And even in modern times did not the poet Blake say: "I fear Wordsworth loves nature, and nature is the work of the Devil. The Devil is in us as far as we are nature"? It has remained for an age of scepticism to substitute investigation for awe. After all, can any course of study or open-air pedagogics bring us into real communion with the world about us? I fear much of the talk about companionship with Nature that pervades our summer life is little better than cant and self-deception, and he best understands the veiled goddess who most frankly admits her impenetrable secrecy. The peace that comes to us from contemplating the vast panorama spread out before us is due rather to the sense of a great passionless power entirely out of our domain than to any real intimacy with the hidden deity. It was John Woolman, the famous New Jersey Quaker, who wrote, during a journey through the wilderness of Pennsylvania: "In my travelling on the road, I often felt a cry rise from the centre of my mind, thus, 'O Lord, I am a stranger on the earth, hide not thy face from me.'"

But I forget that I am myself travelling on the road; and all this long disquisition is only a chapter of reminiscences, due to the multitudinous singing of the thrushes on this side and that, as we—I and my great dog—trod the high cathedral aisles. After a while the sound of running water came to us above the deeper diapason of the pines, and, turning aside, we clambered down to a brook which we had already learned to make the terminus of our walks. Along this stream we had discovered a dozen secret nooks where man and dog might lie or sit at ease, and to-day I stretched myself on a cool, hollow rock, with my eyes looking up the long, leafy chasm of the brook. Just above my couch the current was dammed by a row of mossy boulders, over which the waters poured with a continual murmur and plash. My head was only a little higher than the pool beyond the boulders, and, lying motionless, I watched the flies weaving a pattern over the surface of the quiet water, and now and then was rewarded by seeing a greedy trout leap into the sunlight to capture one of the winged weavers. Surely, if there is any such thing as real intimacy with Nature, it is in just such secluded spots as this; for the grander scenes require of us a moral enthusiasm which can come to the soul only at rare intervals and for brief moments. From these chosen mountain retreats, one might send to a scientist, busy with his books and instruments and curious to pry into the secret powers of Nature, some such an appeal as this:—

> Brother, awhile your impious engines leave;
>   Nor always seek with flame-compelling wires
> Out of the palsied hand of Zeus to reave
>   His dear celestial fires.
>
> What though he drowse upon a tottering bench,
>   Forgetful how his random bolts are hurled!
> Are you to blame? or is it yours to quench
>   The thunders of the world?
>
> Come learn with me through folly to be wise;
>   Think you by cunning laws of optic lore
> To lend the enamelled fields or burning skies
>   One splendour lacked before?
>
> A wizard footrule to the waves of sound
>   You lay,—hath measure in the song of bird
> Or ever in the voice of waters found
>   One melody erst unheard?
>
> Ah, for a season close your magic books,
>   Your rods and crystals in the closet hide;
> I know in covert ways a hundred nooks,
>   High on the mountain side,
>
> Where through the golden hours that follow noon,
>   Under the greenwood shadows you and I
> May talk of happy lives, until too soon
>   Night's shadows fold the sky.

And while like incense blown among the leaves
   Our fragrant smoke ascends from carven bowl,
We'll con the lesser wisdom that deceives
   The Questioner in the soul,

And laugh to hoodwink where we cannot rout:—
   Did Bruno of the stubborn heart outbrave,
Or could the mind of Galileo flout
   The folly of the Grave?

So it seemed to me that the lesser wisdom of quiet content before the face of Nature's mysteries might be studied in the untrained garden of my hermitage. But I have been dreaming and moralising on the little life about me and the greater life of the world too long. So lying near the level of the still pool I began to read. The volume chosen was the most appropriate to the time and place that could be imagined,—Thoreau's *Walden*; and having entered upon an experiment not altogether unlike his, I now set myself to reading the record of his two years of solitude. I learned many things from that morning's perusal. Several times I had read the *Odyssey* within sight of the sea; and the murmur of the waves on the beach, beating through the rhythm of the poem, had taught me how vital a thing a book might be, and how it could acquire a peculiar validity from harmonious surroundings; but now the reading of Thoreau in that charmed and lonely spot emphasized this commonplace truth in a special manner. *Walden* studied in the closet, and *Walden* mused over under the trees, by running water, are two quite different books. And then, from Thoreau, the greatest by far of our writers on Nature, and the creator of a new sentiment in literature, my mind turned to the long list of Americans who have left, or are still composing, a worthy record of their love and appreciation of the natural world. Our land of multiform activities has produced so little that is really creative in literature or art! Hawthorne and Poe, and possibly one or two others, were masters in their own field; yet even they chose not quite the highest realm for their genius to work in. But in one subject our writers have led the way and are still pre-eminent: Thoreau was the creator of a new manner of writing about Nature. In its deeper essence his work is inimitable, as it

205

is the voice of a unique personality; but in its superficial aspects it has been taken up by a host of living writers, who have caught something of his method, even if they lack his genius and single-ness of heart. From these it was an easy transition to compare Thoreau's attitude of mind with that of Wordsworth and the other great poets of his century who went to Nature for their in-spiration, and made Nature-writing the characteristic note of modern verse. What is it in Thoreau that is not to be found in Byron and Shelley and Wordsworth, not to mention old Izaak Walton, Gilbert White of Selborne, and a host of others? It was a rare treat, as I lay in that leafy covert, to go over in memory the famous descriptive passages from these authors, and to con-trast their spirit with that of the book in my hand.

As I considered these matters, it seemed to me that Thoreau's work was distinguished from that of his American predecessors and imitators by just these qualities of awe and wonder which we, in our communings with Nature, so often cast away. Mere descrip-tion, though it may at times have a scientific value, is after all a very cheap form of literature; and, as I have already intimated, too much curiosity of detail is likely to exert a deadening influence on the philosophic and poetic contemplation of Nature. Such an influence is, as I believe, specially noticeable at the present time, and even Thoreau was not entirely free from its baneful effect. Much of his writing, perhaps the greater part, is the mere record of observation and classification, and has not the slightest claim on our remembrance,—unless, indeed, it possesses some scientific value, which I doubt. Certainly the parts of his work having per-manent interest are just those chapters where he is less the minute observer, and more the contemplative philosopher. Despite the width and exactness of his information, he was far from having the truly scientific spirit; the acquisition of knowledge, with him, was in the end quite subordinate to his interest in the moral significance of Nature, and the words he read in her obscure scroll were a language of strange mysteries, oftentimes of awe. It is a con-stant reproach to the prying, self-satisfied habits of small minds to see the reverence of this great-hearted observer before the supreme goddess he so loved and studied.

Much of this contemplative spirit of Thoreau is due to the soul of the man himself, to that personal force which no analysis of character can explain. But, besides this, it has always seemed to me that, more than in any other descriptive writer of the land, his mind is the natural outgrowth, and his essays the natural expression, of a feeling deep-rooted in the historical beginnings of New England; and this foundation in the past gives a strength and convincing force to his words that lesser writers utterly lack. Consider the new life of the Puritan colonists in the strange sur-roundings of their desert home. Consider the case of the adven-turous Pilgrims sailing from the comfortable city of Leyden to the unknown wilderness over the sea. As Governor Bradford wrote, "the place they had thoughts on was some of those vast & un-peopled countries of America, which are frutfull & fitt for habita-tion, being devoyd of all civill inhabitants, wher ther are only salvage and brutish men, which range up and downe, little other-wise than ye wild beasts of the same." In these vast and unpeopled countries, where beast and bird were strange to the eye, and where "salvage" men abounded,—men who did not always make the land so "fitt" for new inhabitants as Bradford might have desired,—it was inevitable that the mind should be turned to explore and re-port on natural phenomena and on savage life. It is a fact that some of the descriptions of sea and land made by wanderers to Virginia and Massachusetts have a directness and graphic power, touched occasionally with an element of wildness, that render them even to-day agreeable reading.

This was before the time of Rousseau, and before Gray had dis-covered the beauty of wild mountain scenery; inevitably the early American writers were chiefly interested in Nature as the home of future colonists, and their books are for the most part semi-scientific accounts of what they studied from a utilitarian point of view. But the dryness of detailed description in the New World was from the first modified and lighted up by the wondering awe of men set down in the midst of the strange and often threatening forces of an untried wilderness; and this sense of awful aloofness, which to a certain extent lay dormant in the earlier writers, did nevertheless sink deep into the heart of New England, and when, in the lapse of time, the country entered into its intellectual renaissance, and the genius came who was destined to give full expression to the thoughts of his people before the face of Nature, it was inevitable that his works should be dominated by just this sense of poetic mystery.

It is this New World inheritance, moreover,—joined, of course, with his own inexplicable personality, which must not be left out of account,—that makes Thoreau's attitude toward Nature something quite distinct from that of the great poets who just preceded him. There was in him none of the fiery spirit of the revolution which caused Byron to mingle hatred of men with enthusiasm for the Alpine solitudes. There was none of the passion for beauty and the voluptuous self-abandonment of Keats; these were not in the atmosphere he breathed at Concord. He was not touched with Shelley's unearthly mysticism, nor had he ever fed

> on the aërial kisses
> Of shapes that haunt thought's wildernesses;

his moral sinews were too stark and strong for that form of mental dissipation. Least of all did he, after the manner of Wordsworth, hear in the voice of Nature any compassionate plea for the weakness and sorrow of the downtrodden. Philanthropy and humanitarian sympathies were to him a desolation and a woe. "Philanthropy is almost the only virtue which is sufficiently appreciated by mankind. Nay, it is greatly overrated; and it is our selfishness which overrates it," he writes. And again: "The philanthropist too often surrounds mankind with the remembrance of his own cast-off griefs as an atmosphere, and calls it sympathy." Similarly his reliance on the human will was too sturdy to be much perturbed by the inequalities and sufferings of mankind, and his faith in the individual was too unshaken to be led into humanitarian interest in the masses. "Alas! this is the crying sin of the age," he declares, "this want of faith in the prevalence of a man."

But the deepest and most essential difference is the lack of pantheistic reverie in Thoreau. It is this brooding over the universal spirit embodied in the material world which almost always marks the return of sympathy with Nature, and which is particularly noticeable in the writers of the past century. So Lord Byron, wracked and broken by his social catastrophes, turns for relief to the fair scenes of Lake Leman, and finds in the high mountains and placid waters a consoling spirit akin to his own.

> Are not the mountains, waves, and skies, a part
> Of me and of my soul, as I of them?

he asks; and in the bitterness of his human disappointment he would "be alone, and love Earth only for its earthly sake." Shelley, too, "mixed awful talk" with the "great parent," and heard in her voice an answer to all his vague dreams of the soul of universal love. No one, so far as I know, has yet studied the relation between Wordsworth's pantheism and his humanitarian sympathies, but we need only glance at his lines on Tintern Abbey to see how closely the two feelings were interknit in his mind. It was because he felt this

> sense sublime
> Of something far more deeply interfused,
> Whose dwelling is the light of setting suns,
> And the round ocean, and the living air,
> And the blue sky, and in the mind of man;

it was because the distinctions of the human will and the consequent perception of individual responsibility were largely absorbed in this dream of the universal spirit, that he heard in Nature "the still, sad music of humanity," and reproduced it so sympathetically in his own song. Of all this pantheism, whether attended with revolt from responsibility or languid reverie or humanitarian dreams, there is hardly a trace in Thoreau. The memory of man's struggle with the primeval woods and fields was not so lost in antiquity that the world had grown into an indistinguishable part of human life. If Nature smiled upon Thoreau at times, she was still an alien creature who succumbed only to his force and tenderness, as she had before given her bounty, though reluctantly, to the Pilgrim Fathers. A certain companionship he had with the plants and wild beasts of the field, a certain intimacy with the dumb earth; but he did not seek to merge his personality in their impersonal life, or look to them for a response to his own inner moods; he associated with them as the soul associates with the body.

More characteristic is his sense of awe, even of dread, toward the great unsubdued forces of the world. The loneliness of the mountains such as they appeared to the early adventurers in a strange, unexplored country; the repellent loneliness of the barren heights frowning down inhospitably upon the pioneer who scratched the soil at their base; the loneliness and terror of the dark, untrodden forests, where the wanderer might stray away and be lost forever, where savage men were more feared than the wild animals, and where superstition saw the haunt of the Black Man and of all uncleanness,—all this tradition of sombre solitude made Nature to Thoreau something very different from the hills and valleys of Old England. "We have not seen pure Nature," he says, "unless we have seen her thus vast and drear and inhuman. . . . Man was not to be associated with it. It was matter, vast, terrific,—not his Mother Earth that we have heard of, not for him to tread on, or be buried in,—no, it were being too familiar even to let his bones lie there,—the home, this, of Necessity and Fate." After reading Byron's invocation to the Alps as the palaces of Nature; or the ethereal mountain scenes in Shelley's *Alastor*, where all the sternness of the everlasting hills is dissolved into rainbow hues of shifting light as dainty as the poet's own soul; or Wordsworth's familiar musings in the vale of Grasmere,—if, after these, we turn to Thoreau's account of the ascent of Mount Katahdin, we seem at once to be in the home of another tradition. I am tempted to quote a few sentences of that account to emphasise the point. On the mountain heights, he says of the beholder:

He is more lone than you can imagine. There is less of substantial thought and fair understanding in him than in the plains where men inhabit. His reason is dispersed and shadowy, more thin and subtile, like the air. Vast, Titanic, inhuman Nature has got him at disadvantage, caught him alone, and pilfers him of some of his divine faculty. She does not smile on him as in the plains. She seems to say sternly, Why came ye here before your time? This ground is not prepared for you. Is it not enough that I smile in the valleys? I have never made this soil for thy feet, this air for thy breathing, these rocks for thy neighbours. I cannot pity nor fondle thee here, but forever relentlessly drive thee hence to where I am kind.

I do not mean to present the work of Thoreau as equal in value to the achievement of the great poets with whom I have compared him, but wish merely in this way to bring out more definitely his characteristic traits. Yet if his creative genius is less than theirs, I cannot but think his attitude toward Nature is in many respects truer and more wholesome. Pantheism, whether on the banks of the Ganges or of the Thames, seems to bring with it a spreading taint of effeminacy; and from this the mental attitude of our Concord naturalist was eminently free. There is something tonic and bracing in his intercourse with the rude forces of the forest; he went to Walden Pond because he had "private business to transact," not for relaxation and mystical reverie. "To be a philosopher," he said, "is not merely to have subtle thoughts, nor even to found a school, but so to love wisdom as to live according to its dictates, a life of simplicity, independence, magnanimity, and trust"; and by recurring to the solitudes of Nature he thought he could best develop in himself just these manly virtues. Nature was to him a discipline of the will as much as a stimulant to the imagination. He would, if it were possible, "combine the hardiness of the savages with the intellectualness of the civilised man"; and in this method of working out the philosophical life we see again the influence of long and deep-rooted tradition. To the first settlers, the red man was as much an object of curiosity and demanded as much study as the earth they came to cultivate; their books are full of graphic pictures of savage life, and it should seem as if now in Thoreau this inherited interest had received at last its ripest expression. When he travelled in the wilderness of Maine, he was as much absorbed in learning the habits of his Indian guides as in exploring the woods. He had some innate sympathy or perception which taught him to find relics of old Indian life where others would pass them by, and there is a well-known story of his answer to one who asked him where such relics could be discovered: he merely stooped down and picked an arrowhead from the ground.

And withal his stoic virtues never dulled his sense of awe, and his long years of observation never lessened his feeling of strangeness in the presence of solitary Nature. If at times his writing descends into the cataloguing style of the ordinary naturalist, yet the old tradition of wonder was too strong in him to be more than temporarily obscured. Unfortunately, his occasional faults have become in some of his recent imitators the staple of their talent; but Thoreau was pre-eminently the poet and philosopher of his school, and I cannot do better than close these desultory notes with the quotation of a passage which seems to me to convey most vividly his sensitiveness to the solemn mystery of the deep forest:

We heard [he writes in his Chesuncook], come faintly echoing, or creeping from afar, through the moss-clad aisles, a dull, dry, rushing sound, with a solid core to it, yet as if half smothered under the grasp of the luxuriant and fungus-like forest, like the shutting of a door in some distant entry of the damp and shaggy wilderness. If we had not been there, no mortal had heard it. When we asked Joe [the Indian guide] in a whisper what it was, he answered,—"Tree fall."

Thoreau's Journal

⟨⟨⟨⟩⟩ Twenty volumes of Thoreau[1] make a pretty large showing for a man who had only a scant handful of ideas, and, in particular, the thought of labouring through the fourteen volumes of the Journal, now for the first time published complete, may well appal the sturdiest reader. It cannot be denied that the bulk of these note-books have no interest except for the confirmed nature-worshipper, and, in part, I suspect, little even for him. Most of the memorable reflections and descriptive passages had already been transferred to the regular books and lectures; what remains is made up largely of trivial daily memoranda, often written down in the field, and then copied out at home for more convenient reference. But there are recompenses for the wary reader who has learnt the art of skipping; scattered at random through the pages he will discover fragments of magic description, shrewd bookish criticisms, glimpses of serene vision, the old familiar thoughts struck out in fresh language. Thus a certain largeness of outlook seems to be added to Thoreau's known feeling toward the humanitarians when we come across these words, written in 1842: "The sudden revolutions of these times and this generation have acquired a very exaggerated importance. They do not interest me much, for they are not in harmony with the longer periods of nature. The present, in any aspect in which it can be presented to the smallest audience, is always mean. God does not sympathise with the popular movements." And for description, where will one turn for a more superbly Rabelaisian picture than this wassail scene of the woods:

From *Shelburne Essays*, Fifth Series (Boston and New York, Houghton Mifflin Company, 1908), pp. 106–31.

[1] *The Writings of Henry David Thoreau.* Walden Edition. Twenty volumes. Boston: Houghton Mifflin Co., 1906.

And then the frogs, bullfrogs; they are the more sturdy spirits of ancient wine-bibbers and wassailers, still unrepentant, trying to sing a catch in their Stygian lakes. They would fain keep up the hilarious good fellowship and all the rules of their old round tables, but they have waxed hoarse and solemnly grave and serious their voices, mocking at mirth, and their wine has lost its flavour and is only liquor to distend their paunches; and never comes sweet intoxication to drown the memory of the past, but mere saturation and waterlogged dulness and distension. Still the most aldermanic, with his chin upon a pad, which answers for a napkin to his drooling chaps, under the eastern shore quaffs a deep draught of the once scorned water, and passes round the cup with the ejaculation tr-r-r-r-oonk, tr-r-r-r-oonk, tr-r-r-r-oonk! and straightway comes over the water from some distant cove the selfsame password, where the next in seniority and girth has gulped down to his mark; and when the strain has made the circuit of the shores, then ejaculates the master of ceremonies with satisfaction tr-r-r-r-oonk! and each in turn repeats the sound, down to the least distended, leakiest, flabbiest paunched, that there be no mistake; and the bowl goes round again, until the sun dispels the morning mist, and only the patriarch is not under the pond, but vainly bellowing troonk from time to time, pausing for a reply.

The scene was written while he was living on the banks of Walden, and afterwards copied, with a few unimportant changes, into his book. It is but one of a hundred examples showing how the essence of his diaries was pressed into that and his other works. It is an example, too, of the peculiarly happy inspiration that other poets than Aristophanes have won from the sullen batrachian song. Thoreau returns to the same theme more than once. "There is the faintest possible mist over the pond holes," he writes six years later, "where the frogs are eructating, like the falling of huge drops, the bursting of mephitic air-bubbles rising from the bottom, a sort of blubbering—such conversations as I *have* heard between men, a belching conversation, expressing a sympathy of stomachs and abdomens." The image of these grotesque revellers haunts him, and has haunted others, as if it were an obscene parody of the fabled singing of the poets at the well of Hippocrene.

214

Et veterem in limo ranæ cecinere querellam—*

the very word *querella* is sacred to the denizens of Helicon.

Such isolated examples of wit and poetry we stumble upon in the Journal, and take our reward for pages of triviality. And, from another point of view, by overlooking the question of immediate interest altogether, we may find a more solid profit in these volumes. As a record written in large of the life of which *Walden* expresses, so to speak, the quintessential meaning, these private and garrulous memoranda have a real value of corroboration. They show the utter sincerity of the man; in their large placid current we perceive the stillness of his nature, and are further assured that his dramatic escape to the woods was not a bit of posing, nor a calculated exploit for "copy," but an experience quite harmonious with the tenor of his days. And this knowledge is precious; for the distinction of Thoreau lies just herein, that what other men were preaching, he lived. In transcendental thought he was, if compared with Emerson, thin and derivative, the shadow of a shadow; in power of description he excelled several of his contemporaries only through greater precision of details—a questionable superiority; and he possessed not a spark of Hawthorne's creative imagination. But he had this one great advantage, that his words come to us freighted with the conviction of experience. "There are nowadays professors of philosophy," he observes in defence of his Walden experiment, "but not philosophers. . . . To be a philosopher is not merely to have subtle thoughts, nor even to found a school, but so to love wisdom as to live according to its dictates, a life of simplicity, independence, magnanimity, and trust. It is to solve some of the problems of life, not only theoretically, but practically."

For the student of the larger intellectual currents Thoreau offers a second advantage, which is made more conspicuous by the publication of the Journal. From his comparative poverty in original ideas and from the independence of his character we can see, better than in the case of Emerson or any other of the group, wherein the transcendentalism of Concord was an echo of the German school, and wherein it differed. No one has yet traced the

* [And frogs in the mud sang the old complaint.]

exact channels by which the formulæ of romanticism migrated from Germany to New England, although it is known in a general way that the direct influence through translations in the American magazines and elsewhere was considerable. Moreover, most of the Concord scholars dabbled at one time or another in the German language. The strongest impulse, no doubt, came indirectly through Coleridge, Carlyle, and the other British Teutonisers, but once here it found a far more suitable soil than in England. Our people had just thrown off the strait-jacket of Puritan religion and were revelling in the always perilous consciousness of spiritual liberty. The situation in Germany at the time of the Romantic School was not altogether dissimilar. Lessing and the Titans of the *Sturm und Drang* had wrestled against the deadening tyranny of the Lutheran Church; they had discarded the formalism of French literary law, and with it pretty much all sense of form whatever; they had, with the help of Kant, broken down the official philosophy of Leibniz and Wolff. On all sides resounded the watchword of *Freiheit*, liberty—except in politics, where neither then nor now have the Germans, as a people, reached any notion of individual liberty submitting to the discipline of self-imposed restraint, without need of the strong hand of Government or the bonds of socialistic regulation. So far as the aim of the Storm and Stress can be described, it might be called a rejection of the eighteenth-century principle of selection for that of universality. The whole of human nature should be embraced and developed, and this development was to come through a setting loose of every impulse and passion of the breast to run its full unhampered course. What that career meant, the *Geniesucht*, the *Unendlichkeitsstreben*, the *ringende Titanenthum*, the *Emancipation des Fleisches*, the *Seelenpriapismus**—may all be seen, by whoever cares to read it, in such a work as Wilhelm Heinse's *Ardinghello*. Out of this blind ferment of freedom came at last the spirit of a new and more compact school, the cultus of the *Ich*, the romantic *I*, as formulated by Fichte, the Schlegels, Schleiermacher, and Schelling, and as practised by Tieck, Novalis, and a small band of contemporaries.

* [The yearning for genius, the striving for infinity, the wrestling titanism, the emancipation of the flesh, the priapism of the soul.]

German romanticism is often defined as a return to mediæval ideals, and for a later period in the movement such a definition is fairly exact. And even in the beginning, although such a master of the school as Friedrich Schlegel preferred to call himself a Grecian, his interest in that land was mainly a sentimental nostalgia for some imagined home of happiness in the past; whereas his kinship, vague at first, and entirely unconscious, was rather with the mediæval Church. Through all the years after the Renaissance, the memory and habit of the Middle Ages had run beneath civilisation like one of those underground rivers, sending up its fountains here and there, even in the disciplined years of the eighteenth century. And when at last the depths had been broken up by the wild license of the Storm and Stress, it reappeared at the surface, its old name forgotten and its current charged with many deposits from its hidden pilgrimage. We are accustomed to find the relationship between romanticism and the Middle Ages chiefly in a common feeling of infinity, in their *Unendlichkeitsstreben*, and this in a way is true. But we must restrict the meaning of the word closely. In the narrower acceptation, the Middle Ages had less of the feeling than the centuries either preceding or immediately following. There is more of the infinite in Virgil's *loca nocte tacentia late** than in Dante's vision of petrified eternity; there is more of the infinite in Shakespeare than in all the mediæval poets put together, more in Plato and Spinoza than in all the intervening schoolmen. What the Middle Ages really strove for was to combine the ideas of personality and limitlessness; the human personality was to be protracted unchanged through unending periods of time, the deity was to be at once human in nature and unbounded in power—a conception of the world which could have arisen only when the feeling for the infinite as something positive in itself and different from a mere quantitative limitlessness had been lost. Necessarily such an effort to contain the infinite within the vessel of the finite brought its penalty—to some minds an unwholesome exaltation and relaxing revery, to others, as to St. Augustine, the anguish of mortal self-contradiction. This was the burden of the *Confessions*: "How shall I call upon my God, God

* [Places widely silent in the night.]

217

and my Lord? For I call him into myself when I call upon him
(*quoniam utique in meipsum eum vocabo, cum invocabo eum*).
And what room is there in me, where my God may enter in, where
God may enter in, God who made heaven and earth?" And this
combat between the thought of a limited and an unlimited personality passed through the Middle Ages, disappeared for a time,
and then returned to be absorbed and modified in the writings of
the Romantic School.

Only so can we understand the *Ich* which Fichte erected into
that tortured system of philosophy, whose chief value is that it gave
a backbone of rigid articulate logic to a body of otherwise flabby
sentiment. The spirit of revolt is the beginning of the movement.
Not only in art does the will or whim (*Willkür*) of the poet suffer
no law over itself, as Friedrich Schlegel avers, but, more mystically,
this liberty is necessary for the expansion of the I into the desired
state of limitless self-satisfaction. Here is no true sense of infinity,
nor yet much talk of God and the soul—these had withered away
under the *Aufklärung*—but an attempt to account for the world
by some juggling with the personal I and the not-I. In place of
the mediæval contrast of a divine Person and a world created out
of nothing by his fiat, Fichte substitutes a formula begotten of
logic on lyricism. Bring together the logical law of identity (A =
A, and not-A is not = A) and the craving of unrestrained egotism, and you get the romantic equivalent for mediævalism: God
is replaced by the human personality, lifted as the transcendental
I above the ordinary I of commerce and society, and the world is
the not-I called into being as a field for its exercise and enjoyment.

Here is room for endless revery, for unbounded exaltations, for
insatiable self-tormentings. This I has in practice no concern with
the reason, which is the faculty of defining and delimiting; it has
no kinship with the will, which means self-restraint; it is the child
of the feelings, which are essentially rebellious to limitations. So
in religion there was a general repudiation of Luther and the
Reformation, as the source of "a dry rational emptiness which
leaves the heart to pine away." To Schleiermacher, the great
preacher of the band, religion was neither reason nor morality,
neither thought nor action, but an emotional contemplation of
the universe by which the soul is thrown into a state of indistin-

guishing revery, and the I and the not-I swoon together into one. The religious feeling, he thought, should "accompany all the doings of a man as if it were a holy music; he should do all *with* religion, nothing *through* religion." And the aim of poetry was the same. It, too, should avoid all that is sharply defined, and should blend all the *genres* into a kind of ineffable music, appealing neither to the thought nor the will. "Poems which sound melodiously and are full of beautiful words, but without any sense or connection"—that, according to Novalis, is the consummation of art.

From the same source spring those peculiar accompaniments of the movement—the so-called romantic irony, the aloofness from society, the sacred idleness. Given this outreaching egotism, together with this contempt of limitations, and inevitably there arises an inner state which is the modern counterpart of St. Augustine's wrestling with the personality of God. Fichte might argue calmly about the world as not-I, but to the inflamed imagination of a Schlegel this division of nature was a disruption of self from self; it became the everlasting, uncompromising discord between the ideal and the real. The only escape from this anguish of dissatisfaction was to ascend into those towers of indifference from which the transcendental I might survey the life of mankind, even its own activities, with unconcerned irony. In art this is the quality by which the artist "appears to smile down upon his own masterpiece from the heights of his spirit"; in life it is the feeling which leads a man to move about in society as in an alien world whose concerns are to him nothing—a mere piece of "transcendental buffoonery." Hence the contempt of business and of the Philistines follows as a kind of seal set upon the romantic soul which is conscious of itself. It cultivates a divine idleness; the summons to loaf and invite one's soul came from over the sea long before the scandalous outbreak of Walt Whitman.

And the theatre of this vagrant aloofness was nature. To the wanderer in the field and on the mountain side, with his spirit bathed in the shifting glamour of colour and form, with no troublesome call upon his reason or his will, this visible music of nature might seem now to be spun like a dream from the depths of his own being and now to be absorbed in silence back into himself.

219

Schelling had modified this mystic revery into a vast metaphysical parallelism. "The system of nature," he said, "is at the same time the system of our spirit"; and again, "Nature is the visible spirit, the spirit is invisible nature." And Novalis, to whom thought was "only a dream of the feelings," held that by a kind of transcendental "magic," to use his famous word, a man might juggle or shuffle spirit and nature together. In his *Lehrlinge zu Sais** romanticism received perhaps its purest expression. "At the well of freedom," says one in that book, "we sit and spy; it is the great magic-mirror wherein serene and clear the whole creation reveals itself; herein bathe the tender spirits and images of all natures, and here we behold all chambers laid open. . . . And when we wander from this view into nature herself, all is to us well known, and without error we recognize every form. . . . It is all a great scroll, to which we have the key." Whereto another prophet in the book replies in the language of Fichte, telling how a man is lord of the world, and how his I, brooding mightily over the abyss of mutable forms, reduces them slowly to the eternal order of its own law of being, *der Veste seines Ichs.*****

Now, of the systematic romanticism of Fichte and Schelling there is little or nothing in the writings of our New England transcendentalists. Many of their ideas may be found in Emerson, but divested of their logical coherence; and as for Thoreau, "metaphysics was his aversion," says William Ellery Channing; "speculation on the special faculties of the mind, or whether the Not-Me comes out of the I or the All out of the infinite Nothing, he could not entertain." Nevertheless, in its more superficial aspects, almost the whole body of romanticism may be found reflected, explicitly or implicitly, in his Journal and formal works. He, too, had sat spying in the well of freedom, and the whole art and practice of his life were a pæan of liberty: "For a man to act himself he must be perfectly free." And this was his mission, to act himself, and to point to others the path of freedom. Calvinism had been discarded in Concord as Lutheranism had been by the romanticists at Berlin. There is little concern in Thoreau with God and the soul, but in its place a sense of individualism, of sublime egotism, reaching out to embrace the world in ecstatic communion. His

* [*The Apprentices at Sais,* a fragment of a novel.]
** [The tribunal of one's own ego.]

religion was on the surface not dissimilar to Schleiermacher's mystical contemplation of the universe; "vast films of thought floated through my brain," he says on one occasion; and the true harvest of his daily life he pronounced "a little star-dust caught, a segment of the rainbow which I have clutched." This revery, or contemplation that spurned at limitations, passed easily into the romantic ideal of music—and that in a very literal, sometimes ludicrous, sense. A music-box was for him a means of consolation for the loss of his brother; a hand-organ was an instrument of the gods; and the humming wires on a cold day—his telegraph harp he called it— seemed to him to convey to his soul some secret harmony of the universe. "The wire is my redeemer, it always brings a special message to me from the Highest." This is the thought that occurs over and over again in the Journal. More particularly in one passage dated September 3, 1851, by Channing, and jumbled together from separate entries in the Journal, he expatiates on this modern harmony of the spheres:

As I went under the new telegraph wire, I heard it vibrating like a harp high overhead; it was as the sound of a far-off glorious life; a supernal life which came down to us and vibrated the lattice-work of this life of ours—an Æolian harp. It reminded me, I say, with a certain pathetic moderation, of what finer and deeper stirrings I was susceptible, which grandly set all argument and dispute aside, a triumphant though transient exhibition of the truth.

There is something bordering on the grotesque in this rhapsodical homage to a droning telegraph wire, but it might be paralleled by many a like enthusiasm of the German brotherhood. Nor was Thoreau unaware of this intrusion of humour into his ecstasy. Like Friedrich Schlegel, he indulges in the romantic irony of smiling down upon himself and walking through life as a *Doppelgänger:*

I only know myself as a human entity; the scene, so to speak, of thoughts and affections; and am sensible of a certain doubleness by which I can stand remote from myself as from another. However intense my experience, I am conscious of the presence and criticism of a part of me, which, as it were, is not a part of me, but spectator, sharing no experience, but taking note of it; and that is no

221

more I than it is you. When the play, it may be the tragedy, of life is over, the spectator goes his way. It is a kind of fiction, a work of the imagination only, so far as he was concerned.

How far this irony carried him in his hatred of Philistinism and his aloofness from society, no reader of his books need be told. The life of the business man he compared to the tortures of an ascetic, and the California gold-fever threw him into a rage of disgust: —"going to California. It is only three thousand miles nearer to hell. . . . The gold of California is a touchstone which has betrayed the rottenness, the baseness, of mankind." Nor did the daily commerce of man with man come off much better. He was not one who would "feebly fabulate and paddle in the social slush." "I live," he says, "in the angle of a leaden wall, into whose alloy was poured a little bell-metal. Sometimes in the repose of my midday there reaches my ears a confused tintinnabulum from without. It is the noise of my contemporaries."—Could an image be more sublimely impertinent?

Often a passage in the Journal bears the stamp of German romanticism so plainly upon it, that we stop to trace it back in memory to Tieck or Novalis or one of the followers of the earlier Storm and Stress. Such are his scattered observations on childhood, on sleep, and the all-enveloping sacrament of silence; such is his constant thought of a new mythology which is to be the end of our study and our art—"all the phenomena of nature need to be seen from the point of view of wonder and awe. . . . Men are probably nearer to the essential truth in their superstitions than in their science." These, I take it, are not cases of translation or plagiarism, but rather of that larger and vaguer migration of thought from one land to another. They show how thoroughly the transcendental philosophy of New England had absorbed the language and ideas of German romanticism, if not its inmost spirit.

And so, one may follow these movements step by step—through irony, aloofness, and sacred idleness, through their flowering in musical revery and communion with nature—and show how they develop on parallel lines always alike on the surface, yet always with some underlying difference more easily felt than named. And this difference is felt more strongly, is indeed then only to be understood, when we go back to that free individualism which is the root of all this varied growth. "Contemplation," says Schleiermacher in his second *Discourse*, "is and always remains something single, separate, the immediate perception, nothing more; to connect and bring together into a whole is not the business of the senses, but of abstract thought. So with religion: it is hers to abide by the immediate experience of the being and activity of the universe, by the individual perceptions and feelings; each of these is a work existing in itself without connection with others or dependence upon them. Of derivation and association religion knows nothing; of all things that may touch her, these are the most contrary to her nature. . . . It is due just to this absolute individuality that the sphere of contemplation is so infinite." Here certainly —and we are at the very heart of German romanticism—is a doctrine which the wise men of Concord would have been the first to repudiate. "Infinity" to Schleiermacher was only another word for endless variety of particulars, amid which the soul of man, itself a momentary atom in the stream, moves in a state of perpetual wonder. The ideal of Emerson was that self-reliance by which the individual, shaking itself free from the mere conformity of manners and tradition, might rise to the community of the higher nature figured by him as the over-soul: "In all conversation between two persons, tacit reference is made as to a third party, to a common nature. That third party or common nature is not social, it is impersonal; it is God." And Thoreau represented friendship by the symbol of two lines divergent on the earth and converging together in the stars. I cannot find the equivalent of this in Schleiermacher. I find rather that, like the rest of the romantics, when he sought for the basis of a man's nature, he turned to pure emotionalism, the very power and faculty by which we are bound within the limits of our individuality. We have seen that to Schleiermacher "the essence of religion is neither thought nor action, but contemplation and feeling." Let us see in what colours he pictures this passive surrender of the soul to the impression of the world. Thus he continues in the *Reden*:

> *Only do not suppose—this is indeed one of the most dangerous errors—that religious contemplation and feeling at their beginning in the first activity of the soul* (des Gemüths) *are severed in any*

223

such way as they necessarily are in our discourse. Contemplation without feeling is nothing, and possesses neither the right source nor the right power; feeling without contemplation is likewise nothing: both are something only when and because they are originally one and unseparated. That first mysterious moment, which comes to us with every sensuous perception before contemplation and feeling have drawn apart, . . . fleeting is it and transparent, like the first exhalation wherewith the dew breathes upon the awakened flowers, demure and tender like the kiss of a virgin, holy and fruitful like the embrace of marriage. Nay, not like this, rather it is all this. Quickly and magically an appearance, an event, unfolds itself to a likeness of the universe. And so, as the beloved and ever-desired form takes shape, my soul flees to her, and I embrace her not as a shadow, but as the holy essence itself. I lie in the bosom of the infinite world; I am in that moment its soul, for I feel all its powers and its infinite life as my own. . . . At the least jar the holy union is blown away, and then first Contemplation stands before me as a separate form; I gaze upon her, and she mirrors herself in the open soul as the image of the departing loved-one in the open eye of the youth. And now first feeling rises up from within him, and spreads like the blush of shame and desire over his cheek. This moment is the highest flowering of religion.

Could anything than this be more essentially at variance with the product of Concord? The nearest approach to it in substance is the hedonism of Pater as expressed in the *Conclusion* to his Renaissance studies. For what in the end is this religion of Schleiermacher's but that culture of the fleeting artistic impression which Pater taught: "Every moment some form grows perfect in hand and face; some tone on the hills or the sea is choicer than the rest; some mood of passion or insight or intellectual excitement is irresistibly real and attractive for us—for that moment only"? It is but the modern decking out of the ancient philosophical heresy of Heracleitus that all things move and flit away, which the English writer places as the motto of his essay. I would not be unappreciative of the great German divine, but I cannot sever his unctuous preaching of emotionalism from the actual emotions which ruled among the coterie to whom his discourses were addressed. When he turns from his image of the bridal of the soul and the universe to the fable of Paradise, and declares that only through the coming of Eve was Adam enabled to lift his thoughts heavenward, when he makes of love the only source of religion, he is, of course, speaking within the acknowledged rights of the preacher. Yet I cannot forget the morbid life of Rousseau, from whom all this *Gefühlsphilosophie* is ultimately derived; I remember more particularly Heinse's yearning for some wilderness apart from the world where he might, like a Platonic sage, pass his life in saintly studies—with Laïs at his side.[1] I am afraid of a religion which accords so easily with this blending of Plato and Laïs, and which serves so well a literature whose principle as announced by Tieck was briefly this: "The decency of our common prosaic life is unallowed in art; in these happy, pure regions it is unseemly; it is among us even the document of our commonness and immorality." I am Puritanic enough to dislike and to distrust these confusions; and it is because I do not find them in Thoreau that I can turn to him after reading much in the *romantische Schule* with a sense of relief, as one passes from a sick-chamber to the breath of the fields. Concord is remote and provincial in comparison with the Berlin and Jena of those days; it lacks the universality and culture of those centres; above all, it lacks the imposing presence of a Goethe and a Schiller, who, however loosely, were still connected with the romantic brotherhood; but it possessed one great offset—character.

"Life shall be the living breath of nature," might have been the motto of Thoreau as it was of a great German. He, too, went out to find the God of history in nature, inasmuch as man is but a part of the whole, a brother to the worm—but the ways of their search led them far asunder. We have seen how on the surface the mystical revery of Novalis's *Lehrlinge zu Sais* is akin to the ideals of Thoreau: yet follow the two to the end. We shall see

[1] This conjunction of Plato and Laïs is taken up from the decadence of Greece itself. The Pseudo-Platonic epigram is well known: "I Laïs who laughed exultant over Greece, I who held that swarm of young lovers in my porches, lay my mirror before the Paphian; since such as I am I will not see myself, and such as I was I cannot."

one of the scholars of Sais journeying through a tropical clime to the shrine of Isis; we shall see him in an ecstasy before that veiled goddess of nature; "then lifted he the light, gleaming veil, and—Rosenblüthchen sank into his arms." It is only Heinse's Plato and Laïs, or Schleiermacher's Adam and Eve if you will, under other names. There is a taint of sickliness in all this. It corresponds too well to the "heavenly weariness" of Novalis himself, as he might be found at the grave of his Sophie, vowing himself to death for lofty ensample of love's eternal faithfulness, and in a short while after discovering his religion incarnate in another woman.

Now there was no Laïs in Thoreau's life, no sentimental identification of a dead Sophie with a living Julie, and above all, no rapturous embrace of both together in the person of the goddess of nature. It may even be granted that the absence of primitive human emotion is so pronounced in his diaries as to render them thin and bloodless. To lay bare the sources of this difference between Thoreau and Novalis it would be necessary to analyse a score of influences silently at work beneath the surface of his culture—the inheritance of Puritan religion, denied indeed, but still making any real return to mediævalism impossible; the British notion of practical individualism expressed in the philosophy of Adam Smith; the lesson of Wordsworth's austerity in the devotion to nature; the spirit of fine expectancy derived from the poets of the seventeenth century, who were Thoreau's chief mental nourishment; the incalculable force of Emerson's personality. It comes at the last chiefly to this: the freedom of the romantic school was to the end that the whole emotional nature might develop; in Thoreau it was for the practice of a higher self-restraint. The romantics sought for the common bond of human nature in the *Gemüth*, Thoreau believed it lay in character. In the *Gemüth* (the word is untranslatable; heart, with the connotation of sentiment, mood, revery, is the nearest equivalent) Schleiermacher found the organ of religion to the absolute exclusion of the reason and the will; there Novalis looked for the inspiration of all art; communion with nature was desirable only because in her, too, might be discovered "all the variations of an endless *Gemüth*";

226

and to this organ of the individual person was reduced in reality the high-sounding *Ich* of Fichte. *Gemüth*—character, *Gefühl*—conduct; in that contrast lay the divergence between German and New England transcendentalism. "What are three-score years and ten hurriedly and coarsely lived to moments of divine leisure in which your life is coincident with the life of the universe?" asks Thoreau in his Journal; but he adds as a corrective: "That aim in life is highest which requires the highest and finest discipline." Man's life, he says elsewhere, "consists not in his obedience, but his opposition, to his instincts," and genius was to him another name for health. This was his resolution and his prayer:

I pray that the life of this spring and summer may ever lie fair in my memory. May I dare as I have never done! May I preserve as I have never done! May I purify myself anew as with fire and water, soul and body! May I gird myself to be a hunter of the beautiful, that nought escape me! May I attain to a youth never attained! I am eager to report the glory of the universe; may I be worthy to do it; to have got through with regarding human values so as not to be distracted from regarding divine values. It is reasonable that a man should be something worthier at the end of the year than he was at the beginning.

And so, despite its provincialism and its tedium, the Journal of Thoreau is a document that New England may cherish proudly. It is the mirror of a life, the record of romanticism striving to work itself out in actual character, and shows thus, as clearly as the far greater writings of Emerson, wherein the originality of the Concord school really lies. The dangers of transcendentalism are open enough—its facile optimism and unballasted enthusiasms—dangers to the intellect chiefly. Any one may point at the incompatibility of Thoreau's gospel with the requirements of society. To follow him, as to follow Walt Whitman, a man must needs shun the responsibilities of the family and State, and walk in solitary ways. Yet, withal, there is brave inspiration in the scornful independence of this botanising vagabond. For the motto of his Journal one might choose the familiar lines of Matthew Arnold:

227

For most men in a brazen prison live,
Where, in the sun's hot eye,
With heads bent o'er their toil they languidly
Their lives to some unmeaning taskwork give,
Dreaming of nought beyond their prison-wall.

             ∽   ∽   ∽

And the rest, a few,
Escape their prison and depart
On the wide ocean of life anew.
There the freed prisoner, where'er his heart
Listeth, will sail;
Nor doth he know how there prevail,
Despotic on that sea,
Trade-winds that cross it from eternity.
Awhile he holds some false way, undebarr'd
By thwarting signs, and braves
The freshening wind and blackening waves,
And then the tempest strikes him. . . .
And he too disappears, and comes no more.

Put out of mind the wild hurtling words Thoreau was so fond of uttering, forget the ill taste into which his narrower circumstances often led him, and there remains this tonic example of a man who did actually and violently break through the prison walls of routine, and who yet kept a firm control of his career. If his aim was to refine his senses so that, like an Æolian harp, he might quiver in response to every impression of mountain and field and river, at least he sought for this refinement by eliminating all the coarser and more relaxing emotions of his breast; by disciplining his will into harmony with the pure and relentless laws of universal being. And if the terms of his practical philosophy may be traced back through the German romanticists to Rousseau's ideal of a return to nature, yet his sympathetic knowledge of hard savage life among the Indians and the tradition of New England's struggle with the wilderness kept him, always in act and generally in words, from sentimental softening of the reality.

Perhaps, in the end, what remains in the mind of the reader is the sense of constant expectancy that plays on almost every page of his works. "Is not the attitude of expectation somewhat divine?" he asks in one of his letters, and always it is morning with him. The clearest expression of this buoyancy of the dawn may be found in the account of A *Walk to Wachusett*, but it is never long absent from the Journal and was a characteristic of his daily life. He walked the fields like one who was on the alert for some divine apparition, and Mr. M. D. Conway has observed that a strange light seemed to shine on his countenance when abroad. This, too, is a trait of the romantic spirit, no doubt; but its quality in Thoreau does not point to Germany. It came to him in part from his birth in a new land, and it was strengthened by his familiarity with the English poets of the seventeenth century. In the works of Henry Vaughan more particularly you will find this note of expectation, rising at times to a cry of ecstasy for which there is no equivalent in the later American. I think of Vaughan as travelling his quiet rounds in his Silurian hills, with an eye open to every impression, and a heart like Thoreau's always filled with the waiting wonder of the dawn. If his mood strikes deeper than Thoreau's, it is because, coming before the romantic worship of the individual, he never cut himself off from the Church and State, but moved in the greater currents of tradition.

Walt Whitman

It is ill dealing with the prophets. They themselves may be approachable, serene, and simple, but about them their disciples soon cast such a mirage of words that the seeker is blinded and baffled, if he is not utterly repelled. And denying what the disciples say, one fears the rebuke of denying the great principles whose names they usurp. You may read in Mr. Burroughs or Mr. O'Connor or Dr. Bucke and feel so strong a repulsion for their idol that only a copious draught direct from the *Leaves of Grass* or the *Specimen Days* will restore your mind to equilibrium. Yet it is fair now to add that, by eliminating himself and allowing Whitman to speak his own words, Mr. Horace Traubel, certainly one of the least tolerable of these enthusiasts, has given us a book of some importance,[1] a daily record of intercourse during four months with his master, when old and paralytic and waiting for the outward tide.

Here we may meet the "good grey poet" just as he was in his little house in Mickle Street, Camden; may sit with him in his chamber in the midst of its indescribable confusion, and hear him talk, "garrulous to the very last." "There is all sorts of débris scattered about," says the diary, "bits of manuscript, letters, newspapers, books. Near by his elbow towards the window a washbasket filled with such stuff. Lady Mount Temple's waistcoat [a gift to Whitman from England] was thrown carelessly on the motley table—a Blake volume was used by him for a footstool: near by a copy of De Kay's poems given by Gilder to Rhys. Various other books. A Dickens under his elbow on the chair. He pushed the books here and there several times this

---

From *Shelburne Essays*, Fourth Series (Boston and New York, Houghton Mifflin Company, 1906), pp. 180–211.

[1] *With Walt Whitman in Camden.* (March 28–July 14, 1888.) By Horace Traubel. Boston: Small, Maynard, & Co., 1906.

evening in his hunt for particular papers. 'This,' he said once, 'is not so much a mess as it looks: you notice that I find most of the things I look for and without much trouble.' " As a matter of fact, his usual method of hunting was to rummage with his stick among the papers on the floor until the desired object came to the surface. Meanwhile, what other chance treasures floated up!—letters from Tennyson, Symonds, Roden Noel, Lord Houghton, Dowden, and many another stout admirer across the sea, all which were passed over to Mr. Traubel and by him duly transcribed for our perusal. What will surprise most readers of the diary is the predominance of this bookish talk; and, except where his own work is concerned, Whitman shows himself a trenchant and just critic—as might be inferred from his essays on Carlyle and Burns. One could wish that he did not so often fall into the trick common among the ill-educated of denouncing criticism while themselves exercising that function. It was, for example, not gracious to complain of Mr. Stedman for weighing him in the critical balance, when he himself was subjecting writer after writer to the same process. And again, in a larger sense, though we may after a fashion understand his distinction, there is almost a touch of insincerity in the constant segregation of himself from literature and the literary class. After all, a book's a book however much there's in 't, and the whole ambition of Whitman's life was in his authorship. More than that, we remember how many times in the *Leaves of Grass* he declares that the justification of America shall be her poets; and what student of the closet would have dared, as he did in his lecture on the *Death of Abraham Lincoln*, to reduce the whole desperate terror of the war to the needs of the literary imagination?—

I say, certain secondary and indirect results, out of the tragedy of this death, are, in my opinion, greatest. Not the event of the murder itself. Not that Mr. Lincoln strings the principal points and personages of the period, like beads, upon the single thread of his career. Not that his idiosyncrasy, in its sudden appearance and disappearance, stamps this republic with a stamp more mark'd and enduring than any yet given by any one man—(more even than Washington's;)—but, join'd with these, the immeasurable value and meaning of that whole tragedy lies, to me, in senses finally dearest to a nation, (and here all our own)—the imaginative and artistic senses—the literary and dramatic ones. *Not in any common or low meaning of those terms, but a meaning precious to the race, and to every age. A long and varied series of contradictory events arrives at last at its highest poetic, single, central, pictorial dénouement. The whole involved, baffling, multiform whirl of the secession period comes to a head, and is gather'd in one brief flash of lightning-illumination—one simple, fierce deed. Its sharp culmination, and as it were solution, of so many bloody and angry problems, illustrates those climax-moments on the stage of universal Time, where the historic Muse at one entrance, and the tragic Muse at the other, suddenly ringing down the curtain, close an immense act in the long drama of creative thought, and give it radiation, tableau, stranger than fiction. Fit radiation—fit close!* How the imagination—how the student loves these things!

I am not sure but a complete critique of Whitman's own methods as a poet, with his wanton neglect of those "climax-moments," might be read in such a passage as this. Certainly, a recollection of this more consciously artistic side of the man should be carried with us when we enter the little Mickle Street house with Mr. Traubel. There we shall see a wearied invalid, lounging nonchalantly and speaking the patois of the pavement, yet withal, if our ears are prepared, still the poet and seer. Other poets have narrowed and grown dogmatic with age, but to Whitman we feel that time has brought only sweetness and breadth; and this perhaps, despite the triviality of much of the record and its childlike egotism, despite the fact that the deeper meanings of Whitman's mind were quite dark to the disciple, is the last impression of Mr. Traubel's book. One pictures the old man as looking like the bust by Sidney Morse, which Whitman seems to have regarded as the best portrait of himself, and which resembles curiously the so-called head of Homer—

> with the broad suspense
> Of *lifted* brows, and lips intense
> Of garrulous god-innocence.

And one observes a little trait often mentioned by the disciple:
—when the conversation takes a more solemn tone, the master
breaks off and turns his eyes to the window, gazing into what vista
of thought, who shall say? It is a pretty symbol of that "with-
drawnness" of spirit, to use his own word, which those nearest to
him never understood. Almost the only signs of petulance during
these days of suffering came when his more fanatical friends
tried to imprison him within the circle of their reforming dogmas.
He would remain fluid to the end.

From this closing scene we may travel back over the earlier
years in the first adequate biography of Whitman[2] yet published.
Mr. Binns, a worshipping young Englishman who still retains
some leaven of common sense, has skilfully thrown into relief the
capital moments of Whitman's career, particularly that obscure
period when he was formulating his new art. We see Whitman,
first as a writer of meagre talent, promising to develop into a
lesser Poe or Hawthorne; then a time of silence, and suddenly, in
the year 1855, in the exact *mezzo cammin* of his life, he prints the
first issue of that extraordinary book, the *Leaves of Grass*, with its
dithyrambic annunciation of the wedding of Romantic individualism with sentimental democracy:

> I celebrate myself, and sing myself,
> And what I assume you shall assume,
> For every atom belonging to me as good belongs to
> you.
>
> I loafe and invite my soul,
> I lean and loafe at my ease observing a spear of
> summer grass.

What happened during those years of gestation? From himself
we know only that one February day in 1848 he received an
invitation to go to New Orleans and edit the *Crescent*; that he
set off with his brother Jeff, and proceeded leisurely through the

---

[2] *A Life of Walt Whitman*. By Henry Bryan Binns. New York: E. P.
Dutton & Co., 1905.—Since the writing of this essay Mr. Bliss Perry's sober
and succinct biography has appeared. Houghton Mifflin Co., 1906.

Middle States, and down the Ohio and Mississippi Rivers; that he lived in New Orleans for some months, and then plodded back northward, up the Mississippi and the Missouri, by the Great Lakes, and down the Hudson to Brooklyn once more, where for a while he worked again as printer and as builder, but intermittently and with his heart elsewhere. We know that during these seven or eight years he was writing and rewriting, casting about for a form proper to his ideas, and that he "had great trouble in leaving out the stock 'poetical' touches." But of the deeper motives at work we hear from himself nothing. Mr. Binns finds in the enlargement of Whitman's mental horizon by travel one of the main causes of his poetical conversion, and with this he connects that shadowy passion which somewhere lies in the background of the poet's experience, alluded to more than once, but never fully revealed. It seems that about this time Whitman formed an intimate relationship with a Southern lady of higher social rank than his own, who became the mother of his child, perhaps, in after years, of his children; and that he was prevented by family prejudice or some other obstacle from marriage or the acknowledgment of his paternity. One would like to connect this incident with the fair portrait over his mantel in Mickle Street—"an old sweetheart of mine," as he once said in the presence of Mr. Traubel, "a sweetheart, many, many years ago." But when asked whether she was still living, he seemed profoundly stirred, and lapsed into his usual reticence. "He closed his eyes, shook his head: 'I'd rather not say anything more about that just now.'" All this is involved in conjecture, yet such an experience would help to explain the emotional intensifying of his self-consciousness to inspire the *Leaves of Grass*.

We may be thankful for these hints from Mr. Binns and Mr. Traubel, but the best commentary on Whitman, apart from this period of gestation, is still his own *Specimen Days*, one of the most remarkable autobiographies ever written, despite a certain tediousness due to its paucity, not poverty, of ideas, and its ejaculatory language. The external elements that moulded his character are here set forth with extreme precision—first of all the sturdy English and Dutch stock, thoroughly Americanised, from which

234

he sprung, and then the old homestead in the garden spot of Long Island. Not far off lay the Great South Bay, and beyond that the sandy bars and the ever-beating Atlantic. All the sights and sounds of the sea entered into the child's heart and spoke in the songs of the man. As a boy, he longed to write a book which should express "this liquid, mystic theme," and in old age his nights were haunted with a vision "of interminable white-brown sand, hard and smooth and broad, with the ocean perpetually, grandly, rolling in upon it, with slow-measured sweep, with rustle and hiss and foam, and many a thump of low bass drums." Of all his poems, the most personal, perhaps the only one filled with passion as the world understands passion, is that incomparable rhapsody, *Out of the Cradle Endlessly Rocking*, which tells how once, in the month of lilacs, he listened by the beach to a mocking-bird complaining of its lost mate, and in the cry of the bird and the lisp of the waves heard the two riddling words of fate:

> Yes, when the stars glisten'd,
> All night long on the prong of a moss-scallop'd stake,
> Down almost amid the slapping waves,
> Sat the lone singer wonderful causing tears.

> He call'd on his mate,
> He pour'd forth the meanings which I of all men
>   know.

> Yes my brother I know,
> The rest might not, but I have treasur'd every note,
> For more than once dimly down to the beach gliding,
> Silent, avoiding the moonbeams, blending myself
>   with the shadows,
> Recalling now the obscure shapes, the echoes, the
>   sounds and sights after their sorts,
> The white arms out in the breakers tirelessly tossing,
> I, with bare feet, a child, the wind wafting my hair,
> Listen'd long and long.

> *Soothe! Soothe! Soothe!*
> *Close on its wave soothes the wave behind,*

235

And again another behind embracing and lapping,
  every one close,
But my love soothes not me, not me.

Low hangs the moon, it rose late,
It is lagging—O I think it is heavy with love, with
  love.

O madly the sea pushes upon the land,
With love, with love.

O night! do I not see my love fluttering out among
  the breakers?
What is that little black thing I see there in the
  white?

Loud! loud! loud!
Loud I call to you my love!

        ◇   ◇   ◇

A word then (for I will conquer it),
The word final, superior to all,
Subtle, sent up—what is it?—I listen;
Are you whispering it, and have been all the time,
  you sea-waves?
Is that it from your liquid rims and wet sands?

Whereto answering, the sea,
Delaying not, hurrying not,
Whisper'd me through the night, and very plainly
  before daybreak,
Lisp'd to me the low and delicious word death,
And again death, death, death, death,
Hissing melodious, neither like the bird nor like my
  arous'd child's heart,
But edging near as privately for me rustling at my
  feet,
Creeping thence steadily up to my ears and laving
  me softly all over,
Death, death, death, death, death.

236

Of formal education Whitman had little, but he was always a miscellaneous reader of books, and he had that peculiar training of the American in those years which came from a variety of occupations. Through the *Specimen Days* we catch glimpses of him working desultorily as type-setter, proof-reader, editor, writer, school-teacher, carpenter—for the most part in Brooklyn, but seeing a good deal of the country, and making himself familiar with all the manifold life of his beloved Mannahatta. It was always the tides of life that attracted him. He had, as he says, a passion for ferries, and spent much of his time on these boats, often in the pilot-houses, where he could get a full sweep of the changing panorama. And the moving stream of Broadway attracted him with a like sympathy; he loved to lose himself in "the hurrying and vast amplitude of those never-ending human currents," or to gaze down into it from the advantage of the omnibus top.

The great event in his life was the war. His brother George had enlisted in the army, and in the battle of Fredericksburg was wounded. Walt immediately went South, found his brother not seriously injured, stayed with the army awhile, and then in Washington made himself a kind of voluntary nurse and friend in the hospital wards. He passed from cot to cot bearing what gifts he could bring, writing letters for the feeble, above all giving of himself out of the bountifulness of his superb physical nature:

> Behold I do not give lectures or a little charity,
> When I give I give myself.

Many a friendless, broken lad was actually raised by his magnetic sympathy out of the despair that meant death; many another found, in his serene countenance, courage for the inevitable end. "Poor youth," he jots down in his notebook of these days, "so handsome, athletic, with profuse beautiful shining hair. One time as I sat looking at him while he lay asleep, he suddenly, without the least start, awaken'd, open'd his eyes, gave me a long steady look, turning his face slightly to gaze easier—one long, clear, silent look—a slight sigh—then turn'd back and went into his doze again. Little he knew, poor death-stricken boy, the heart of the stranger that hover'd near." Such were the notes that went

237

unchanged into the *Specimen Days*—mere hasty scribblings, yet showing now and then a rare literary art. To me the final moral impression from these memoranda is the comforting assurance— much needed in these days of realistic fiction—that human nature is not entirely bestialised by war. Whitman describes the horrors of the field after a battle with pathetic vividness, but above all he causes one to feel the great wave of idealism that swept over the country, bringing the hearts of men into unison, and lifting them out of themselves into a larger purpose. And with this goes the physical impression of endlessly marching troops, of interminable shadowy processions through the lonely roads of Virginia and in the streets of Washington.

To Whitman himself there came a deepening and purifying of his nature. He gave generously, prodigally, of his sympathy, and received his reward in the sure possession of peace; but under the physical strain something broke within him. From the age of fifty-four to his death at seventy-three (1892), he was an invalid, suffering more or less from paralysis. He travelled somewhat, but most of the time he was at his home in Camden, or visiting at a farmhouse in the adjacent country. Henceforth his notes are largely made up of his communings with nature—scraps hastily written down out of doors, and palpitating at times with the immediate intoxication of the world's beauty. And this is the end of the record:

Finally, the morality: "Virtue," said Marcus Aurelius, "what is it, only a living and enthusiastic sympathy with Nature?" Perhaps, indeed, the efforts of the true poets, founders, religious, literatures, all ages, have been, and ever will be, our time and times to come, essentially the same—to bring people back from their persistent strayings and sickly abstractions, to the costless average, divine, original concrete.

Artistically this return to nature meant for Whitman a revolt against the poetical conventions. He observed—as who has not? —a certain hollowness in almost all the poetry of the day, owing to the fact that it was not rooted in the realities of modern life. The rhythm was merely pretty, and had lost its vital swing; the primitive habits which had made it a bond of union by the

238

clapping of hands and the beating of feet were too far in the past to lend it any communal force.[3] And the spirit of verse was

[3] Mr. Bliss Perry in his Biography emphasises the fact that Whitman was not alone in this metrical revolt. In particular he calls attention to the remarkable parallel between Whitman's work and Samuel Warren's rhapsody, *The Lily and the Bee*, which was published in England in 1851, promptly republished by Harpers, and reviewed in *Harper's Monthly* of November, 1851. The rhapsody describes a day and night passed in the Crystal Palace, but its real subject, avowed by the author, is "Man—a unity":

"In dusky, rainless Egypt now!
Mysterious memories come crowding round—
From misty Mizraim to Ibrahim—
Abraham! Joseph! Pharaoh's Plagues!
Shepherd Kings! Sesostris!
Cambyses! Xerxes! Alexander! Ptolemies! Antony! Cleopatra!
Cæsar—
Isis! Osiris! Temples! Sphinxes! Obelisks! Alexandria!
The Pyramids.
The Nile!
Napoleon! Nelson!
—Behold, my son, quoth the Royal Mother, this ancient
wondrous country—destined scene of mighty doings—
perchance of conflict, deadly tremendous, such as the
world has never seen, nor warrior dreamed of.
Even now the attracting centre of world-wide anxieties.
On this spot see settled the eyes of sleepless Statesmen—
Lo! a British engineer, even while I speak, connects the
Red Sea with the Mediterranean, Alexandria and Cairo
made as one—

       ❧ ❧ ❧

"A unit unperceived,
I sink into the living stream again!—
Nave, transept, aisles and Galleries,
Pacing untired; insatiate!
Touchstone of character! capacity! and knowledge!
Spectacle, now lost in the Spectators; then spectators in the
spectacle!
Rich; poor; gentle; simple; wise; foolish; young; old; learned;
ignorant; thoughtful; thoughtless; haughty; humble; friv-
olous; profound!"

Whitman was a great reader of the magazines and no doubt saw this poem just at the time when he was beating about for his own new style. Both in form and spirit this is a really remarkable parallel. There needs but a touch of genius to fit the lines in with the most characteristic of Whitman's.

equally a thing of the past. It was essentially a product of feudalism, and Tennyson was the last pale flower, exquisite indeed, but
fragile and useless, of a civilisation which had shown its luxuriance
in Shakespeare. In these traditions of form and spirit the poet
was swathed until he sang no longer as a free individual man in
touch with the universal currents of life, but was an empty echo
of an outworn age, a simulacrum (this was the word Whitman
applied to Swinburne) of vanished emotions. To restore poetry
to its dominion over the present, therefore, Whitman would
first of all abrogate the accepted rules of rhythm, and would
allow his lines to swing, so he thought, with the liquid abandon
of the waves and the winds. Feudalism should give place to
democracy; there should be no more distinctions, but all things
should be equally good and significant, the body with the soul, vice
with virtue, the ugly with the beautiful, the small with the great.
And he, Walt Whitman, would chant himself, lustily and unashamed, as a "simple separate person." So he would lead the
people of America back to the *costless average, divine, original
concrete.* Unfortunately, in breaking away from much that was
undoubtedly a sham, he forgot too often those eternal conventions which grow out of the essential demands of human nature.
Rhythm is such a convention, and where his broken prose is of
a kind to strain the ear in the search for cadences which are not
to be found, he simply, as Ben Jonson said of Donne, deserves
hanging for not keeping accent. To bawl out that things unlike are
like, is not to make them so, and a manly egotism, if too noisy, may
sink into mere fanfaronade. For page after page Whitman is rather
a preacher of poetry than a poet; and this perhaps may be his
final condemnation, that he is persistently telling us how the true
poem of to-day should be written instead of making such a poem.
Preaching has its uses and may arouse the loftiest emotions, but its
uses and emotions are not those of poetry. The simple truth is
that a large number of Whitman's so-called poems are not only
sermons, but dull and amorphous sermons. If they arouse in
certain enthusiasts any sensation beyond that of a prosaic homily, it
is because these generous readers bring with them the residual
emotion arising from his work as a whole. Consider a few lines
from the *Salut au Monde:*

What do you see Walt Whitman?
Who are they you salute, and that one after another
    salute you.

∾ ∾ ∾

I see the places of the sagas,
I see the pine-trees and fir-trees torn by northern
    blasts,
I see granite bowlders and cliffs, I see green
    meadows and lakes,
I see the burial-cairns of Scandinavian warriors,
I see them raised high with stones by the marge
    of the restless oceans, that the dead men's
    spirits when they wearied of their quiet graves
    might rise up through the mounds and gaze
    on the tossing billows, and be refreshed by
    storms, immensity, liberty, action.
I see the steppes of Asia,
I see the tumuli of Mongolia, I see the tents
    of Kalmucks and Baskirs,
I see the nomadic tribes with herds of oxen
    and cows, etc., etc.

Now it so happens that a contemporary of Whitman, who like-wise undertook in his own way to vivify the enfeebled rhythms, and who sought, by returning to the spirit of Greece, to escape from mediæval feudalism, who wrote also much of his own feelings and was withal on occasion an undisguised preacher—it happens that Matthew Arnold in *The Strayed Reveller* has treated a very similar theme:

    They see the Centaurs
    In the upper glens
    Of Pelion, in the streams,
    Where red-berried ashes fringe
    The clear-brown shallow pools,
    With streaming flanks, and heads
    Rear'd proudly, snuffing
    The mountain wind.
    ∾ ∾ ∾

They see the Scythian
On the wide stepp, unharnessing
His wheel'd house at noon.
He tethers his beast down, and makes his meal—
Mares' milk and bread
Baked on the embers;—all around
The boundless, waving grass-plains stretch, thick-
    starr'd
With saffron and the yellow hollyhock
And flag-leaved iris-flowers.

Is it not plain, even from these fragmentary quotations, that Matthew Arnold has here accomplished what Whitman proposed as a poetical task? that he has transferred to the reader the actual vision instead of asserting what he himself had seen? And a good deal of Whitman's poetry is of this rudimentary sort. I find jotted down in the margins of my *Leaves of Grass* a dozen or more of such comparisons. There are lines in *Autumn Rivulets* which might be taken for the first rough draft from which Landor or Wordsworth elaborated his image of the inland shell; "Sail, sail thy best, ship of Democracy," sounds like a sketch for Longfellow's "Thou, too, sail on, O Ship of State"; Shelley's *West Wind* is there in embryo, and clumsily distorted stanzas of Gray and Horace. In a larger sense much of his verse is little more than a lusty preaching of what other men have dealt with creatively. His proclamation of health is good in its way, but long before him Scott had assimilated that doctrine into the breathing characters of his novels. I find no harm in Whitman's insistence on unashamed physical love, only surprise now and then to hear the language of the gutter from the pulpit; but for poetry I prefer Byron's creative assumption of that doctrine in the story of Haidée. Is not all the theory of Whitman's *Children of Adam* to be found there, turned to beautiful uses, in that picture of the two lovers brought together by mother Nature in the cavern by the starlit bay? Indeed, I am not sure but we might go further back and discover the modern sermon distilled by Lucretius into one perfect sensuous verse:

Et Venus in silvis iungebat corpora amantum.*

Were this all, Whitman might be dismissed to Messrs. Traubel & Burroughs, and to his excitable British champions, without further ado; but it is by no means all. Again and again when Whitman forgets his doctrine and hearkens to his inspiration, he shows himself a poet in the simplest acceptation of that term. There are single lines here and there, such as the oft-quoted "White arms out in the breakers tirelessly tossing," which have a magical power of evoking an image or the memory of subtle sounds and odors. There are phrases, such as his "vigorous, benevolent, clean," that almost condense a system of morals into an epigram; paragraphs that hold the true poetic emotion and stand out from their context like those half-evolved figures of Rodin struggling from their matrix; short poems, such as *The Singer in the Prison*, that might take their place unabashed in any anthology; long poems, such as *Out of the Cradle* and *When Lilacs Last*, that show a grandiose, if somewhat stumbling, craftsmanship. And it should be observed that his rhythm in these successful passages is by no means so lawless as he himself and others have supposed. Occasionally it resembles the movement in the short rhymeless lines of Matthew Arnold, but in general it is markedly dactylic. Perfect hexameters abound:

> Shouts of demoniac laughter fitfully piercing and
> pealing

and

> Alternate light and day and the teeming spiritual
> darkness.

From these the variation is gradual—

> Only the lull I like, the hum of your valvèd
> voice. . . .

* [And Venus in the woods would unite the bodies of lovers.]

> Curious in time I stand, noting the efforts of
> heroes. . . .
> In a far away northern county in the placid pastoral
> region—

to a solution of the verse into pure prose. The prevalent effect is that of a hexametric cadence such as probably preceded the regular schematisation of the Homeric poems, now following its own inner law at the expense of external form, and now submitting to no law at all, but sprawling in mere uncouth ignorance.

And when he succeeds, Whitman stands naturally with the great and not the minor poets. Take, for instance, these three familiar poems by Browning and Tennyson and Whitman on the same theme, and Whitman, though not at his highest here, is still not out of place:

> Fear death?—to feel the fog in my throat,
> The mist in my face,
> When the snows begin, and the blasts denote
> I am nearing the place,
> The power of the night, the press of the storm,
> The post of the foe;
> Where he stands, the Arch Fear in a visible form,
> Yet the strong man must go. . . .
> I was ever a fighter, so—one fight more,
> The best and the last!
> I would hate that death bandaged my eyes, and
> forbore,
> And bade me creep past!
> No! let me taste the whole of it, fare like my peers
> The heroes of old,
> Bear the brunt, in a minute pay glad life's arrears
> Of pain, darkness and cold.
> For sudden the worst turns the best to the brave,
> The black minute's at end,
> And the elements' rage, the fiend-voices that rave,
> Shall dwindle, shall blend,
> Shall change, shall become first a peace out of pain,
> Then a light, then thy breast,
> O thou soul of my soul! I shall clasp thee again,
> And with God be the rest!

❧ ❧ ❧

Sunset and evening star,
    And one clear call for me!
And may there be no moaning of the bar,
    When I put out to sea,

But such a tide as moving seems asleep,
    Too full for sound and foam,
When that which drew from out the boundless
        deep
    Turns again home.

Twilight and evening bell,
    And after that the dark!
And may there be no sadness of farewell
    When I embark;

For tho' from out our bourne of Time and Place
    The flood may bear me far,
I hope to see my Pilot face to face
    When I have crossed the bar.

❧ ❧ ❧

Whispers of heavenly death murmur'd I hear,
Labial gossip of night, sibilant chorals,
Footsteps gently ascending, mystical breezes, wafted
        soft and low,
Ripples of unseen rivers, tides of a current flowing,
        forever flowing,
(Or is it the plashing of tears? the measureless
        waters of human tears?)

I see, just see skyward, great cloud-masses,
Mournfully slowly they roll, silently swelling and
        mixing,
With at times a half-dimm'd sadden'd far-off star,
Appearing and disappearing.

(Some parturition rather, some solemn immortal
        birth;
On the frontiers to eyes impenetrable,
Some soul is passing over.)

245

Browning's lines are beaten out with a superb vigour, but in substance they express only the crude individualism of a man who sees nothing beyond his personal emotions, who will contend for these face to face with the Arch Fear, that great contemner of persons, and thinks to carry them into the silence of the grave. Tennyson, the poet of universal law, has caught up into one luminous throbbing image the merging of the soul into the great tides of being from whence it sprung, while still the idea of personality is not entirely lost, but changed into a kind of mystic symbol. It is notable that Whitman, who posed before the world as the upholder of rank egotism, shows less of this quality in the presence of death than either of his great contemporaries. Here all thought of self is lost in a vague *rapport*, as he would say, with the dim suggestions of whispering, cloud-wrapped night; here is a perception of spiritual values far above the anthropomorphism of Browning, and a power of evoking a poetical mood, when once we have trained our ear to bring out his rhythms, as strong, though not as permanent, as Tennyson's. In this note of almost pantheistic revery, the lines may represent a departure from Whitman's earlier manner, but in another respect they exhibit the most constant and characteristic of his qualities—the sense of ceaseless indistinct motion, intimated in the sound of ascending footsteps and of the unseen flowing rivers, expressed more directly in the shifting clouds and the far off appearing and disappearing star.

And this sense of indiscriminate motion is, I think, the impression left finally by Whitman's work as a whole,—not the impression of wind-tossed inanities that is left by Swinburne, but of realities, solid and momentous, and filled with blind portents for the soul. Now the observer seems to be moving through clustered objects beheld vividly for a second of time and then lost in the mass, and, again, the observer himself is stationary while the visions throng past him in almost dizzy rapidity; but in either case we come away with the feeling of having been merged in unbroken processions, whose beginning and end are below the distant horizon, and whose meaning we but faintly surmise:

> All is a procession,
> The universe is a procession with measured and
>   perfect motion.

The explanation of this effect is in part simple. The aspect of nature never forgotten by Whitman in town or field is the sea, and always the sea in motion. He is on the beach listening "As the old mother sways her to and fro singing her husky song," and looking out upon the "troops of white-maned racers racing to the goal." The endless rush of the ferries is in the substance of his verse as it formed a part of his life, and the quick pulsations of Broadway are equally there:

> Thou of the endless sliding, mincing, shuffling feet!
> Thou, like the parti-coloured world itself—like in-
>   finite teeming, mocking life!
> Thou visor'd, vast, unspeakable show and lesson!

And the world itself is an Open Road,—"the long brown path before me," he calls it, "leading wherever I choose." Only as adding to the freedom and spaciousness of this sliding panorama can the "cataloguing" portions of Whitman's book find any justification.

From these material images it is an easy transition to the vision "Of the progress of the souls of men and women along the grand roads of the universe." Out of the infinite past he beholds himself climbing, as it were, up the long gradations of time:

> Rise after rise bow the phantoms behind me,
> Afar down I see the huge first Nothing, I know I
>   was even there,
> I waited unseen and always, and slept through the
>   lethargic mist,
> And took my time, and took no hurt from the fetid
>   carbon. . . .

> Cycles ferried my cradle, rowing and rowing like
>   cheerful boatmen,

247

> For room to me stars kept aside in their own rings,
> They sent influences to look after what was to hold
> me.

And in the future, the soul, like Columbus dreaming of ever new worlds, perceives for itself other unending voyages:

> As if some miracle, some hand divine unseal'd my
> eyes,
> Shadowy vast shapes smile through the air and sky,
> And on the distant waves sail countless ships,
> And anthems in new tongues I hear saluting me.

It was the same symbolism in the *Passage to India* ("Passage to more than India!" as the refrain becomes) which led Whitman to speak of that poem to Mr. Traubel as containing, in the jargon of Mickle Street, "the essential ultimate me" and "the unfolding of cosmic purposes."

To most men, when their eyes within are opened, that spectacle brings a feeling of painful doubt. The mere physical perception of innumerable multitudes jostling forward with no apparent goal, contains an element of intellectual bewilderment for the observer. His own identity is suddenly threatened, and the meaning of his existence becomes as obscure to him as that of the alien individualities that crowd his path. And when this spectacle, as it does with some men, passes into an intuition of vast shadowy fluctuations in the invisible world, the bewilderment grows to a sense of terror, even of despair. It is the tonic quality of Whitman—the quality for which his sane readers return to him again and again—that his eyes were opened to this vision, and that he remained unafraid. All the vociferousness of his earlier poems is little more than a note of defiance against the thronging shapes that beset him. But I think it was something more than his obstreperous individualism that saved him in the end. Look into his face, especially in the noble war-time picture of him called the Hugo portrait, and you will be struck by that veiled brooding regard of the eyes which goes with the vision of the seer. He felt not only his personal identity entrenched behind walls of

248

inexpugnable egotism, but he was conscious, also, of another kind of identity, which made him one with every living creature, even with the inanimate elements. He was no stranger in the universe. The spirit that gazed out of his own eyes into the unresting multitude looked back at him with silent greeting from every passing face. And it was chiefly through this higher identity, or sympathy, that he cast away fear. He chants its power in a hundred different ways—now crudely pronouncing himself this person and that, and again merely declaring that all persons are the same and equally good to him, now denying all distinctions whatsoever. He gave it a mystical name:

> Through me the afflatus surging and surging,
>   through me the current and index.
> I speak the *pass-word primeval*; I give the sign of
>   *democracy*.

The word has been caught up by certain of his disciples and made the pass-word for admission into Whitman clubs and the key to unlock the society of the future. As the poet of democracy he is supposed to have relegated all preceding literatures and religions to the dust heap, and to have inaugurated a new era of civilisation. Now, undoubtedly he did represent in a way the political and physical aspects of America before the war—its large fluctuations of population, its sense of unfulfilled destiny. But for the problems confronting the actual militant democracy I cannot see that his poems have any answer. "Salvation can't be legislated" was the phrase with which he warned off the labour agitators and heralds of reform who sought his assistance in the later years. I fear that the working-man to-day who should undertake to follow his doctrine of *insouciance* would soon learn that loafing may be something very different from an invitation to the soul. There may be inspiration for the self-reliant individual in Whitman, but even more than Emerson's his philosophy is one of fraternal anarchy, leaving no room for the stricter ties of marriage or the state. It is curious that throughout his works you will find scarcely an intimation of the more exclusive forms of love or friendship which furnish the ordinary theme of poetry. In that universe of unresting motion into which he gazed he could discover neither time nor place for the knitting of those more enduring unions. Camarado! was his word, the cry from one man to another as they meet in the streaming procession, walk together for a little way with clasped hands, and then with the kiss of parting separate, each to his own end. This, and no political programme, is, as I understand it, the meaning of the pass-word primeval, democracy.

Only with Whitman's experience of the war, and his daily familiarity with death, do we catch the first note of that deeper mysticism which looks through the illusion of change into the silence of infinite calm. I have been struck by the fact that it was the battle-fields of Virginia that first revealed to him the stars and their infinite contrast with this life of ours. He is describing "these butchers' shambles" in his *Specimen Days*, when suddenly he seems to have become aware of the full glory of the sky: "Such is the camp of the wounded—such a fragment, a reflection afar off of the bloody scene—while all over the clear, large moon comes out at times softly, quietly shining. Amid the woods, that scene of flitting souls—amid the crack and crash and yelling sounds—the impalpable perfume of the woods—and yet the pungent, stifling smoke—the radiance of the moon, looking from heaven at intervals so placid—the sky so heavenly—the clear-obscure up there, those buoyant upper oceans—a few large placid stars beyond, coming silently and languidly out, and then disappearing—the melancholy, draperied night above, around."—It was out of such material as this, written hastily in little pocket note-books, that the *Drum-Taps* were later constructed. One of the poems, the earliest in which this pathetic fallacy of the sky appears, connects Whitman with Homer:

> I see before me now a travelling army halting,
> Below a fertile valley spread, with barns and the
> orchards of summer,
> Behind, the terraced sides of a mountain, abrupt, in
> places rising high,
> Broken, with rocks, with clinging cedars, with tall
> shapes dingily seen,
> The numerous camp-fires scatter'd near and far,

some away up on the mountain,
The shadowy forms of men and horses, looming,
    large-sized, flickering,
And over all the sky—the sky! far, far out of reach,
    studded, breaking out, the eternal stars.

It is a picture, roughly-limned, yet comparable in its own way with that scene in the *Iliad* which Tennyson has translated so magnificently:

And these all night upon the bridge of war
Sat glorying; many a fire before them blazed:
As when in heaven the stars about the moon
Look beautiful, when all the winds are laid,
And every height comes out, and jutting peak
And valley, and the immeasurable heavens
Break open to their highest, and all the stars
Shine.

Almost, in such passages as these, it would seem as if the familiarity with death had drawn for Whitman the last curtain of initiation; almost he stands like Emerson's young mortal in the hall of the firmament,—"On the instant, and incessantly, fall snow-storms of illusions. He fancies himself in a vast crowd which sways this way and that. . . . Every moment, new changes, and new showers of deceptions, to baffle and distract him. And when, by and by, for an instant, the air clears, and the cloud lifts a little, there are the gods still sitting around him on their thrones,—they alone with him alone." To that diviner glimpse Whitman never quite attained, and this is well, for in attaining it he would have passed beyond the peculiar inspiration which makes him what he is. He had been haunted by the idea of death as a boy, and had associated it with the breaking of the sea-waves on the beach. It was the supreme symbol of change, beautiful and beneficent, purging and renewing, yet still a gateway into new roads, and never a door opening into the chambers of home. Such a character it retains, indeed, in the later poems, but its ministration strikes nearer the heart of things:

Word over all, beautiful as the sky,
Beautiful that war and all its carnage must in time
    be utterly lost,
That the hands of the sisters Death and Night
    incessantly softly wash again, and ever again,
    this soil'd world:
For my enemy is dead, a man divine as myself is
    dead,
I look where he lies white-faced and still in the
    coffin—I draw near,
Bend down and touch lightly with my lips the white
    face in the coffin.

Even in his chant, *When Lilacs Last in the Dooryard Bloom'd*,
it is notable that he instinctively chooses for his picture the dead
President on that long westward journey, with the crowds thronging to behold the passing train. He is still haunted by the thought
of endless progress and procession, although in the same poem is
to occur that wonderful hymn to the Deliverer:

Come lovely and soothing death,
Undulate round the world, serenely arriving,
    arriving,
In the day, in the night, to all, to each,
Sooner or later delicate death.

Prais'd be the fathomless universe,
For life and joy, and for objects and knowledge
    curious,
And for love, sweet love—but praise! praise! praise!
For the sure-enwinding arms of cool-enfolding
    death.

Dark mother always gliding near with soft feet,
Have none chanted for thee a chant of fullest wel-
    come?
Then I chant it for thee, I glorify thee above all.

He lacked the rare and unique elevation of Emerson from whom
so much of his vision was unwittingly derived, but as a compensa-

tion his temperament is richer than the New England poet's, and
his verbal felicity at its best more striking. I do not see why Americans should hesitate to accept him, with all his imperfections and
incompleteness, and with all his vaunted pedantry of the pavement, as one of the most original and characteristic of their poets;
but to do this they must begin by forgetting his disciples.

Charles Eliot Norton

One of the mottoes prefixed to the second volume of these letters[1] is a sentence from Sainte-Beuve, which would read in English something like this: "The illustrious writers, the great poets, scarcely exist without having about them other men, themselves essential rather than secondary, great in their incompleteness, the equals in the inner life of thought with those whom they love, whom they serve, and who are kings by right of art." The words could not be more fitting if they had been written with Norton in mind, so perfectly do they express his relation to the artists of his generation. We think of him first, perhaps, as the friend of Ruskin and Carlyle, of Longfellow and Lowell, and of the other writers who were giving lustre to the Victorian and—may we say?—Cantabrigian age, and we recall the epitaph he once playfully suggested for himself: "He had good friends, whom he loved"; but we do his memory wrong if we regard him as a mere parasite or shadow, of those greater reputations. He was more than friend and audience; he was counsellor and, at times, judge. One of the few notes of personal resentment in his correspondence is a protest against a passage in Ruskin's *Præterita* which had represented him as seeking unasked the society of the more famous man. Ruskin, indeed, meant to cast no slur, and in the same book adds the most generous praise of his "first tutor":

Norton saw all my weaknesses, measured all my narrownesses, and, from the first, took serenely, and as it seemed of necessity, a kind of paternal authority over me, and a right of guidance—

From A *New England Group and Others*, Shelburne Essays, Eleventh Series (Boston and New York, Houghton Mifflin Company, 1921), pp. 97–113.

[1] *Letters of Charles Eliot Norton*. With Biographical Comment, by his daughter Sara Norton and M. A. De Wolfe Howe. Boston: Houghton Mifflin Co., 1913.

254

*though the younger of the two—and always admitting my full
power in its own kind.*

Something of that "rectorial power" he had with whomsoever
he lived, whether individual or community, and from it came his
honour and a measure, too, of bitter reproach. His letters, as they
are now published in selection, have other claims to attention,
but their greatest value is in the clear revelation of the man himself
to those who knew him not at all or, like the writer of this essay,
knew him but slightly, and of the source of the authority which
made him among his more productive contemporaries an *égal au
dedans*. The opportunity to set forth the nature of that power
brings a peculiar pleasure, not without a sense also of humility,
to the present editor of the journal which Norton helped to found
and into which so much of his character entered.[2]

As for the work of the editors of these volumes it is sufficient to
say that there is not a word of their own about Norton, nor is there
a letter of his included, which would have given offence to his
scrupulous taste in such matters; and, on the other hand, there is
no evidence that anything has been omitted which is necessary to
the understanding of the man and his position. Possibly the interest of the volumes would not have been diminished if an even
stricter selection had been exercised in the earlier letters. Norton
came to maturity rather late, and it is the gravity of his judgment
more than any adventitious aids of fancy or cleverness that holds
our attention.

His letters in this respect are curiously unlike those of Lowell,
with which one naturally compares them. After the first crude
effervescence of youth Lowell charms us with his grace and dazzles
us with the fecundity of his invention; we say that never was there
a fellow like this to amuse and entertain. But somehow the interest
does not quite hold to the end; we are a little irked to find that he
never entirely controlled his own faculties; we never touch bottom
with him, not so much because of the depth of his mind as because of the drift of its currents. With Norton it is just the reverse.
We begin by thinking him, comparatively at least, a trifle dull;

[2] Written in 1913 when I was editing the *Nation*.

but as we read on we are caught by the sheer integrity of his language; we are impressed by the feeling that here was a man of utter veracity, who never swerved aside to be funny or wise or profound or original, but was concerned to say with unflinching precision just what he felt and thought. No doubt these virtues have a negative side and denote a certain slowness of imagination and a certain lack of higher spontaneity in the writer, but at the worst we are not annoyed by the attempt to conceal such deficiencies under a sham sprightliness, and at the best we forget them by reason of other positive qualities. There is nothing in this correspondence in any way equivalent to the winged phrases in which Lowell describes to Norton the effect of Emerson's Phi Beta Kappa oration: "It began nowhere and ended everywhere, and yet, as always with that divine man, it left you feeling that something beautiful had passed that way—something more beautiful than anything else, like the rising and setting of stars," etc. Nor was it within the compass of Norton's pen to write any one of a dozen of those improvisations in which Lowell fairly takes your breath away with the audacity of his wit. But neither was it within the scope of Lowell's intelligence to give finality to one of the commonplaces of experience with just such grave and pondered beauty of expression as that which Norton used to Leslie Stephen on the death of his brother: "It is one of those changes which alter the whole habit and aspect of life,—shutting up so many chambers to which nobody else has a key, increasing the solitary and silent part of life which grows so disproportionate to the rest as we grow old." In the end we suspect that most readers will say, as they close the second of these volumes: Here is the larger man and the deeper nature, and here, after all deductions, are the finer letters.

But it must not be supposed that Norton was pedantic or priggish in his correspondence, or sent out an epistle with the solemn consideration of a judge handing down a decision. He is familiar and easy enough on occasion, and at times strong and picturesque. Especially during and after his third long visit abroad his letters and journal gain in substance by the occasional portraits of men and reports of conversations. Naturally, Carlyle is prominent in these, and he is presented as abounding in the kind of humorous exaggeration by virtue of which Norton always defended him against his detractors.[3] One day it is Carlyle discoursing on Browning:

> So *he went on till some one asked him if he had seen Browning lately. "Na," said he, with a twinkle in his eye, "but I've read the whole of his new poem,* The Ring and the Book, *in four volumes, from beginning to end, without omitting a word, and a most extraordinary production it is;—a work of great ingenuity and full of verra strikin' sentences. I met Browning, indeed, in Piccadilly the other day, and I told him I'd read his poem from the first word thereof way to the last, and he said to me, quickly, 'Well! Well?' and I replied that I thought it a book of prodigious talent and unparalleled ingenuity; but then, I suppose trusting to the sincerity of my own thoughts, I went on to say that of all the strange books produced on this distracted airth, by any of the sons of Adam, this one was altogether the strangest and the most preposterous in its construction; and where, said I, do ye think to find the eternal harmonies in it? Browning did not seem to be pleased with my speech, and he bade me good morning."*

At another time it is Carlyle's swift judgment of Sumner, whom he defines as "the most completely nothin' of a mon that ever crossed my threshold,—naught whatsoever in him or of him but

---

[3] *Haud inexpertus loquor.* There lies before me now a letter from Norton, dated 8 April, 1904, which illustrates this point:

"I am truly obliged to you for sending to me a copy of your interesting paper on *The Spirit of Carlyle,* which I might not have had the pleasure of seeing had it not been for your kindness. . . .

"You will not be surprised at my thinking that you do Froude more than justice, and that in your estimate of his work you hardly recognize how false an impression Froude conveys of the actual life and relations of Carlyle, for it ought to be held in mind that whatever tendency to mysticism may have controlled Carlyle's conception of life, his actual relations to it were of the simplest character. These actual and natural relations have been distorted by Froude to such a degree that the true impression of the man as he lived is hardly to be obtained from his volumes. The intensity of his domestic affections, the tenderness of his sympathies, his fidelity in the discharge of all duties to his family, were almost as exceptional as his literary genius. He exposed himself to great misapprehensions by his humorous extravagances and by his exaggerated utterances of feeling; but he had one of the simplest and soundest of hearts, and he had a capacity for quick and tender sympathy such as I have known in few other men. . . ."

wind and vanity." And again it is Carlyle on Carlyle, expressing a fundamental truth about himself which some of his critics have still to learn:

> While we were sitting by the fireside, before we left the house this afternoon, he said, speaking of himself,—"I've been much misunderstood in my time, and very lately now I was readin' an article on Froude's view of Ireland in the last number of Macmillan, written by a man whom ye may have seen, one ——, a willow pattern of a man, very shrill and voluble, but harmless, a pure herbivorous, nay, graminivorous creature, and he says with many terms of compliment that there's 'a great and venerable author' who's done infinite harm to the world by preachin' the gospel that Might makes Right, which is the verra precise contrary to the truth I hold and have endeavoured to set forth, which is simply that Right makes Might. And I well remember when, in my younger days, the force o' this truth first dawned on me, it was a sort of Theodicee to me, a clew to many facts to which I have held on from that day."

But it is Norton himself we come to seek in this correspondence, rather than Carlyle or another, and Norton's place as the last representative of a remarkable generation—*ultimus Novorum Anglicanorum*. Some day we shall appreciate New England literature at its true value. But before that day we must learn to distinguish between what is provincial and what is merely local. If anything is provincial it is to incorporate such men as the old Scottish poets in the main body of English literature, as is commonly done in manuals of the subject, and to relegate the Massachusetts writers to an appendix, if they are mentioned at all, as though they were foreign to the spirit of the language in which they wrote. In one of his letters from London, Lowell tells of a Scotsman who "had the ill-manners" to compliment him on his English: "Why, I shouldn't know you weren't an Englishman. Where did you get it?" Lowell's was the reproof valiant. "I couldn't resist," he says, "and answered with a couple of verses from a Scottish ballad—

> I got it in my mither's wame,
> Whaur ye'll get never the like!

He will never compliment me again, I fear." Whatever justification there may be for separating off the New England group would
lie rather in their facile cosmopolitanism. It is true that they
showed symptoms of a weakening at the root by their too ready
submission to influences from Germany and Spain and Italy, but
in the main they were faithful inheritors of one of the dominant
British traditions. Through all the changes that inevitably came
with the passage of two hundred years, they still remembered the
voice of Bunyan and Baxter and Marvell and Herbert and Wither
and the others to whom their fathers had hearkened at the time of
the great exodus. They created no one piece quite of the first rank
in the realm of the imagination, but the body of their work, when
the final account is made, will stand out honourably in the general
production of the Victorian era, and the spirit which directed them
and which rises from their books as a kind of fine and fragrant exhalation, will be recognized as one of the very precious things in
the history of the world.

And Norton himself was fully aware of the beauty and meaning
of that tradition into which he was born. No doubt, in the course
of his long life he said many hard things about America, speaking
sometimes not altogether wisely. Like others of his generation, he
was caught up by the enthusiasm of the years when the country
was moved to its depths by a passionate idea, and had it not been
for ill health he would have fought in the Civil War with the
soldiers of his State. But after the war he was never in sympathy
with certain marked tendencies of democracy and never hesitated
to express his opinion. "I have been too much of an idealist about
America," he wrote, near the end of his life, "had set my hopes too
high, had formed too fair an image of what she might become.
Never had nation such an opportunity, she was the hope of the
world." This disillusion was in part due to his fastidious social
sense, sharpened by the contrast of America with the large opportunities he had enjoyed. Society was to him "the very rarest and
best thing that the world proper can give us. It is the thing that
our modern materialism is largely killing out,—that is, in its highest
form, the society that bears witness to leisure and culture, and good
breeding, made up of men who, though versed in affairs, are still
idealists and lovers of poetry." This was the idea he had in mind,

no doubt, when he began a lecture on the word "gentleman" before a large class with the grave pleasantry: "None of you, probably, has ever seen a gentleman." Such sentiments and words were not always taken kindly, and when, as at the time of the Spanish War, he did not hesitate to expose publicly the mixture of hypocrisy and thoughtlessness that entered into the popular furor, resentment against him became almost a mark of loyalty to the country. Opinions may vary in regard to his tilt with Senator Hoar; there are those who still think he was rightly rebuked for "the habit of bitter and sneering speech"; but these, we may believe, are not many. Reading the letters of Norton and Senator Hoar side by side, most of us to-day will feel that honour and truth are rather on the side of Norton, and his address to the Cambridge Club, which, in a garbled report, called forth the storm of reproach, will seem the memorable utterance of a calm and virile patriotism. Nor should it be forgotten that the address ended with the strong words, *"Nil desperandum de republica."* Norton himself did, in fact, never despair. Many times in his letters he expresses his faith in the essential soundness of the people. It is notable that the architecture of the World's Fair at Chicago was to him a magnificent achievement and a greater promise, and that from the city itself he could draw happy auguries for the future of America. A Brahmin of New England who can admire Chicago is not quite lost to virtue.

But withal, whether for his credit or discredit, it must be admitted that Norton stood before the country and exercised the office of critic as the product of a particular time and place. He was of Cambridge, the earlier Cambridge which was, with Concord, one of the eyes of New England, the Greece of Greece, so to speak; and this position he never forgot. Several times in his letters he refers to the exceptional character of the generation in which his own life began. "I believe, indeed," he says once, writing at the end of the century, "that the very pleasantest little oasis of space and time was that of New England from about the beginning of the century to about 1825 [he himself was born in 1827]. The spirit of that time was embodied in Emerson, in Longfellow, in Holmes, and in Lowell. It was an inexperienced and youthful spirit, but it was a happy one; it had the charm of youth, its hope, its simplicity, its sweetness." He might have added, as his reader no doubt added, that he, too, was one of the bearers of that spirit—*sacra fero ingenti percussus amore**—though, for the hopefulness of youth, he brought other qualities. Innumerable forces of inheritance made him what he was. His ancestor, John Norton, named for his more noted uncle, one of the four famous Johns (Cotton, Norton, Wilson, and Davenport), took charge of the parish of Hingham in 1678. In the same year he published a poem, being nothing other than a *Funeral Elegy, Upon that Patron of Virtue, the truly pious, peerless & matchless Gentlewoman, Mrs. Anne Bradstreet*. In 1897 our Norton edited the poems of the matchless gentlewoman, and in his introduction wrote of her with more than his usual freedom and intimacy:

> It struck me that there would be something of quaint appropriateness in my writing, at this long interval, in regard to her whose praises he [John Norton] had sung, and that the act would not be without a certain piety toward my ancestor. And, further, I reflected, that as I could trace my descent in one line directly from Governor Thomas Dudley, the father of Mrs. Bradstreet, and as portraits of her brother, Governor Joseph Dudley, and his wife, looked down on me every day while I sat at breakfast and dinner, she, as my Aunt many times removed, might not unjustly have a claim upon me for such token of respect to her memory as had been asked of me. . . . She cherished in herself and in her children the things of the mind and of the spirit; and if such memory as her verses have secured for her depend rather on the circumstance of a woman's writing them at the time when she did, and in the place where she lived, than upon their poetic worth, it is a memory honourable to her, and it happily preserves the name of a good woman, among whose descendants has been more than one poet whose verses reflect lustre on her own. (Through one of her children she is the ancestress of Richard Henry Dana; through another, of Oliver Wendell Holmes.)

From a daughter of John Norton, married to John Quincy, was descended John Quincy Adams. In the direct male line came Andrews Norton, who in 1811 was appointed a tutor at Harvard and later professor of sacred literature. In 1821 he married

* [Smitten with a mighty love, I carry sacred offerings.]

Catharine Eliot (whence the relationship with President Eliot), and soon bought the house with some fifty acres of land in Cambridge known as Shady Hill. In that quiet home, which was to welcome so many of the great scholars and writers of the world, and whose gracious courtesies and dignity so many Harvard men still cherish in memory as a possession equal in value to any learning, Charles Eliot Norton, one of four children who grew to maturity, was born, and there, after many years and many labours, laid down his life.

By every right of tradition Norton belonged with the group of scholars and poets who just preceded him in birth, and he belonged with them also by virtue of his own accomplishments. When we consider the work of that generation it seems as if we saw the energy of a strong people, nourished through long discipline and austere abstentions, now suddenly freed from repression and displaying itself in manifold, and all too brief, expansion. Each man had his particular share in that activity: to one it was the exercise of wit, to another the sentiment of home and hearth, to another the comfort of religion, to another the re-creation of aboriginal life, to another the critical judgment, to another the symbolism of a brooding imagination, to another the freedom of nature, to another the justification of the untrammelled spirit. Now it must be admitted that in none of these fields was Norton quite pre-eminent; even as a critic his writing falls below Whipple's, who was nevertheless in every way a smaller man than he. It is not unlikely that the melancholy which shows itself occasionally in his letters was in some small measure due to the consciousness of these deficiencies. So he writes one day to Lowell: "Except for George [William Curtis], I have been very solitary. From year to year I seem to myself to grow more and more silent, and to express less of what is in my soul. I should like to have the power of expression,—at least long enough to give form and utterance to a few of the deepest conceptions of Life and its significance and uses which come to one as one grows old and draws the lessons from his own experience." It is true, as he says, that he never embodied his wisdom of experience in literary form, but this wisdom is precisely what he stood for among his contemporaries, and just because we feel this in his letters we shall treasure them. He was, in

262

the best sense of the word, the man of culture, the ripe scholar, to whom the lessons of the past had become a personal experience. To the multiform flowering of the time he brought the note of sound cosmopolitanism.

But he brought also with that culture, and this was his largest gift, a peculiar virtue of inheritance. More than any other man of his group, he represented the naked New England conscience and its tenacity of character. It may seem that his powers were manifested chiefly in negation. To the individual, and particularly to the young student who showed promise of achievement, he could be generous of help and encouragement. But in relation to the community at large he stood undeniably as critic and check; and this attitude was often deeply resented. What has this man done, people would ask in a tone of cavilling rebellion, that he should set himself up as judge over others? Well, the question was not unnatural; yet is not character always in some way negative? Is it not of its very essence to act as a check upon the impulsive temperament, and even upon the ranging enthusiasms of the soul? And especially in the hour of expansive liberty that came to New England when it had broken from the bondage of religion, it was desirable that the principle of restraint, broadened indeed by contact with the world, but not weakened or clouded, should have had its voice and embodiment. On the ship which brought Norton home from Europe in May of 1873 Emerson also sailed, and we have in Norton's journal a record of his wonderful conversation, with the journalist's comment and criticism. For one who reflects on the later course of New England and America these are memorable pages:

Emerson was the greatest talker in the ship's company. He talked with all men, and yet was fresh and zealous for talk at night. His serene sweetness, the pure whiteness of his soul, the reflection of his soul in his face, were never more apparent to me; but never before in intercourse with him had I been so impressed with the limits of his mind. His optimistic philosophy has hardened into a creed, with the usual effects of a creed in closing the avenues of truth. . . . He refuses to believe in disorder or evil. Order is the absolute law; disorder is but a phenomenon. . . .

But such inveterate and persistent optimism, though it may show only its pleasant side in such a character as Emerson's, is dangerous doctrine for a people. It degenerates into fatalistic indifference to moral considerations, and to personal responsibilities; it is at the root of much of the irrational sentimentalism in our American politics. . . .

Never were truer words put on paper. The pure whiteness of Emerson's soul is, when all has been reckoned up, the finest thing that New England has given to the world; but in the society for which he ministered as a high priest of ecstatic vision, there was a place also, an indispensable place, for the questioner who stood for the traditional New England conscience and sense of evil. We shall do well to honour Norton in our memory as one who through all spiritual temptations kept his feet firmly planted on the bedrock of character.

The winds of folly blew about him as they blow about us, the dust of pedantries smote his eyes, cant and sentimentalism fouled his air, but he held to his course unmoved, cherishing always in his heart what is lovely and of good report, a faithful teacher, to whom were well applied the words of the poet who had been the chief study of his life:

Felice te, che sì parli a tua posta.*

* ["Happy thou that thus speakest at thy pleasure." *Inferno*, XVI, 81. (Trans. by C. E. Norton.)]

Henry Adams

⟨～～⟩ The display of a copy of *The Education of Henry Adams* has been a kind of hall-mark of distinction for any private library, ever since the book was printed and distributed to a few friends of the author in 1907. Even to have read its jealously guarded pages was something to boast of, and the initiated were wont to wag their heads over its revelations as over some exotic drink which they were expected to admire, but which teased their palate by its strange flavour. And now the volume is published to the world, and one wonders what the world will make of it—perhaps nothing. Yet simply as the record of an unusual life it is certainly entertaining above the average, and would be doubly so were it half as long. The virtue of cynicism is its point, and only the genial can afford to be diffuse. Mr. Adams was nothing if not cynical; had he learned the rare art of compression, he might have produced a work worthy of a place beside the autobiographies of Gibbon and Franklin.

No other man of this country, save his brothers, one of whom, the late Charles Francis Adams, has followed his example, had quite such material at his disposal. Son of the elder Charles Francis Adams, grandson of a President, and great-grandson of the mighty John of Revolutionary fame, his conscience was a kind of historical epitome. As private secretary of his father at the British court during the Civil War, he saw the inside of that society and government towards whose public manifestation his family had lived in a state of hereditary feud. As a member of the Harvard faculty for seven years, he is said to have introduced the first historical seminary into an American college. As an author, not to mention his privately printed *Mont-Saint-Michel and Chartres* (recently re-

From *A New England Group and Others*, Shelburne Essays, Eleventh Series (Boston and New York, Houghton Mifflin Company, 1921), pp. 117–140.

published by the authority of the American Institute of Architects) and his unacknowledged novels *Esther* and *Democracy*, he produced a history of the United States under Jefferson and Madison notable for its original and broad use of sources, for its judicious characterizations, and its sustained interest. As a citizen of Washington, where his later and some of his earlier years were spent, he saw familiarly the working of a government which he admired no more than he did that of London. As a friend, he was close to John Hay and Clarence King, great men in this field, the latter especially, though little known to the world, yet by the few idolized as the *deus præsens* of social joy and wisdom.

Not many men of the past generation enjoyed such opportunities of watching the drama of life, and perhaps none of them excelled him in the power of penetrating beneath the surface of things; and this power is none the less amazing when, as often happened with him, the lifted curtain, behind which we looked for the revelation of some well-staged scene of history, exhibited only the disarray of planless confusion. That indeed is the moral of the book—if moral it may be called—the baffled sense of mystery behind the veil of apparent design. "King and Hay and Adams could neither of them escape floundering through the corridors of chaos," he says, with an ungrammatical reminiscence of Longfellow, "that opened as they passed to the end."

But this is to anticipate. What we have to note now is the pungent interest of Adams's comments on the figures thrown up in flashes of light beside him as he journeyed through these shadowy corridors. Sometimes it is a whole society that furnished him with a discharge of epigrams. First it is the people among whom he was born, and who stamped their traits upon his own soul:

Resistance to something was the law of New England nature; the boy looked out on the world with the instinct of resistance; for numberless generations his predecessors had viewed the world chiefly as a thing to be reformed, filled with evil forces to be abolished, and they saw no reason to suppose that they had wholly succeeded in the abolition; the duty was unchanged. That duty implied not only resistance to evil, but hatred of it. Boys naturally look on all force as an enemy, and generally find it so, but the New

Englander, whether boy or man, in his long struggle with a stingy
or hostile universe, had learned also to love the pleasure of hating;
his joys were few.

Beside this one might set his summary characterization of the
opposite type as he came into contact with it as a Harvard under-
graduate: "Strictly, the southerner had no mind; he had temperament. He was not a scholar; he had no intellectual training; he
could not analyse an idea, and he could not even conceive of admitting two; but in life one could get along very well without ideas,
if one had only the social instinct." To complete the gallery I may
quote his report of a national trait which had exercised the wit of
Shakespeare and Swift and Horace Walpole and a long succession
of observers of human nature as minted in Great Britain.

*The English themselves [he remarks while in London] hardly
conceived that their mind was either economical, sharp, or direct;
but the defect that most struck an American was its enormous
waste in eccentricity. Americans needed and used their whole
energy, and applied it with close economy; but English society was
eccentric by law and for sake of the eccentricity itself. The com-
monest phrase overheard at an English club or dinner-table was
that so-and-so "is quite mad." It was no offense to so-and-so; it
hardly distinguished him from his fellows; and when applied to a
public man, like Gladstone, it was qualified by epithets much more
forcible. Eccentricity was so general as to become hereditary distinction. It made the chief charm of English society as well as its chief
terror.*

The epigrammatic flavour is sufficient to lend some freshness to a
truism as old as Hamlet's clown, but Adams's further query
whether this eccentricity is a sign of strength or weakness, and
his remarks on its working when brought into conflict with the
plainer methods of his father and Thurlow and William Evarts,
add a quality of reflection that is not at all trite. Nor did his
keen understanding forsake him when dealing with individuals, as
might be instanced by his characterizations of the men just named,
or of such other politicians as Grant and McKinley and their
Cabinets. Of mere anecdote the pages contain comparatively little,

although here and there a good story gets entangled in his web of comment. Those who have some knowledge of Henry Reeve, the solemn, bulky, busy, doctrinaire editor of the *Edinburgh Review,* and of the Grotes, will be amused by this rencontre: "Every one," says Adams, "had heard of Mrs. Grote as 'the origin of the word grotesque.' Every one had laughed at the story of Reeve approaching Mrs. Grote, with his usual somewhat florid manner, asking in his literary dialect how her husband the historian was:—'And how is the learned Grotius?' 'Pretty well, thank you, Puffendorf!' One winced at the word, as though it were a drawing of Forain." Best of all, best of all at least for the lover of literature who tempers his enthusiasms with a grain of hard-headed cynicism, is Adams's account of meeting with Swinburne at the home of Lord Houghton, and this pendant to it of a later date:

> *Ten years afterwards Adams met him [Swinburne] at the Geneva Conference, fresh from Paris, bubbling with delight at a call he had made on Hugo:—"I was shown into a large room," he said, "with women and men seated in chairs against the walls, and Hugo at one end throned. No one spoke. At last Hugo raised his voice solemnly, and uttered the words:—'Quant à moi, je crois en Dieu!' Silence followed. Then a woman responded as if in deep meditation:—'Chose sublime! un Dieu qui croit en Dieu!' "*

But it is not as a gallery of character etchings or as a repertory of stories that Mr. Adams's book mainly interests us; it is always the observer more than the observed that holds our attention, the effect being much the same as if we were reading a novel of Henry James, in which we are less concerned with the narrated acts of a group of men and women than with the colour these actions will take in the mind of some outside spectator, revealed or half-revealed. With both the novelist and the biographer the impelling motive is curiosity rather than sympathy; but with a difference. In James we feel more the detachment of a mere psychological experimenter, the unconcern of one who creates a world of complex emotions and wills for the somewhat chilly pleasure of taking apart what he has so carefully put together; whereas in Adams there is always present the eager desire to discover in the drama some elusive truth which, if found, would give a meaning to its unfolding scenes. The autobiography is well named *The Education of Henry Adams*, though we surmise from the beginning that no lesson will ever be learned, and that the learner has set himself to decipher a text in a foreign tongue without grammar or lexicon in his hands.

In a way the text before him was not one of his own choice, but forced on him by birth and inheritance. This breed of New England, of whom he was so consciously a titled representative, had once come out from the world for the sake of a religious and political affirmation—the two were originally one—to confirm which they were ready to deny all the other values of life. For the liberty to follow this affirmation they would discard tradition and authority and form and symbol and all that ordinarily binds men together in the bonds of habit. But the liberty of denying may itself become a habit. The intellectual history of New England is in fact the record of the encroachment of this liberty on the very affirmation for which it was at first the bulwark. By a gradual elimination of its positive content the faith of the people had passed from Calvinism to Unitarianism, and from this to free thinking, until in the days of our Adams there was little left to the intellect but a great denial:

Of all the conditions of his youth which afterwards puzzled the grown up man, this disappearance of religion puzzled him most. The boy went to church twice every Sunday; he was taught to read his Bible, and he learned religious poetry by heart; he believed in a mild Deism; he prayed; he went through all the forms; but neither to him nor to his brothers or sisters was religion real. Even the mild discipline of the Unitarian church was so irksome that they all threw it off at the first possible moment, and never afterwards entered a church. The religious instinct had vanished, and could not be revived, although one made in later life many efforts to recover it. That the most powerful emotion of man, next to the sexual, should disappear, might be a personal defect of his own; but that the most intelligent society, led by the most intelligent clergy, in most moral conditions he ever knew, should have solved all the problems of the universe so thoroughly as to have quite ceased making itself anxious about past or future, and should have persuaded itself that all the problems which had convulsed human thought from earliest recorded time, were not worth discussing, seemed to him the most curious social phenomenon he had to account for in a long life.

So the original affirmation had been swallowed up in its own defences, while the negative impulse grew "to a degree that in the long run became positive and hostile." But with this intellectual negation there remained almost in full force the moral impulse which from the first had been so intimately associated with a negative separatism. This is the key we must hold in our hands if we would enter into the inner life of Henry Adams and the other New Englanders of his generation, taking the word broadly—we must, if possible, put ourselves into the state of men whose conscience was moving, so to speak, *in vacuo*, like a dispossessed ghost seeking a substantial habitation. Adams "tended towards negation on his own account, as one side of the New England mind had always done." In this vacuum various minds sought relief in various ways, connecting themselves naturally with the contemporary currents of European thought. Emerson, as the purest spirit of them all, would rest in the bare liberty of prophesying, in the security of an intuition content in itself and careless of all preceding experience as formulated in law and custom. He was *par excellence* the pure Romantic, yet withal a New Englander at heart, not a German. John Fiske, if we may extend the limits of a generation so far, looked to the new discoveries of scientific evolution to give substance to the vague cosmic deity which had swum into the place of the Christian Jehovah. Most significant of all in some respects for our present subject is the case of Charles Eliot Norton. With him New England scepticism merges into the contented agnosticism of his British friends, particularly of Leslie Stephen, while the sting of conscience takes the form of distress at the licence of an agnostic society. So he writes, in one vein to Goldwin Smith:

Possibly I regret less than you do the giving up of the old faith, and the being compelled to renounce as hopeless every attempt to solve the problems which excite our curiosity. The position toward the universe in which we find ourselves seems to me on the whole the manliest which has been attained. We are thrown back on our

*own resources to make the best of our lives. A new sense of respon-
sibility is aroused in us, and, by the narrowing of the limits of our
hopes and expectations, we find ourselves more capable of using
our faculties for legitimate and rational ends.*

But when the conscience of Norton is speaking we hear words
very different from those of his reason just quoted. So, for instance, he writes to Leslie Stephen:

*It looks as if the world were entering on a new stage of experi-
ence, unlike anything heretofore, in which there must be a new discipline of suffering to fit men for the new conditions. I fear that
America is beginning a long course of error and of wrong, and is
likely to become more and more a power for disturbance and for
barbarism. The worst sign is the lack of seriousness in the body of
the people; its triviality, and its indifference to moral principle.*

Norton was not consistent, you will say; and rightly. There is a
question to ask of a man who finds a new source of responsibility
in a creed destructive of the very principle of authority, yet la-
ments the lack of responsibility in a world that acts in accordance
with such a creed; there is a beautiful inconsistency in the heart of
one who professes complete agnosticism, yet spends his life in the
devoted study of Dante. It is the inconsistency of a conscience that
has outlived faith and not found philosophy, the will of New
England working out in its own peculiar manner the problem of
the nineteenth century. To Adams the question of meaning in
the world came with a somewhat different emphasis. Norton was
the product of a long line of theologians, and doubt, when it crept
in, took primarily the form of philosophical scepticism. But Adams
was not born into the Brahmin caste. From the beginning, as seen
in his great-grandfather and in his ancestral cousin, the revolt
against traditional authority had been rather in the field of politics,
and it was in his blood, so to speak, that his agnosticism should
strike first upon the belief in a providential purpose in history.
That indeed is the stimulus of what he calls his education. His inquiry was to branch out into a wider sphere, and in the end was to
make its return to a medieval mysticism, as Norton's did to a
medieval æstheticism; but in his earlier years he was sufficiently ab-

sorbed in seeking some theory to explain the sequence of historical events. What was the meaning of this opposition which his for-bears and his father had maintained against the settled institutions of government? To whose profit did it accrue, or was there any profit to be found anywhere? In what way had the world grown wiser and truer from this struggle and from all the struggles of men since the beginning of time? Where should he put his finger on the thread of progress in the terrible tangle of human misadventure?

He began his inquiry—at least in old age, looking back over his experience, he seemed to himself to have begun it—when as a boy he watched the political manœuvres of the Abolitionists. At home he "lived in the atmosphere of the Stamp Act, the Tea Tax, and the Boston Massacre"; only now "the Slave Power took the place of Stuart Kings and Roman Popes." He observed his father and Charles Sumner and their clique play the game of politics against the entrenched aristocracy of Boston; he saw from the inside the working of the coalition which sent Sumner to the Senate and made George Boutwell the Democratic governor of Massachusetts; he thought their ends noble, such as his great-grandfather would have approved, but he knew that their means were ignoble; and he wondered. "Thus before he was fifteen years old, he had man-aged to get himself into a state of moral confusion from which he never escaped."

Formal instruction gave him no clue to the labyrinth. "Four years of Harvard College, if successful, resulted in an autobio-graphical blank, a mind on which only a water-mark had been stamped." He got no wisdom from his teachers, none from his fellow students, though these included such promising names as Alexander Agassiz, Phillips Brooks, H. H. Richardson, and O. W. Holmes. "The chief wonder of education," he remarks, "is that it does not ruin everybody connected with it, teachers and taught." That is the world-old ingratitude of the scholar, commonly pro-nounced most vigorously by those who have profited most from instruction; it falls naturally from the lips of Henry Adams, and perhaps with him means something. At any rate he left college still "watching vaguely for a path and a direction." Travel might bestow what the class-room had withheld. He travelled. In Rome, more than once, he sat at sunset on the steps of the church of

Santa Maria di Ara Cœli—there where Gibbon had mused on the fall of empire—sat, and reflected, and concluded nothing:

Rome was a bewildering complex of ideas, experiments, ambitions, energies; without her, the Western world was pointless and fragmentary; she gave heart and unity to it all; yet Gibbon might have gone on for the whole century, sitting among the ruins of the Capitol, and no one would have passed, capable of telling him what it meant. Perhaps it meant nothing.

We need not follow Adams through all the stages of his historical education. One great lesson in negative wisdom he was to learn in London, while helping his father to unravel the machinations of Palmerston and Lord John Russell and Gladstone against the government of the United States. He was to observe men sensitive to any imputation of untruth and otherwise highly moral, yet in public speaking one thing while in private acting another, men whose courage, as it seemed to him, lay in subterfuge and whose honour went no further than indignation. "If one could not believe them, Truth in politics might be ignored as a delusion"; and he had ample grounds for not believing any word of Gladstone at least, the most righteous of them all. What was to be made out of such a contradiction in terms by a student of life who "liked lofty moral principles and cared little for political tactics"? "Here, then, appeared in its fullest force, the practical difficulty in education which a mere student could never overcome; a difficulty not in theory, or knowledge, or even want of experience, but in the sheer chaos of human nature."

That difficulty was not diminished when he returned to Washington and saw a blunt plain soldier like Grant entangled in the most questionable business. For one moment, indeed, at the time of our Spanish War, he felt a sense of possible purpose working itself out in history. To him, if to no one else, "still living in the atmosphere of Palmerston and John Russell, the sudden appearance of Germany as the grizzly terror which, in twenty years, effected what Adamses had tried for two hundred in vain,—frightened England into America's arms,—seemed as melodramatic as any plot of Napoleon the Great." But his satisfaction was more temperamental than intellectual—than intelligent, one might say—and in the embroglio of foreign intrigue that followed, and that wrecked the health of his dearest friend, John Hay, he was forced to see again only the conflict of blind wills and the shifting combinations of chance.

If Adams's observation of history in the making, supplemented by his study of history in the past, led to these sceptical conclusions, a sudden event of a more personal sort seemed, as it were, to rend the veil of cosmic charity and to show him that the foolishness of human affairs was but a little centre of chaos encompassed by a vast and malignant chaos of nature. Called from London to Italy by a telegram, he found his beloved sister, a woman of forty, for whom life had been gay and brilliant, dying in extreme torture from a miserable accident. As he sat by her bedside and watched the agony of her dissolution, while out of doors the world was glowing with the sensuous joys of an Italian summer, it seemed to him that now for the first time he beheld Nature face to face; and what he saw in that vision was to haunt him for the rest of his years:

Impressions like these are not reasoned or catalogued in the mind; they are felt as part of violent emotion; and the mind that feels them is a different one from that which reasons; it is thought of a different power and a different person. The first serious consciousness of Nature's gesture—her attitude towards life—took form then as a fantasm, a nightmare, an insanity of force. For the first time, the stage-scenery of the senses collapsed; the human mind felt itself stripped naked, vibrating in a void of shapeless energies, with resistless mass, colliding, crushing, wasting and destroying what these same energies had created and laboured from eternity to perfect. Society became fantastic, a vision of pantomime with a mechanical motion; and its so-called thought merged in the mere sense of life, and pleasure in the sense. The usual anodynes of social medicine became evident artifice. Stoicism was perhaps the best; religion was the most human; but the idea that any personal deity could find pleasure or profit in torturing a poor woman, by accident, with a fiendish cruelty known to man only in perverted and insane temperaments, could not be held for a moment. For pure blasphemy, it made pure atheism a comfort.

God might be, as the Church said, a Substance, but he could not be a Person.

In those hours of biting agony, while the individual life so dear to him was wrestling unequally with the unsympathetic powers of death, Adams saw the destiny of mankind merged into the destiny of the sum of things. At an early period he had added to his reading of history a faithful study of science, and as he had sought for a thread of providential guidance in the one, so, under the influence of the newly based theory of evolution, he looked for signs of design and progress in the non-human order of creation. At first the two fields of inquiry had lain apart, but now, as I say, they appeared as phases only of the one problem which engaged his passionate attention. But the search baffled him, baffled him the more as it became more complex. As in history he thought he saw the evil persisting unchanged along with the good, so in the field of science he beheld the lower order of existence continuing on with the higher and throwing an element of stable confusion into progressive mutation. More than that. When he went beyond the material of biology into the dark background of inorganic forces he learned that the physicists themselves acknowledged only an inexpressible mystery. In Germany he heard Haeckel avowing that "the proper essence of substance appeared to him more and more marvellous and enigmatic as he penetrated further into the knowledge of its attributes,—matter and energy,—and as he learned to know their innumerable phenomena and their evolution." In France he heard the clearer and more authoritative voice of Poincaré making the same confession of ignorance: "[in science] we are led to act as though a simple law, when other things were equal, must be more probable than a complicated law. Half a century ago one frankly confessed it, and proclaimed that nature loves simplicity. She has since given us too often the lie. To-day this tendency is no longer avowed, and only so much of it is preserved as is indispensable so that science shall not become impossible." Then, turning to England, he read such words as these: "In the chaos behind sensation, in the 'beyond' of sense-impressions, we cannot infer necessity, order, or routine, for these are concepts formed by the mind of

275

man on this side of sense-impressions. . . . Briefly, chaos is all
that science can logically assert of the supersensuous." Thus as
the "unknowable" came nearer to man's inquiry it seemed to put
on positive and menacing hues; the pronouncements of the most
advanced physical thinkers echoed to Adams what he had learnt
from his own study in history—chaos in the background here and
there. And if he went to the pseudo-science of psychology he was
faced with another "sub-conscious chaos below the mind"; man's
"normal thought," he learned, "was dispersion, sleep, dream, inconsequence; the simultaneous action of different thought-centres
without central control. His artificial balance was acquired habit.
He was an acrobat, with a dwarf on his back, crossing a chasm
on a slack-rope, and commonly breaking his neck." Here was a
question that sprang from something very far from idle curiosity.
Had Adams not witnessed the terror of the mystery, when this
thing called chaos had suddenly lurched forward out of its background of mystery and enveloped his little oasis of well-loved order?

What was the proper attitude towards this enigma? Was it that
no one can reach beyond himself? "All that Henry Adams ever saw
in man was a reflection of his own ignorance"—such was his
political discernment far back in his London days; should that be
the final verdict of all his seeing? In a way he had acquired what
ages ago had been proclaimed by Socrates as the beginning of
wisdom: not to think we know what we do not know. Into this
sea of negation he had sailed from the ancient moorings of his
people; but not even the New Englander of the nineteenth century could rest in pure negation. Emerson, like Socrates, had
found no difficulty in combining scepticism with an intuition of
pure spirituality, though, unlike Socrates, to maintain his inner
vision intact he shut his eyes resolutely on the darker facts of
nature. That serene indifference to evil was the last thing possible
to Adams. Another New Englander, nearer to Adams in date,
John Fiske, had accepted the most rigid deductions of biological
evolution, and then on Darwin's law of natural selection, which
for humanly felt good and evil substituted a conception of blind
unfeeling mechanism, had superimposed the conception of a
cosmic deity unfolding the world to

one far-off divine event,
To which the whole creation moves.

Whatever may be said of such a philosophy, it was meaningless
to Henry Adams; he could not marry the faith in a benignant
pantheistic will with the sort of chaos that lurked for him behind
every door of our ignorance. Still another New Englander, Charles
Eliot Norton, as we have seen, was content to profess a complete agnosticism of theory along with an unswerving belief in
human responsibility—to what? Alas, that "what" was the little
irksome word that Adams could not get out of his mind.

The answer, or the direction towards an answer, came to him
as he walked the halls of the Paris Exposition of 1900. There,
at least, under the guidance of his scientific friend, Langley, if
he saw nothing that pointed to a rational design at the end of
things, he beheld in the great gallery of machines a symbol of
what science had substituted for design. "The planet itself seemed
less impressive, in its old-fashioned, deliberate, annual or daily
revolution, than this huge wheel, revolving within arm's-length at
some vertiginous speed, and barely murmuring,—scarcely humming an audible warning to stand a hair's-breadth further for
respect of power,—while it would not wake the baby lying close
against its frame. Before the end, one began to pray to it; inherited
instinct taught the natural expression of man before silent and
infinite force. Among the thousand symbols of ultimate energy, the
dynamo was not so human as some, but it was the most expressive." Force, he would say, blind whirling force, strapped and
bound in iron, is supreme over all:

Dinos has driven out Zeus and rules as king.

We should need, in fact, a living Aristophanes to celebrate this
step of a New Englander's education. Other men of the century
had discovered this same god, but their worship had taken strangely
different forms. "Power is power," says Tolstoy, reading for himself the lesson of history at the conclusion of his *War and Peace*,
"that is, Power is a word, the true meaning of which is to us in-

comprehensible"; and then, as a good humanitarian, he personifies this Unknowable in the instinctive soul of the People. Nietzsche, too, had found only *Macht* at the heart of the world, but he worshipped this Power not at all in the impulse of the People—quite the contrary; and some of his interpreters have deified a *Schrecklichkeit* very different from the pity of Tolstoy. Perhaps the true lesson of our age would be to learn why and how this modern Janus of Power has tricked us into believing that he has only one face. But Adams was too knowing to bow the knee with Tolstoy, and too timid to salute with Nietzsche. He took another way.

Norton, as we have seen, had found agnosticism compatible with devotion to Dante, being able at least to sympathize with the energetic moral sense and the æsthetic vision of that poet; and Adams, like him, turned at last for consolation to the age of Dante, if not to Dante himself, though with a difference. From the Exposition, "caring but little for the name, and fixed only on tracing Force, Adams had gone straight to the Virgin at Chartres, and asked her to show him God, face to face, as she did for St. Bernard." What the Virgin revealed to him is told clearly enough in the autobiography, but for its fullest elucidation one should read that extraordinary disquisition on the art and poetry and philosophy and religion of the twelfth and thirteenth centuries which he entitles *Mont-Saint-Michel and Chartres*. In the Virgin Mother of God, to whose honour the cathedrals pointed their arches towards heaven, before whose throne the windows were made to glow like the jewels of a queen, for whose delight romance wove its shimmering web of words, to whom great scholars sacrificed their learning, our far-travelled New Englander saw at last the one symbol of Force comprehensible to the human heart, if not to the human brain. "The Puritans," he says, "abandoned the New Testament and the Virgin in order to go back to the beginning, and renew the quarrel with Eve"; our latest Puritan rediscovers woman on her medieval throne, and chants to her in modern speech the ancient pæan to Alma Venus Genetrix. It would be a pretty business to unravel the various motives that had impelled him on this devious way from the sturdy, if unloving, protestantism of his race. He himself makes much of the motive of love as the aspect of infinite power which man can understand.

That may be; but I suspect that another attribute of the Virgin meant even more to his mind. Read, if you will, his charming pages on her interventions and miracles; you will observe that they were almost without exception performed to override the course of law and justice, and you will learn that behind her woman's pity there was another quality which Adams, at any rate, does not hesitate to glorify as equally feminine:

The fact, conspicuous above all other historical certainties about religion, that the Virgin was by essence illogical, unreasonable, and feminine, is the only fact of any ultimate value worth studying, and starts a number of questions that history has shown itself clearly afraid to touch. . . . She was imposed unanimously by all classes, because what man wanted most in the Middle Ages was not merely law or equity, but also and particularly favour. . . . The individuals rebelled against restraint; society wanted to do what it pleased; all disliked the laws which Church and State were trying to fasten on them. . . . If the Trinity was in its essence Unity, the Mother alone could represent whatever was not Unity; whatever was irregular, exceptional, outlawed; and this was the whole human race.

Conscience was the last tie of New England to its past. Was it the perfect irresponsibility of the Virgin, human no doubt, feminine perhaps, certainly not Puritan, that gave to our tired sceptic the illusion of having reached a comfortable goal after his long voyage of education? There is a fateful analogy between the irresponsibility of unreasoning Force and unreasoning love; and the gods of Nietzsche and of Tolstoy are but the two faces of one god. To change the metaphor, if it may be done without disrespect, the image in the cathedral of Chartres looks perilously like the ancient idol of Dinos decked out in petticoats.

If we regard Adams's scholarship, his imagination, his verbal dexterity, his candour, his cynical vivacity, his range of reflection, we must give him a high place in the American literature of the past generation, a higher place probably than his present limited popularity would indicate. But one winces a little at acknowledging that the latest spokesman of the Adamses and of New England ends his career in sentimental nihilism. From Harvard College,

279

which to Adams had been only one stage in the way of disillusion, the boy John Fiske had written: "When we come to a true philosophy, and make *that* our stand-point, all things become clear. We know what things to learn, and what, in the infinite mass of things, to leave unlearned; and the Universe becomes clear and harmonious." The tragedy of Adams's education is that of a man who could not rest easy in negation, yet could find no positive faith to take its place. From one point of view he may appear to be the most honest and typical mind of New England in its last condition; yet withal some manlier voice, some word of deeper insight that yet faces the facts of life, we must still expect to hear from the people of Mather and Edwards and Channing and Emerson.

A 3
B 4
C 5
D 6
E 7
F 8
G 9
H 0
I 1
J 2